Exploring Language

Shirley Russell

Consultant: Peter Buckroyd

OXFORD

OXFORD
UNIVERSITY PRESS

Oxford University Press is a department of the University of Oxford.
It furthers the University's objective of excellence in research, scholarship,
and education by publishing worldwide in

Oxford New York

Auckland Cape Town Dar es Salaam Hong Kong Karachi
Kuala Lumpur Madrid Melbourne Mexico City Nairobi
New Delhi Shanghai Taipei Toronto

With offices in

Argentina Austria Brazil Chile Czech Republic France Greece
Gautemala Hungary Italy Japan South Korea Poland Portugal
Singapore Switzerland Thailand Turkey Ukraine Vietnam

Oxford is a registered trade mark of Oxford University Press in the
UK and in certain other countries

British Library Cataloguing in Publication Data

Data available

ISBN 978-019-8325840

10 9 8 7 6 5 4 3 2 1
Printed in Great Britain by Bell and Bain Ltd., Glasgow

Contents

Acknowledgements

Shirley Russell's grateful thanks go to editor Jan Doorly for her unflagging help and support, and to consultant Peter Buckroyd for his constant encouragement and constructive advice.

The author and publisher are grateful for permission to reprint the following copyright material:

Martin Amis: extract from *Yellow Dog* (Jonathan Cape, 2003), reprinted by permission of The Random House Group Ltd.

Jeremy Clarkson: 'It's got the wrong trousers, Gromit' in 'Car', *The Sunday Times*, 10.6.2007, copyright © Jeremy Clarkson/NI Syndication 2007, reprinted by permission of News International Syndication Ltd.

Giles Coren: 'Special Timex Indiglio. For you good price', *The Times*, 16.6.2007, copyright © Giles Coren/NI Syndication 2007, reprinted by permission of News International Syndication Ltd.

David Crystal: extract from *Listen to Your Child: A Parent's Guide to Children's Language* (Penguin, 1986), copyright © David Crystal 1986, reprinted by permission of Penguin Books Ltd.

Norman Fairclough: extract from *Language and Power* (Longman, 1989), reprinted by permission of Pearson Education.

Alex Gallway: Letter to the Editor: *The Times*, 6.6.2007, copyright © The Times/NI Syndication 2007, reprinted by permission of News International Syndication Ltd.

James Herriot: extracts from *Vets Might Fly* (Michael Joseph, 1976), reprinted by permission of David Higham Associates.

Katherine Hibbert: 'No Trace of Corn' (Book Review), in 'Culture', *The Sunday Times*, 10.6 2007, copyright © The Sunday Times/NI Syndication 2007, reprinted by permission of News International Syndication Ltd.

Mark Hodkinson: 'Roger Federer's fifth win equals "living legend"', *Daily Telegraph*, 9.7.2007, reprinted by permission of Telegraph Media Group Ltd.

Antony Jay and Jonathan Lynn: extract from 'A Conflict of Interest' first broadcast 31.12.1987, from *Yes, Prime Minister*, copyright © Antony Jay and Jonathan Lynn, reprinted by permission of Alan Brodie Representation Ltd.

Anthony Jones and Jeremy Mumford: extracts from *Children Using Language* (NATE, 1971), reprinted by permission of the National Association for the Teaching of English (NATE).

Joe Joseph: 'Modern Morals', *The Times*, 24.1.2007, copyright © The Times/NI Syndication 2007, reprinted by permission of News International Syndication Ltd.

Cosmo Landesman: 'It ain't got that swing' (Film Review) in 'Culture', *The Sunday Times*, 10.6.2007, copyright © Cosmo Landesman/NI Syndication 2007, reprinted by permission of News International Syndication Ltd.

Ben Laurance: 'Backpeddlar' from 'In Gear' column, *The Sunday Times*, 20.5.2007, copyright © Ben Laurance/NI Syndication 2007, reprinted by permission of News International Syndication Ltd.

Michael Lee: 'Booze is "Ruin of Britain"', *The Sun*, 11.5.2000, copyright © The Sun/NI Syndication 2000, reprinted by permission of News International Syndication Ltd.

Darren Lewis: 'Roger the Great', *Daily Mirror*, 9.7.2007, reprinted by permission of the Mirror Group.

Jenny McCartney: 'It's so uncool not to be in the brand band', *Sunday Telegraph*, 10.6.2007, reprinted by permission of Telegraph Media Group Ltd.

Marianne Macdonald: 'Have you met my beautiful friend?', *The Times*, 27.7.2007, copyright © The Times/NI Syndication 2007, reprinted by permission of News International Syndication Ltd.

Ben McIntyre: 'English grows into strange shapes when transplanted into foreign soil', from 'Books', *The Times*, 24.3.2007, and from article about climate change, *The Times*, 7.7.2007, both copyright © Ben McIntyre/NI Syndication 2007, reprinted by permission of News International Syndication Ltd.

Michael McTear: *Children's Conversation* (Basil Blackwell, 1985), reprinted by permission of Wiley-Blackwell.

W. Somerset Maugham: extract from 'An Appointment in Samarra' in *Sheppey* (Heinemann, 1933), reprinted by permission of A. P. Watt Ltd on behalf of the Royal Literary Fund.

Peter Mayle: extract from *A Year in Provence* (Hamish Hamilton, 1989), copyright © Peter Mayle 1989, reprinted by permission of Penguin Books Ltd.

Caitlin Moran: extract from 'Re:re:re: Tuesday – your last e-mail was a right roffle', *The Times*, 23.4.2007, copyright © Caitlin Moran/NI Syndication 2007, reprinted by permission of News International Syndication Ltd.

Matthew Parris: 'Evil Plotters? More like sad and crackpot', *The Times*, 7.7.2007, copyright © Matthew Parris/NI Syndication 2007, reprinted by permission of News International Syndication Ltd.

Melanie Phillips: 'A criminal absence of will', *Daily Mail*, 19.2.2007, reprinted by permission of Solo Syndication Ltd.

Monica Porter: 'Is e-mail killing literacy?', *Daily Mail*, 26 October 1999, reprinted by permission of Solo Syndication Ltd.

Nigel Powell: 'Don't Panic', *The Sunday Times*, 20.5.2007, copyright © The Sunday Times/NI Syndication 2007, reprinted by permission of News International Syndication Ltd.

Melanie Reid: 'Prepare to be ostracised, all you smokers of England', *The Times*, 11.6.2007, copyright © The Times/NI Syndication 2007, reprinted by permission of News International Syndication Ltd.

Carol Sarler: 'I say use, you say usage, let's call the whole thing off' from 'Thunderer' column, *The Times*, 15.1.2007, copyright © The Times/NI Syndication 2007, reprinted by permission of News International Syndication Ltd.

Julian Savulescu: extract from 'Sex selection: The case for', *MJA* 1999: 171, 373-375, copyright © 1999 *The Medical Journal of Australia*, reprinted by permission of the Australasian Medical Publishing Company.

Jane Shilling: 'Men and Women on an equal footing? Only in fiction', *The Times*, 4.5.2007, copyright © Jane Shilling/NI Syndication 2007, reprinted by permission of News International Syndication Ltd.

Miriam Stoppard: 'Dr Miriam gets to the heart of...', *Daily Mirror*, 10.5.2007, reprinted by permission of the Mirror Group.

Shelley von Strunckel: extract from 'In the Stars', 'Style' Magazine, *The Sunday Times*, 10.6.2007, copyright © Shelley von Strunckel/NI Syndication 2007, reprinted by permission of News International Syndication Ltd.

Norman Tebbit: quoted in *The Cambridge History of English Language, Vol. 4*, edited by Suzanne Romaine (Cambridge University Press, 1999), reprinted by permission of Lord Tebbit.

Theakston advertisement, reprinted by permission of T&R Theakson Ltd.

Robert Troup: extract from 'Girl Talk' from the Paramount Picture *Harlow*, words by Bobby Troup, music by Neal Hefti, copyrght © 1965, renewed 1993 by Famous Music LLC and Bobby Troup Music, reprinted by permission of the Hal Leonard Corporation and Bobby Troup Music. International copyright secured. All rights reserved.

Peter Trudgill: *Sociolinguistics: An Introduction to Language and Society* (Penguin, 1974, revised edition 1983), copyright © Peter Trudgill 1974, 1983, reprinted by permission of Penguin Books Ltd.

Sarah Vine: 'Too much Home Front? Oh, do grow up!', *The Times*, 5.7.2007, copyright © The Times/NI Syndication 2007, reprinted by permission of News International Syndication Ltd.

Ben Webster: 'Your hybrid powertrain's got snagged on your isofix... it's gonna cost you', *The Times*, 3.2.2007, copyright © The Times/NI Syndication 2007, reprinted by permission of News International Syndication Ltd.

The Week: extract from 'Health Scare of the Week', *The Week*, 10.2.2007, reprinted by permission of The Week Ltd.

Editorial: 'Sack Charlie', *The Sun*, 10.5.2007, copyright © The Sun/NI Syndication 2007, reprinted by permission of News International Syndication Ltd.

Profile on Estuary English: 'Ain't nuttin' to wor' abaht, me old mate', *The Sunday Times*, 7.6.1998, copyright © The Sunday Times/NI Syndication 1998, reprinted by permission of News International Syndication Ltd.

We have made every effort to trace and contact all copyright holders before publication. If notified, the publisher will rectify any errors or omissions at the earliest opportunity.

Introduction to the Study of Language

You probably remember GCSE English as a relatively cosy subject, focused mainly on what people (including yourself) were writing or saying. On content, to put it another way.

Now, you are being asked to focus on the way in which that content is being expressed: on style, in other words.

Not only is this switch of attention disconcerting in itself, it also brings new problems in its wake. Suddenly, you're being faced with what seems an awful lot of abstruse technical terms you've never met before, whose meaning you certainly don't understand at first sight: *lexis*, for example, meaning vocabulary, or even more simply, words.

'Do I really have to write stuff like this?' you may ask. The answer, I'm afraid, is 'Yes'. For two good reasons.

1 Specialist terms may seem a pain at first, but they act as a kind of shorthand and, once you've learned to use them, they save you a lot of effort. Don't use them, and you have to waste time spelling out what they mean.

2 Examiners love them. See Assessment Objective 1 of your AS course, which demands that you.

> Select and apply a range of linguistic methods, to communicate relevant knowledge using *appropriate terminology* and coherent, accurate written expression.

In other words, it isn't enough to write good sense about a text in ordinary language. If you want to impress your examiners, you *must* use the appropriate specialist terms.

The ingredients of language

The first set of specialist terms you need to know are broad, general ones, used to break language down into its different features.

The specialist term for these features is the *ingredients of language*, and for your convenience they are listed below:

- **lexis:** the words themselves that make up the text or discourse
- **grammar:** the way individual words are structured and arranged together in sentences
- **structure:** the way the content of a text is organized (this is sometimes referred to as discourse structure, *discourse* being simply an earlier term for text)
- **semantics:** the meaning conveyed by the lexis; semantics can be broadened out to include *pragmatics*, the technical term for the unwritten rules that allow us to imply what we mean in social contexts rather than state it directly.

In the case of written texts only, you will also need to discuss:

- **graphology:** the way in which written texts are presented on paper or some other background; their spatial arrangement and layout, the type and size of their lettering, etc.

In the case of spoken texts only, you will also be expected to discuss:

- **phonology:** the use of vocal elements to add extra force to what is being said
- **prosodic features:** the individual parts or ingredients of language that, taken together, make up the texts you will be asked to analyse and comment on.

Note

While each of the above ingredients may be found in a text, each may not always be sufficiently important for you to comment on. Every text is different, and what strikes you in one may not be so interesting in another.

What you *must not* do is simply make a list of the ingredients without saying anything useful about them. The examiners already know what ingredients are in a given text: what they want *you* to do is tell them something useful about them.

Activity

1 Which two alternative specialist terms are used to denote a passage of speech or writing?

2 What do you understand by the term lexis?

Analysing the ingredients

Knowing how to break language down into its different ingredients is fine as far as it goes, but that isn't very far. What we need to do now is break these individual ingredients down in their turn, so that we know how to talk about them in the necessary detail.

Since lexis is the bedrock of every text, it seems logical to start with that. 'What kind of words has the speaker/writer chosen?' should be our first question, and this will introduce us to another important specialist term: **register**.

The concept of register

English has a huge range of vocabulary, basically Anglo-Saxon but with large inputs from French, Latin and Greek, and lesser ones from every country colonized in the days of the British Empire. This richness allows us to create many different varieties of language, or registers, appropriate to many different subjects and kinds of audience.

The diagram below will give you some idea of their range, starting from the most widely used **common register** (the sort of conventional language we use in polite social situations, known as **Standard English**); moving down to the informal spoken registers of **colloquial English** and **slang**; and moving upwards at the other end of the scale to registers that have nothing much in common with any of the first three: the **bureaucratic register** (often known as **officialese**), and the even more remote and impersonal registers of professions such as science, medicine, and the law: the **learned registers**.

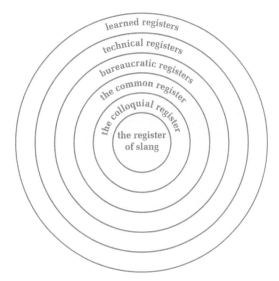

Registers and connotations: the right word in the right place

Words are used to **denote** things: *lad*, for instance, as used in the **common register**, simply denotes a male not yet arrived at adulthood – a *boy* or *youth*. But words carry **connotations** also; ideas and emotions that are conjured up in the listener's or reader's mind when a particular word is used. *Lads* used in utterances like *Awa' the lads* or *The lads done good* is quite different in meaning, carrying a heavy overlay of pride and of male bonding – to football supporters, for example.

In the same way, words that start from a similar central idea or meaning, such as *men and women*, can morph into other words with very different connotations in the various registers outlined above.

- Learned registers: *human beings, mankind, humanity, the human genome*
- Technical registers: *companies, managers, personnel, engineers*
- Bureaucratic registers: *the general public, social groups/classes, society*
- Common register: *men and women, ladies and gentlemen, folk(s), people*
- Colloquial register: *lads and lasses, blokes and birds, chavs, geezers, tarts*
- Register of slang: *guys* (fill in others from your own experience).

The progression through the registers from most familiar to most impersonal and remote should be clear to see.

The relationship between register and grammar

Fortunately for A level students, there is nearly always a match between words and grammar within the different registers (a **lexo-grammatical correspondence**, in technical terms).

As a rule of thumb, if the lexis is conventional, the grammar will be conventional also: sentences will be well-formed and grammar conventionally correct. (Don't worry if you don't know much about grammar at this point – you'll catch up with it later.)

If the lexis is the informal one of colloquial English or slang, sentences will often be broken up and fragmentary, and grammar not conventionally correct, e.g. *Well out of order they was, the blighters. That Rooney – he's wicked man, innit.* The colloquial and slang registers are generally spoken rather than written, and so will always be less 'correct' in the textbook sense.

In the learned registers, the sentence structure will be as unfamiliar to the ordinary speaker/writer as the Latinate vocabulary. Speakers and writers will often choose to use the impersonal pronoun *it* for their subject rather than the more personal *you*; they will also often prefer to use the *passive voice* in place of the more usual active one, e.g. *It will be seen/observed that...* rather than *you will see*. This creates a dispassionate tone more appropriate to the rational discussion of intellectual subjects than ordinary language.

To sum up: the more complex the ideas, the more complex the lexis and sentence structure are likely to be.

Critiques of registers in use

A: Degree in café deportment

Peter Mayle examines the behaviour of female university students in the French town of Aix.

Aix is a university town, and there is clearly something in the curriculum that attracts pretty students. The terrace of the Deux Garçons is always full of them, and it is my theory that they are there for education rather than refreshment. They are taking a degree course in café deportment, with a syllabus divided into four parts.

One: the arrival

One must always arrive as conspicuously as possible, preferably on the back of a crimson Kawasaki 750 motor cycle driven by a young man in head-to-toe black leather and three-day stubble. It is not done to stand on the pavement and wave him goodbye as he booms off down the Cours to visit his hairdresser. That is for *gauche* little girls from the Auvergne. The sophisticated student is too busy for sentiment. She is concentrating on the next stage.

Two: the entrance

Sunglasses must be kept on until an acquaintance is identified at one of the tables, but one must not appear to be looking for company. Instead, the impression should be that one is heading into the café to make a 'phone call to one's titled Italian admirer, when – *quelle surprise!* – one sees a friend. The sunglasses can then be removed and the hair tossed while one is persuaded to sit down.

Three: ritual kissing

Everyone at the table must be kissed at least twice, often three times, and in special cases four times. Those being kissed should remain seated, allowing the new arrival to bend and swoop around the table, tossing her hair, getting in the way of the waiters and generally making her presence felt.

Four: table manners

Once seated, sunglasses should be put back on to permit the discreet study of one's own reflection in the café windows... to check important details of technique: the way one lights a cigarette, or sucks the straw in a Perrier *menthe*, or nibbles daintily on a sugar lump. If these are satisfactory, the glasses can be adjusted downwards so that they rest charmingly on the end of the nose, and attention can be given to the other occupants of the table.

Peter Mayle, *A Year in Provence*

Sample critique

The lexis here is drawn largely from the common register: *bend, swoop, tossing*, for example; familiar words describing familiar actions. The words are simple, clear and so well chosen that the girl's body language comes vividly to life. But Mayle wants to convey more than simple physical behaviour. He wants to show that what is going on here is an elaborate display of artificial manners, contrived movements and gestures designed to make an effect on anyone who might be watching. And thanks to the richness of the English language, he can do this simply by the introduction of words with more mannered and artificial connotations: *deportment, conspicuously, sophisticated* and *technique* being the most important. Look up the definitions of these words and you will see that each suggests an overlay of the simple and unaffected by something more carefully contrived.

Sentence structure is also fairly simple, most having only one or two clauses. What longer sentences there are tend to consist of a build-up of phrases rather than convoluted dependent clauses (clauses that depend for their meaning on the main clause they are attached to; see page 68), e.g. *Those being kissed should remain seated, allowing the new arrival to bend and swoop around the table, tossing her hair, getting in the way of the waiters…*

Unusually for sentence structure in the common register, however, the writer adopts the use of the impersonal subject, *one*. This is another way in which the writer heightens the sense of social exclusiveness. Compare *I wouldn't like to seem too eager* with *One wouldn't like to seem too eager*.

B: Health scare of the week

The danger posed by sun beds has significantly increased over the last decade, says The Guardian. A survey has shown that, in response to a public demand for a faster tan, an increasing number of salons are using extra-strong lamps that emit between two and three times as much harmful UV light as the equivalent models ten years ago. In Scotland, 83% of the sun beds surveyed had UV outputs that exceeded the limit laid down in the British and European standard. In addition, the introduction of coin-operated machines has increased the likelihood of abuse: it has led to people using them for longer, and less control over the age of users. Previous studies have indicated that people who begin using sun beds in their teens and twenties are 75% more likely to develop malignant melanomas, the deadliest form of skin cancer, than those who begin using them later in life.

The Week, 10 February 2007

- -

Sample critique

The lexis here belongs to the formal end of the common register: words like *posed, significantly, equivalent* and *exceeded* all have a certain weight and seriousness while being sufficiently part of everyday language to be easily understood by the average reader. *Emit*, rather than the less formal *give off*, trembles on the brink of being technical, and specialist terms like *UV light* and *malignant melanomas* are used to give precision to the piece, but on the whole, the lexis is just what you would expect when averagely educated writers write for averagely educated readers.

Sentence structure matches lexis in this extract, taking the form for the most part of straightforward statements, as in sentences 1, 3 and 4, and when dependent clauses and phrases are used, they follow logically from the main clause without a break, as in sentences 2 and 5.

There are no personal subjects here, as there might be in a more down-market publication than *The Week*. Compare *A survey has shown* with a formulation such as *Investigators from the Sun have discovered that...*

The colloquial register

Formality disappears as we move away from the common register into the informal, colloquial one. Polite modes of address such as *madam* and *sir* give way to more friendly and personal ones such as *mate*; words with a French or Latin flavour are junked in favour of one- or two-syllable English ones; sentences probably become shorter and more brusque. Compare *If I might have your attention, ladies and gentlemen* with *Listen up, you lot.*

Activity

Read the following letter to a newspaper and comment on what you think it reveals about language issues in Britain today:

Failing to find what I wanted in a menswear shop, I looked around for an assistant. A young man approached me. 'Aw wi, mai?' he enquired. Appalled, I made an excuse and left.

The ultra-colloquial register: Slang

The colloquial register slides almost imperceptibly into the register of slang, so that it may seem difficult to arrive at a clear definition of either: *mate* may become *sunshine*, for example, as a term of address; *chap* or *bloke* may morph into *guy* or *man* or *dude* (used to address women as well as men), but where do we put a word like *chav*? Does it belong to the colloquial register, or is it slang? It's a matter of perception to some degree, as with most questions of language use: *bird*, for instance, may be slang to one person, a colloquialism to another. Look more closely, however, and you will see that good slang has something that the 'blokiness' register doesn't have: originality.

Slang is characterized by the use of newly coined words, such as *dumbing down, nerd, geek, yo*; or newly coined meanings for existing words, such as *man, my man, cool, wicked, sick* (both these last being 'cool' replacements for boring old *good*), *whatever floats your boat*, etc.

Two of the most important new arrivals on the scene are simply new takes on some of the most basic words in the English language: *Whatever* and *Yeah, right*. These are simple, but devastating when uttered in the bored tone perfected by certain teenagers, and so much better than the old-fashioned *Who do you think you're kidding?*

Jeremy Clarkson (that middle-aged teen) envies his children's access to expressions like these when he at their age had only *groovy*. He thinks that 'the word "whatever" as in "I heard what you just said and I can't be bothered to even think of a response" is one of the greatest additions to the English language.' *Yeah, right* works in much the same way, conveying an enormous degree of cynical disgust and disbelief in two little words. Coinages like these spread like bush fires through the media and turn up all over the world in a matter of days.

Activity

The phrase *I'm like* in place of *I said* is enormously popular at the moment. So is the emphatic use of the little adverb *so*, as in, 'I'm *so* not looking forward to the party'. What do you think they contribute to the range of English expression?

The ultra-formal registers

As they move upmarket from the common pool of Standard English, registers become more specialized and adopt increasingly large numbers of words drawn from Latin and Greek.

The lexis of the first of these registers, often referred to as *officialese*, or even more pejoratively, *jargon*, is the one that is most disliked and the hardest to justify.

Officialese – the kind of language in which officials of one kind or another talk to us – contains some elements of ordinary vocabulary but is notorious for its use of abstract, impersonal words that are difficult to pin down. When social workers write phrases such as *the structural transformation of multi-agency support systems and services*, for instance, they presumably have some idea of what they mean, but the general public doesn't, and becomes cross. Witness this letter to the *Times*:

> Sir,
>
> Which of the two following signs do you think would mean most to the average motorist: 'Bird Flu Control Zone' or 'Avian Influenza Surveillance Zone'? And which do you think the bureaucrats have chosen to erect on the roads of Suffolk? Well done, Sir Humphrey.
>
> The *Times*, 6 February 2007

Activity

1 Extract the main points from the pieces of writing below.
2 Write a paragraph summarizing the writers' criticisms of this use of language:
   i in the common register
   ii using more colloquial language.
   Adjust the sentence structure of each paragraph to suit the lexis.
3 Comment on the writer's use of the word *fags* in A; the writer's use of *ripped off* in B; the writer's use of *internal lines of communication* in C.

> A Of all the things that keep you sleepless in this restive world, good money says that the 'conditionalities' in Iraq are not among them. And yet that is precisely how Des Browne, the Defence Secretary, referred to the problems of the region last week.
>
> Meanwhile, on Sky News, a pundit was speaking in 'generalistic' terms, while back at the BBC a motive had turned into a 'motivation', the tax on a packet of fags became a 'taxation' and a perfectly coherent formula was transformed into a 'formulation'.
>
> Carol Sarler, The *Times*, 15 January 2007

B Do you know an A-pillar from an isofix; a hybrid from tiptronic transmission? If not it could prove to be expensive the next time you take your car to the garage for repairs or servicing.

Mechanics are increasingly using arcane terminology that baffles their customers and makes them suspect that they are being ripped off, according to a survey by Direct Line insurance.

Ben Webster, The *Times*, 3 February 2007

C In his annual review, the chief economist of the Chartered Institute of Personnel and Development suggests that if Human Resources departments need to open up internal lines of communication and aim to kill off incomprehensible management-speak so as to get managers and employees talking sensibly together, HR could start by rebranding as 'people managers'.

'People are people. They are not human resources and are not simply personnel. They have skills and capabilities but they also have needs and emotions that need to be looked after,' he said.

Mr Philpott said the spread of jargon was hindering the ability of British managers to communicate initiatives and improve the productivity of their staff. It was also undermining trust. 'If employees don't know what you're saying to them they often interpret it as not in their interests.' He pointed to the widespread use of 'modernization' in the pubic sector by managers trying to reform working practices. It could convey 'something good', he said. 'But because of the way it is conveyed in terms of management reform-speak, it sounds like a threat.'

D Some newer financial advisers pitch their appeal to well-heeled women. Bramdiva, the wealth management company launched by Nicola Horlick, the fund manager, uses its female-friendly approach as its central selling proposition. 'A lot of women are sick of going to people who patronize them or shower them with jargon,' she says.

The technical register

The characteristic lexis of this register also tends to be abstract and personal, but because the words used describe concrete objects and techniques, their meaning can be more easily understood by laymen (people without any expert knowledge of a subject). Consider, for example:

A micro-chip is located in the head of the key which automatically deactivates the immobiliser when the key is inserted in the ignition lock.

When the topic is more complex, however, so of course is the terminology, which then needs in-depth explanation for non-experts to understand. You would need to be very well up in photography, for instance, to cope with statements like this:

The use of extension rings and bellows generally demands extra exposure time, which must be increased according to the inverse square law – for example, a triple extension will need nine times the normal exposure.

> **Note**
>
> The common register often adopts specialist terms from the technical and other registers, while still remaining the common register. A motoring journalist, for example, may use a number of technical terms to demonstrate his or her knowledge while writing predominately in the common register:
>
> This brings big power for sure but not without big problems, too: throttle response becomes slack, engine noise is dulled and steering feel and handling prowess have to be compromised simply to safely direct so much power or, more specifically, torque through the steered wheels.

The learned registers

The varieties of language at the furthest remove from the **common register** – e.g. those of **science** and the **law, philosophy** and **medicine** – are used by people who have had long years of study in their professions. All are full of **specialist terms** derived from Latin and Greek elements, e.g.

* *genotype* – the genetic constitution of an individual (from Greek *genos*)
* *tort* – a breach of duty leading to liability for damages (from Latin *tortum*)
* *hypothesis* – a suggested explanation of a group of facts (from Greek *hypotithenai*)
* *dyspepsia – indigestion* (from Greek *dys* = diseased, faulty and *pepsis* = stomach).

You may ask why subjects already as heavy as these should be saddled with the extra difficulty of Latin and Greek terminology. The answer is that it isn't really a matter of choice. The lexis of science and the law must be exact and fixed, so that its users anywhere in the world, at any time, can be sure of what it means. Because Latin and Ancient Greek are 'dead' – i.e. no longer spoken anywhere as living languages – they cannot change their meanings as words in English do, and so are ideal for the purpose.

Choosing the appropriate register

Nobody actually tells us which register to use in which contexts; we pick it up as we go along by listening to other people and noticing their reactions. We learn as children not to use rude words like *poo* in front of adults; as adolescents, not to ask teachers *What's going down, man?*; as adults, not to call employers by their first name without being asked. We learn, in other words, to conform: to adapt the way we speak or write to suit the person we're addressing and the situation we're in.

> **Activity**
>
> 1 Discuss the use of the following registers, taken from Professor Randolph Quirk's textbook, *The Use of English*.
>
> Bye bye, your Holiness. See you!
> Hi, John; I'm just phoning to say your sister has croaked.
> Professor Crowell, I think I understand your first two points, but could you explain that last fucker?

(continued)

2 You've just broken up with your closest friend/had a terrific argument with someone in your group.

  a Explain what happened to the following people:

  - your friends
  - your parents
  - a tutor.

  b Discuss any differences you notice in your use of language in the three accounts.

3 Explore the range of the informal register by:

  a listening carefully

  b taking notes of the way you find yourself speaking in the following contexts:

  - at home with your family (Do you have any special words that outsiders would not understand? Do you always speak in complete sentences?)
  - attempting to wheedle something out of your reluctant mother or father
  - talking to friends of your own sex
  - talking to friends of the opposite sex
  - taking part in sport or a game of some kind.

4 **a** Now explore the formal register by working with another student or students in the following simulated situations:

  - an interview with your head teacher or pastoral tutor
  - a committee meeting
  - an interview with a prospective employer.

  b Discuss any noteworthy differences you have discovered between the formal and informal registers.

5 Write a letter of application for a job or a university place. Discuss the lexis, sentence structure, and grammar used in your letter.

The electronic registers

The new kids on the block – **e-mails** and **text messaging** – belong to the informal range of registers. They have more in common with unstructured spoken English than with the formal written mode, partly because nobody is sure yet what conventions to use in e-mails. The old *Dear Sir, Yours faithfully*, etc. of business letters, for instance, looks odd in the electronic setting, but as yet there is no consensus as to what should replace them. Informal e-mails certainly aim at a conversational style, trying to convey an impression of feeling through the use of *emoticons* – groups of characters that are meant to look like a face turned on its side, e.g.:

:-) or :)   'smiley faces', indicating that the writer is amused, or trying to amuse, or being ironical and making fun of what he or she is saying

:-(or :('unsmiley faces', indicating regret, disappointment, disapproval, unhappiness

;-)   a winking smiley face, indicating 'don't take this seriously'

;->   a mischievous smiley face, indicating that the writer is up to something.

With such appealing little ways of getting close up and personal, no wonder people spend far more time than they should on opening their e-mails, even when they should be at work. E-mails are becoming a serious addiction.

The ways in which electronic methods of communication are changing the language are discussed in Chapter 4, Language and Technology.

1 Text Varieties

Guidelines for the analysis and evaluation of prose

A **discourse** is the expression of a person's ideas, attitudes or feelings. For the purpose of English language studies, every discourse, spoken or written, is a **text**. Novels, films, plays, poems, advertisements, conversations – all are texts for you to examine from the following points of view:

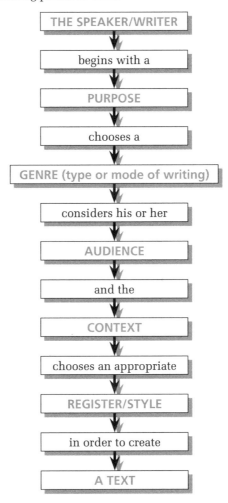

THE SPEAKER/WRITER

begins with a

PURPOSE

chooses a

GENRE (type or mode of writing)

considers his or her

AUDIENCE

and the

CONTEXT

chooses an appropriate

REGISTER/STYLE

in order to create

A TEXT

Purpose

Most people who speak or write for a public audience are driven by a purpose. They feel a need to do one or more of the following:

- advise or instruct their audience (readers or listeners), so produce **instructive** or **informative** texts
- persuade others to share their particular philosophy of life – social, political, sexual or religious – and so produce **persuasive** texts
- entertain their audience, so set out to write texts that will **entertain** and/or amuse.

Writers of texts may be motivated by just one purpose, in which case their style will tend to be homogeneous (all of a piece), or by several, in which case these will be flagged up by variations of tone and style. There is usually one main, over-arching purpose, however, and the overall style will generally reveal what it is.

Instructive texts

When writers set out simply and purely to instruct, the writing will have the characteristics illustrated in Example A below.

Example A

Q: How do I connect my Wi-Fi enabled laptop to my home broadband?

A: First, ensure that your router supports Wi-Fi. Not all do, so you may have to upgrade. Look for one that supports the standard known as G, rather than newer Draft-N models, which are more expensive… Configure your connection to the router with the Windows wireless network set-up wizard (see tinyurl.com/5ulf3). It's crucial to secure your connection – see InGear tips at tinyurl.com/2fufm8.

Nigel Power, *Sunday Times,* 20 May 2007

- -

This text has the following features that are typical of instructive texts:

- there is a formal manner and impersonal tone, but use of personal pronouns *I* and *you* create a sense of relationship between writer and reader
- instructions are given in chronological order
- the lexis is necessarily technical because related to the IT field, and may be repetitive because focused on the same subject throughout
- the mood is imperative as opposed to indicative (see page 23), because an expert is telling someone what to do
- verbs are dynamic (concerned with action) and take the form of directives: *ensure, look for, configure, see.*

Instructive texts that are longer than this will usually be laid out with bullet points or numbered paragraphs to make each step in the process clear – this is vital when cooking from a recipe or assembling a piece of flat-pack furniture, for example.

When the writer wants to entertain as well as instruct, the mood is more relaxed:

Example B

Always try a bike before you buy. Preferably try several. If the dealer cavils when you ask to take one for a spin before committing yourself, take your money elsewhere…

A racing bike? Novices will find the bum-in-the-air riding position makes it hard to look around for traffic. And skinny tyres and potholes don't mix. Mudguards and a rack are practical but will negate the advantage of having spent a month's wages to be able to boast that you have the most anorexic two-wheeler in town.

Ben Laurance, *Sunday Times*, 20 May 2007

- -

The mood is still imperative, the verbs dynamic, but the tone achieved by the use of the second-person pronoun *you* is friendly and the use of colloquialisms such as *skinny* and *bum-in-the-air* makes the discourse seem closer to speech than to technical writing (particularly since the lexis contains no purely technical terms at all). The writer's use of humour (the description of a lightweight bicycle as *anorexic*) also adds to the informal style, since humour is avoided as an irrelevant distraction in purely instructive texts.

Activity

1 Use the following headings to write a short magazine article about renewing a passport. Write in the style of either A or B above. You may need to research the relevant details.
   - When do I have to renew my passport?
   - What is the best way to renew?
   - What if I've only got a few weeks before I fly?
   - Will I have to be interviewed when I renew?
   - Does the interview apply to children as well?
   - What are the rules for passport photographs?
   - What do I do if a passport is lost or stolen?

2 Comment on your use of lexis and grammar to create the appropriate tone and relationship with your audience.

Persuasive texts

Writers vary in the methods they use to persuade audiences to agree with them. Some, like the author of A below, write in a personal tone and a manner close to speech. They use inclusive pronouns like *me, us* and *we* to build a relationship of intimacy and trust with the audience, and their writers wear their hearts on their sleeves by using emotive words and phrases that both express their feelings and play on ours.

Example A

Most of the letters I receive here at the Daily Mirror on gender selection of babies are from parents who desperately want a boy.

If this test were available, lots of girls would be aborted and that would be bad for all of us, believe me.

Nature is clever enough to make sure there are 100 girls for every 103 boys. And that's the way it has been for millions of years.

If that delicate balance is disturbed we would have a society dominated by war-like males and their influence would go undiluted by peace-loving females.

By and large, wars aren't started by women, they're started by power-hungry men.

In societies where men really outnumber women there's more crime, more violence, more fighting, more killing and more murders.

This week we had an example of that effect when Peter Medlicott shot a policeman – enraged because he jumped to the assumption that his girlfriend was cheating on him with their lodger.

Road rage is another good example of what can happen when anger and fury take hold of a person. Brain research has shown that when a man is consumed by anger his instinct to inflict serious harm on his victim bypasses the cerebral cortex – the part of the brain which can reason, calm, and inhibit basic instincts.

In this situation a man reverts to his primitive brain – also called the reptilian brain because it persists in reptiles and, way back, formed the basis of our own brains – which doesn't think, it just lashes out. Think enraged alligator or shark.

Women, as a rule, don't possess these monstrous, overpowering, killer instincts that get out of hand in the heat of the moment.

We get angry, but we rarely kill. We prefer revenge. And that is a dish best eaten cold.

Dr Miriam Stoppard, *Daily Mirror*, 10 May 2007

- -

Others, like B below, rely on the power of rational argument: they write in an impersonal manner, keeping their readers at an emotional distance by largely using the third-person singular and plural – *girls, boys, families, women, the female child,* etc. – and keeping their tone of voice dispassionate by referring to statistics rather than expressing feeling.

Example B

Some critics claim that allowing sex selection implies that, in general, one sex is superior to the other – to do so is sexist… It devalues girls. However, it does not, any more than choosing to play Australian Rules football rather than soccer implies the former is 'better' in some general sense. Boys and girls are different, and this difference matters to different families in different ways.

Sex selection is more likely to harm women in Asia. There, sex selection is already common. The male-to-female ratio has risen to close to 1.2 in China and some urban parts of India. This situation has worsened since the advent of prenatal sex determination. It was estimated in 1990 that, globally, there are 100 million women 'missing' (died prematurely) as a result of various forms of discrimination. It has been claimed that sex selection would 'foster the already existing bias against the female child'.

Yet, even in Asia, it is not clear that sex selection should be banned. Disturbed sex ratios may not be a bad thing. Advantages which have been postulated include increase in influence of the rarer sex, reduced population growth and interbreeding of different populations. Most importantly, a false belief in the inferiority of women is not a product of sex selection – sex selection is the product of that belief. Education and improving social and employment arrangements for women are more important in correcting these false beliefs than preventing sex selection.

Julian Savulescu MB BS PhD, Director, Ethics Unit, Murdoch Institute, University of Melbourne. From an article published on the Internet by *The Medical Journal of Australia*

Activity

1 Write an argument in the style of A on page 15, in favour of keeping the voting age at 18.

2 Write an argument in the style of B above, in favour of reducing the voting age to 16.

Informative texts

Informative texts cover an enormously wide range of topics and styles. They also frequently overlap with other kinds when their writers set out to amuse or stimulate or give a little gentle instruction in topics their audience knows little about.

When writers want to impart information purely for its own sake, they keep themselves and their opinions in the background, and use ordinarily polite and conventional lexis and formal sentence structure. They don't attempt to build an intimate relationship with their audience but focus directly on their subject instead, as Katharine Hibbert does in the book review below.

Before I Die is the story of Tessa, a 16-year-old with leukaemia who has a to-do list to complete before she dies. Number one is losing her virginity. The rest of the list is no less controversial.

As a first novel by an unknown author, *Before I Die* is also remarkable for the stir it has created among publishers and the speed with which it arrives in bookshops. [Jenny] Downham wrote the final full stop in February; the book will be on sale next month…

Having to improvise plays for reluctant audiences is what Downham credits with teaching her to create characters and tell stories. It also revealed teenagers' interests. 'Whenever we turned up at a youth club, we'd ask: "What do you want to see a show about?" They'd always say sex, then they'd say drugs, so we'd have to find a way of doing that.'

Downham's realistic, honest treatment of such tricky topics sets her novel apart from teen magazines' glamorous but often censorious and patronising approach.

Katharine Hibbert, *Sunday Times*, 10 June 2007

In contrast, the review of the film *Ocean's 13* that follows mixes information with subjective opinion. The writer, Cosmo Landesman, sets out to persuade us that the film is not worth watching, displays his own pretensions to cool by criticizing those demonstrated by the characters, and attempts to amuse and entertain us with his parody of slick American slang.

… watching Ocean's 13 is like watching a vain man preen in front of a mirror for about two hours. It's a film that thinks it's really stylish and hip. Hey, ladies, check out all that hunky Hollywood talent (Clooney, Pitt). Hey, guys, dig the Vegas glitz, Clooney suits and Brad's smile – he's the only man who can wink with his lips.

But it's all as fake as the smile of a Vegas hooker. Ocean's 13 celebrates a kind of cool that only the moronic readers of lowbrow men's mags would think was attractive.

Cosmo Landesman, *Sunday Times,* 10 June 2007

- -

Some writers present their information blended with a large dose of persuasion. They use the same kind of emotive appeals as advertisers, disguising them with a gloss of fine words. Advertising a house in London SW19 for sale at £1,349,500, one estate agent describes it like this:

A Most Imposing Residence

This wonderfully spacious detached residence is perfectly located for Wimbledon Park. Its double reception rooms and substantial garden make it a stunning home for entertaining and to provide a superior family lifestyle.

- -

The language being used here might be described as **pragmatic**. On the surface, it appears to be simply factual: words like *imposing* might be taken to refer to the large scale of the property. Put it together with *wonderfully spacious, a stunning home for entertaining*, and, most revealing of all, *a superior family lifestyle*, however, and it becomes clear that the real message of the text, never openly stated but clearly implied, is that this is just the kind of house that people who wish to impress other people ought to buy. The underlying appeal, in other words, is to snobbery.

Look at estate agents' details on expensive houses and you will find that low-key descriptions are thin on the ground. Those on offer are *fantastic, stunning, gorgeous, fabulous, stylish, luxurious, sought-after, enviable, outstanding, splendid, unique, sumptuous, superb, truly striking* and *ideally located.* Hyperbole (exaggerated language) is often the signal of a hard sell.

Some apparently informative texts manage to use quite a number of words without saying anything much at all, and these are very hard to separate from writing whose main purpose is just to entertain.

Cancer: Jun 21–Jul 22

Nobody would argue that the changes streaming through almost every area of your life aren't just exciting, but constitute an improvement. Your instincts say that, too. Still, you'd prefer to have a few hard facts. But they're in short supply and become even more so from Friday until early July while the communication planet, Mercury, is retrograde in Cancer. You'll be contending with the same mix-ups as others, but many will highlight personal issues that you've been ignoring or were unaware of. Unappealing as dealing with yet more questions may be, the resulting insights will form the foundation for the wonderful ways in which your life will ultimately be rearranged.

Shelley von Strunckel

- -

There is only one objectively true statement in this horoscope: *hard facts [are] in short supply.* The rest of the text uses language pragmatically, appealing to readers' hunger to know what the future has in store for them, and relying on their willingness to bend what is happening in their lives to suit what is being determined by the stars. Things as simple and everyday as buying new shoes or having an unexpected invitation can easily be tweaked into becoming part of the *changes streaming through… your life.* Note the use of dynamic verbs like *streaming* to emphasize the suggestion of excitement, and the use of apparently specialized knowledge in the pseudo-technical statement *the communication planet, Mercury, is retrograde in Cancer.* The writer excuses herself from giving any real information about the future by claiming that future events depend on personal issues that the reader is either *unaware of* or is deliberately *ignoring.*

Entertainment texts

The field here is extremely broad. Any writer can set out to entertain simply by writing amusingly about his or her pet likes or dislikes. Jeremy Clarkson is a popular example of this with his newspaper columns and articles on cars and everything else under the sun.

The key to this kind of writing seems to be either to discuss quite serious topics in a totally unserious way, or to discuss some minor difficulty or problem that irritates most ordinary human beings on a daily basis – opening magazines or shirts wrapped in cellophane, for example – and blowing it up into monstrous proportions.

Expect to find some or all of the following features.

- **Tone:** a pleasantly friendly manner with use of personal pronouns to create a sense of relationship.

- **Structure:** a lengthy, rather rambling introduction which may have apparently little to do with the main topic.
- **Lexis:** the use of hyperbole; a mix of informal and conventional language, with perhaps some trendy slang or modern clichés like *any time soon*; some over-the-top metaphors, similes and/or analogies; some puns or other types of word-play.
- **Grammar:** a mix of sentence structures ranging from lengthy (full of piled-up phrases or strings of adjectives) to grammatically incomplete ('minor') sentences.

A Given the choice of trying on a pair of trousers in a shop, or being beaten to death by an African tribe that wants to eat my genitals, I would take the tribe.

The first pair you try never fit. Not even close. You wheeze and you pant and you suck your stomach in until bits of it are pushing against your cerebral cortex and your eyes are 5in in front of your face, but it's no good. So, in a space the size of Alec Guinness's box, you take them off again, put your own strides back on and paddle across the shop in stockinged feet to get a bigger pair. Which aren't in stock. So you go bigger still and end up with something that has a waistline broadly similar in circumference to the rings of Saturn...

Get this straight, ladies. This. Is. Not. Fun. Any man who tells you he enjoys trying on clothes – and you can trust me on this – is not the sort of man who finds you sexually attractive. Even if you are Uma Thurman.

Jeremy Clarkson, *Sunday Times*, 10 June 2007

B When you pass someone smoking in the street, or meet someone who has just had a cigarette, you recoil at the smell of their clothes and their breath... it feels quite offensive: an unwelcome whiff from some grim past.

And that, dear smokers, is the great alienation that you face. In the reborn, smoke-free England, prepare to become perceived as a relic. You've been left behind. Worse than that, you must be prepared to be regarded as, well... ever so slightly down-market.

As you stand outside your pub or your club or your restaurant, or even your friend's dinner party, you will find you have become part of a sad, excluded, sheepish army of no-hopers, the huddled masses who loiter, sucking deeply on their drug of choice.

I'm not being judgmental, you understand; I'm reporting accurately the extraordinary pariah-like situation of those who continue to smoke in Scotland. When it comes to branding yourself as indelibly working-class, smoking has become as bad as being obese. One smoking friend of mine, a lawyer, says she's going to start wearing a shell suit so she doesn't stand out from the crowd.

And it's not just the company that smokers are forced to keep, it's the surroundings. Away from the high streets, where chairs and tables outside have helped create a (long overdue) mood of café culture, Scotland has sprouted a forest of shabby plastic awnings, scuffed beer gardens with patio heaters, and Perspex shelters that look like bus stops. Littered with fag butts, these are not the places for the fashionable to be seen...

So will snobbery be the unexpected weapon of the antismoking lobby in England? I expect it will. The organisation Ash hopes that four million people... will stop because of the ban. When smokers find they must enter the kingdom of chavdom, expect that figure to rise.

Melanie Reid, *The Times*, 11 June 2007

Spoken texts

Texts in the speech mode draw more on what might be called the poetic side of language: they use such devices as intonation, pitch, volume and rhythm to work on their listeners' emotions and reinforce the meaning of the words themselves. If we were to read the following aloud to a person with little or no knowledge of English, for example, it's likely that he or she would feel its emotional pull:

> Who bends not his ear to any bell which upon any occasion rings? But who can remove it from that bell which is passing a piece of himself out of this world? No man is an island, entire of itself; every man is a piece of the continent, a part of the main. If a clod be washed away by the sea, Europe is the less, as well as if a promontory were, as well as if a manor of thy friend's or of thine own were: any man's death diminishes me, because I am involved in mankind, and therefore never send to know for whom the bell tolls; it tolls for thee.
>
> John Donne, *Devotions Upon Emergent Occasions*, 1624

Speakers have various rhetorical devices they can deploy when they want to impress or move us. They use, for example:

- the subjunctive mood: *Let this be clear to all* (instead of 'I want this to be clear'); *Where there is discord, may I bring harmony* (instead of 'I hope I will be able to bring harmony'; there is a yearning quality to the subjunctive that helps to persuade an audience that the speaker is sincere and working towards a finer, better world

- striking images and symbols with universal meaning: *the **light** of goodness; the **torch** of freedom*

- patterning of sound through assonance and/or alliteration: *Learn our language; brave any danger*

- parallel phrasing: *We shall pay any price, bear any burden, meet any hardship*

- antithesis: *We shall support any friend, oppose any foe*

- parallel phrasing with antithesis: *Ask not what your country can do for you – ask what you can do for your country*

- inclusive pronouns: ***We** happy few, **we** band of brothers; **My** fellow citizens; **You** can do it if **you** B & Q it*

- triads (speaking in 'threes'): *We shall restore pride in the NHS, we shall improve education, we shall create jobs for all; My priority is Education, Education, Education.*

In passages of ordinary conversation, the key terms to note are **dialect**, **sociolect**, and **idiolect**. These can be defined as follows.

- **Dialect:** a regional or social variety of a language differing in pronunciation, grammar, or vocabulary from the standard written language of the country in which it exists. Estuary English, for example, began as a regional dialect (that of people living near the Thames in Essex and north Kent), but has developed into a much wider social dialect through the influence of media stars like Jonathan Ross and high-profile footballers like David Beckham.

- **Sociolect:** the term used to describe a dialect spoken by a particular social class; most educated, conservatively minded, middle-class people speak either a pure or a slightly modified version of Standard English, for instance. Those who want to be thought to have 'street-cred' alternate between this and Estuary English according to the company they're in – listen to recordings of Tony Blair speaking off the cuff to hear this in action.

- **Idiolect:** the term used to describe the speech patterns peculiar to individual speakers of any dialect. You may think your idiolect differs a lot from that of your parents because you use terms like *cool, stuff like that, I was like* and so on, but if everyone in your peer group is using them too, is it really an idiolect or a dialect common to the teen group?

If you are asked to discuss a passage of spoken English (an **illocutionary discourse**), be aware that you may be reading either the speaker's own words, or words that he or she is **represented** as saying (i.e. a writer has put them into someone else's mouth).

For example, in the review of *Ocean's 13* on page 17, the writer makes fun of the (in his eyes) crudely commercial appeal of the film by parodying its producers' attitudes in their own American idiom:

> It's a film that thinks it's really stylish and hip. Hey, ladies, check out all that hunky Hollywood talent (Clooney, Pitt). Hey, guys, dig the Vegas glitz, Clooney suits and Brad's smile – he's the only man who can wink with his lips.

Admittedly, his meaning would be clearer if he had flagged it up by using quotation marks to show where the quoted words begin and end ('*Hey, ladies... wink with his lips*'), but he is writing for the *Sunday Times* and can be reasonably sure that his readers will catch on.

Other things to look out for in a speech discourse are:

- **lexis:** formal or informal
- **grammar:** minor/incomplete sentence structures, e.g. *Could do. Not sure. See you*; deviations from standard forms, e.g. *I already <u>done</u> it. Give us <u>them</u> books*; use of fillers, e.g. *We did some Jane Austen and <u>stuff</u>. <u>Like</u> I hate reading*; non-fluency indicators, e.g. *er, um*; use of inclusive pronouns and phrases, e.g. *you, we, people like us, all of us*
- **stylistic features:** hyperbole, analogies, metaphors and similes, symbolism.

Genre

A **genre** is the term used to describe a **category** to which a given text may be said to belong. Examples of genres include fairy stories and nursery rhymes; the novel, drama, poetry, dramatic monologue, literary criticism, biography, autobiography; newspaper editorials and articles; advertisements and product literature; cartoons and comic strips; soap opera and other scripts; publicity leaflets and fliers; charity appeals; transcriptions of speech.

To qualify for inclusion in a particular genre, a text must have some readily distinguishable features that clearly mark it off from texts in other genres. Another characteristic of a genre is its traditional quality – it will be found to have existed over a considerable period of time. Ask even a toddler how a fairy story begins and you will hear 'Once upon a time'.

Audience

The writing of any text is shaped by the writer's awareness of the audience targeted: what he or she estimates to be its level of knowledge, intelligence, and interest. If the target audience is made up of the writer's peers, the lexis and style can be specialized and/or technical. If the audience is wide and drawn from a random sample of the general public, the writer will tailor lexis and style to a slightly lower level, cutting out esoteric or highly specialized terminology. If addressing a less well educated or younger audience, lexis will be kept simple and concrete, and sentence structure uncomplicated and short.

Context

Context can be defined as the situation created by a writer's purpose and the nature of the audience being addressed. It is context that determines the meaning of whatever is being said. If an architect describes a building as *imposing*, for example, this will mean something like *impressive in physical scale and appearance*. Used by an estate agent, its meaning changes to something like *Will impress the hell out of your friends and acquaintances*. The form of the word does not change; the meaning does. When we look at the way in which context alters meaning, we are said to be working in the area of **pragmatics**.

In the same way, consider what the BBC usually calls 'very strong language'– obscene words, to you and me. As the radio critic Paul Donovan reveals, a recent play called *Black Watch* contained *152 f***s, 61 c***s, and a colourful array of other vulgarities, including 'shit' (enunciated as 'shite', since the speakers are Scots), 'fanny', 'poof', 'prick', 'shag', and so on.* Yet he found none of it offensive because of its military context: *The language emerges as the natural discourse of servicemen seeing their comrades die in the desert and knowing their famous regiment is dying back home…*

In other words, just as context is determined by **purpose** and **audience**, so context in its turn determines the **variety** of language and **style** to be used.

Language variety and style

Look again at the pieces by Dr Miriam Stoppard and Julian Savulescu on pages 15 and 16, and you will see how each writer has used lexis, grammar, and tone to suit the intended audience and context.

Stoppard's style is conversational (*believe me*), her tone warm and sincere; she uses the kind of simple, non-technical lexis she feels appropriate to readers of popular newspapers, and she avoids both the use of statistics and close logical argument – see the non-sequitur (argument that doesn't follow strictly logically) at line 12. She considers no opposing arguments or evidence, and simply expects her audience to agree with the one-sided account she gives.

Savulescu, on the other hand, writes in the remote, impersonal tone of the dispassionate expert presenting scientific fact. There is no attempt to build a relationship with his audience of fellow scientists because he can rely on their being interested in objective truth rather than in stories of 'human interest'.

How to categorize texts

1 Group according to **purpose**

- to instruct
- to persuade
- to inform
- to entertain

2 Group according to **audience**

- the general public
- fellow experts in a particular field of knowledge
- people interested in acquiring some of the speaker/writer's expertise
- wealthy people or people who might buy a product

3 Group according to **manner**

- formal or informal
- friendly and conversational in tone, or distant, reserved, remote

4 Group according to **genre**

- advertisements and product literature; publicity leaflets, cartoons and comic strips, etc.

5 Group according to **mode**

- spoken (i.e. transcript of speech discourse, phone call, conversation, lecture, play/soap opera script, etc.)
- electronic (e-mail or text message)
- written (encompassing newspaper articles, editorials, diary entries, fairy stories, etc.)
- multi-modal (containing two or more of transcribed speech acts, writing, graphics, electronic messaging, etc.)

6 Group according to **stylistic features**

Look at the choice of lexis. Is it simple, everyday; does it include colloquialisms or slang; is it formal, polite; technical, specialized; esoteric, learned; full of hyperbole? Look at the grammar. Check whether any of the aspects described in the following table are significant enough for you to mention.

Stylistic feature	Examples
sentence structure	Lengthy, complete, with several clauses and phrases; short, abrupt, incomplete (or 'minor') sentences
nouns	Highly abstract (e.g. *evidence, general opinion*); mainly concrete (e.g. *scientists, ordinary people*)
pronouns	Impersonal, third-person singular or plural, e.g. *it can be seen*; *they claim*; personal, inclusive, e.g. *I, you, we, our* etc.
adjectives	Many; sparse; highly coloured; low-key
adverbs	Used to intensify/emphasize, e.g. *madly jealous*, *bitterly angry*, *achingly poignant*, *quickly forgotten*
verbs	In the **indicative mood**, verbs are used to make statements and assertions, e.g. I *am*/he *is*/they *are* ready; Brown *will announce it* tomorrow. In the **imperative mood**, verbs are used to give commands, e.g. *Behave!, Shut up!*, etc. The indicative and imperative moods deal in certainty. They state what is, was, or will be, or what the speaker wants someone to do. Verbs in the **subjunctive mood**, in contrast, have nothing certain about them; they are used to express only what the speaker *wishes* or *hopes* may happen in the future, not what definitely will, e.g. *May we learn* from our *mistakes*. The **subjunctive** can also be used to exhort or encourage people to do what a speaker wants them to do, instead of ordering them, e.g. *Let us work together to make this country great again*

(continued)

modal verbs	These are used: <ul><li>**to express intention:** *Will* indicates intention for yourself, *shall* indicates your intention for other people, e.g. *I will smoke, whatever you say; You shall go to the ball, Cinders, in spite of your wicked stepmother*</li><li>**to point out necessity:** *You must learn to spell 'accommodation'*</li><li>**to warn of obligation:** *You ought to/should pay off your credit card*</li><li>**to ask for permission:** *May I/Can I borrow some money?*</li><li>**to suggest possibility:** *I can stop smoking if I want to; I may go to Glastonbury again this year*</li></ul>
prosodic features	Use of rhythm, intonation (remember the voice rises towards a comma and falls towards a full-stop); pitch (indicated perhaps by vertical arrows in a transcript); stress; use of patterned sound, alliteration, assonance
rhetorical features	Irony; repetition; parallel phrasing; antithesis; triads; imagery and symbolism

7 Group according to **graphology**

Is the text printed, or handwritten to make it more personal and 'real'? Is the handwriting simple or sophisticated? Is the typography (the size, style and colour of the print) appropriate for the purpose of the text? Does the overall layout make an effective impact?

8 Group according to **representation**

Texts can also be categorized by their use of what might be termed **representation** – the technique of revealing things about a character through the words given to him or her to speak.

- **Lexis**, for instance, can be used to indicate social class, merely through the connotations of the words being used. Middle- and upper-class people might be made to call their children 'darling' and might address a ticket-collector, say, as 'my good man'
- **Deviant grammar** may be used to represent a particular way of speaking
- **Deviant spellings** may represent a departure from received pronunciation: *Wot abahrt them suitcases, then?*
- **Pseudo-phonetic spellings** can also be used to indicate a character's regional origins: *Ee ba goom* suggests a Yorkshire upbringing; *I ken verra weel whit tae dae* suggests a Scottish one. Such spellings can also be used to represent emotions like excitement (*YEEAH!*), longing (*Pleeeeease!*), or disgust (*YUUUK!*).

Overview

Your task is to discuss how well overall the features mentioned above help the writer to succeed in what he or she set out to do.

Activity

Study the texts A–E on the following pages. These texts illustrate different varieties of language use.

Discuss various ways in which these texts can be grouped, giving reasons for your choice.

It's so uncool not to be in the brand band

by Jenny McCartney

Everywhere one looks, corporate brands are intent upon turning themselves into people, and people are busily transforming themselves into brands. Chains such as Pret a Manger and Starbucks spend vast amounts of money on appearing relaxed and approachable, flaunting their frayed blue jeans even as their beady little corporate eyes are checking out the annual profits. Pret's website informs any customer with a problem 'Our MD Clive Schlee hasn't got much to do: hassle him!' At one stage, indeed, Pret was so eager to be matey that it even forced its own sandwiches to chat directly to the public: signs beneath fillings that were about to be discontinued would read: 'I'm leaving! It's not because I've been bad… just to make way for something new,' a surreal little message that always left me with the impression that somewhere, a big tub of Brie and Cranberry filling was quietly weeping its creamy heart out.

Starbucks, on the other hand, is like one of those hustling hippies on university campuses, always trying to flog you an extra 'experience', such as a mellow jazz CD or outsize company mug. Yet chain stores are, by necessity, too big and innately obsessive to be cutting-edge: they can do no more than dab on a hint of zeitgeist. That is why brand consultancies are constantly sniffing after the elusive essence of 'cool', yearning for a fresh dash to invigorate their brands. For brands cannot stay still: they must keep subtly evolving or face consumer rejection. The profits of Marks and Spencer, for example, have recently been boosted considerably by a sly tweaking of its brand to take in a fondness for luxury and green concerns. If M&S were a person it would now be an awfully nice, reliable eco-worrier with a penchant for cashmere pashminas and double-chocolate tiramisu.

This text is a conversation between three women in a hairdressing salon. They are discussing possible names for the baby the stylist will be having in two months' time.

Key:

(.) indicates a brief pause

Numbers within brackets indicate length of pause in seconds

Words between vertical lines are spoken simultaneously

Stylist (S)

Client (C)

Junior (J)

(continued)

C: you must be getting a bit tired now Sam (.) aren't|you|

S: |tired|(.) yeah (.) I am a bit

C: exciting though (3) I bet (.) wondering|what|

S: |oh yeah|(1) wondering what he'll be like when he comes out of here *[patting her tummy]* (.) get me some more foils will you please Yvonne

C: so you're still sure it's a boy

S: yeah I am (.) yes (2) I always have been right from the start (2) I don't know why

C: have you got a name yet (.) or are you still|trying to decide|

S: |still trying to| agree more like (3) when I find one I like Alan doesn't (.) and then he says one and I say no (1) can't have that (.) so we keep arguing|and getting|nowhere

C: |mind you| |(.) it is difficult (1) especially now there's so many new names to choose|from|

S: |oh|I|know

C: |some of which are hideous in my opinion

S: I like archie myself (1) I really fancy it (2) it's got a really nice feel about it for me

C: um

S: you don't like|archie then|

C: |it sounds a|bit old-fashioned to me (.)|that's all|

S: |better than|all these jasons and darrens these days though (1) names for kids who're always in trouble (4) what do you think Yvonne

J: I like justin (2) it's really classy I think

C: you know the other kids would call him arch though

S: really (2) I never thought of that (.) I wouldn't like that

C: well (.) you know what kids are like (1) they either shorten a name or make it longer and you can't make archie|longer (.) so|

S: |what would|you choose then

C: I don't think you can beat the old names myself (2) john or richard (2) or daniel

Giles Coren

Special Timex Indiglo. For you, good price

Hey, pssst! You want buy watch? I have very nice watch. Is famous Timex watch. Very cheap. Thousand dollar. You make me offer I give you good price. Is make lovely souvenir of Albania. You want try on? Is made by famous Timex company. Is have one careful owner. Actually is not very careful. Is invade Afghanistan, which anybody, example Soviet Union, will tell you is not very careful. Also is invade Iraq on spurious pretext, inflame worldwide Muslim hostility, bring world to brink of Armageddon. So is not very careful.

Also is not very careful because is lose watch from not having properly fastened during walkabout in my country, which is only country in world where is have popularity rating higher than three-legged camel…

And previous owner is lose not only watch. Is mislay also somewhere world confidence in America...

But is still very nice watch. Is have hours, minutes, seconds, everything. Is have also date. If it is seem sometimes previous owner does not know what day it is, is not fault of watch. Is made by famous Timex company, so is not saying is Thursday when in fact is Tuesday, or things like this. Although personally I am never hear of Timex. I am hear of Rolex. I am hear of Seiko. But I am never hear of Timex. Apparently is cheapo cheapo brand from 1970s…

Is no tracking device or security number attaching to watch. Only is small engraving, 'George W Bush President January 20, 2001', which is why is available cheap. Only five hundred dollar. If more popular president is engraving on back, such as Richard Nixon or Grover Cleveland, is make too expensive…

Hundred dollar. I give you good price. Fifty dollar. Ten dollar?

***Romeo and Juliet* Act II Scene 2**

Juliet: 'Tis but thy name that is my enemy:
Thou art thyself, though not a Montague.*
What's Montague? It is not hand nor foot
Nor arm nor face nor any other part
Belonging to a man. O, be some other name.
What's in a name? That which we call a rose
By any other word would smell as sweet;
So Romeo would, were he not Romeo call'd,
Retain that dear perfection which he owes
Without that title.

* You would still be yourself if you were not a Montague

(continued)

E

"A *lot* can happen in 20 minutes," said the white-coated bloke as he sipped his Theakstons. From his garb I thought him to be either doctor, or cricket umpire. Being in a pub by the village green I naturally assumed the latter. *"Rain ſtopped play then?"* I guessed from the damp ſplodges on his coat. "SIGHLIN DAHN! *Whiċh means I can grab a quick pint."* "So, what's with the twenty minutes?" "Well, Theakstons ċheċk their beer every twenty minutes, you know. Temperature, ABV, raw materials and so forth. I've seen whole teams scuttled out in that time." We supped, ruminatively. *"I reċkon you can taſte that twenty minutes in every sip."* I ventured. *"Oh yes,"* he replied. *"It's worth every second, a bit like the rain, whiċh I don't believe will ċlear for at leaſt another twenty minutes. And, if Theakstons teſt their beer every twenty minutes, ſhouldn't we do the same?"* The logic was indiſputable, and, deſpite the hint of sunſhine sneaking through the window, the umpire's decision was final.

PECULIERLY FINE COMPANY

2 Language and Gender

The first edition of this book (1993) pointed out that women received less public respect than men (even from other women), and were paid less for doing the same or equally important work. Since we absorb the attitudes and values of our society through the words we learn as we grow up, it further suggested that language might be partly responsible for this gender imbalance.

Obsolescent sexist terms

It's difficult to get excited these days about gender-marked terms. Some, like *spinster* and *old maid*, haven't been used for years, since many unmarried women live with their partners, and many others, apparently unattached, wouldn't exactly qualify as *maids* in the virginal sense of the word.

Certain words classed as semantically derogatory (i.e. demeaning to women) may also seem hardly worth making a fuss about. *Dinner ladies, cleaning ladies* and *lollypop ladies* may not in fact be derogatory terms at all, but well-meaning attempts to show respect by the people who use their services.

Activity

Our cleaning lady comes for two hours a week.

Our cleaning woman comes for two hours a week.

Discuss which term you would prefer to use.

Mistress is another term traditionally taken to be demeaning to women. Whereas its symmetrical opposite, *master*, radiates the control and power men have over others, *mistress* implies a weaker and therefore inferior position.

Activity

1 Look up all the definitions of the word 'mistress' given in the complete edition of the Oxford English Dictionary.

2 Discuss whether 'mistress' should be automatically assumed to be a term derogatory to women.

Madam, from an old-fashioned viewpoint, can also be seen as a derogatory word, since it, unlike its symmetrical opposite, *sir*, has unsavoury connotations. In an age when the sale of sex is taken for granted, in the Western world at any rate, its connotations today are as much of power and wealth as of sexual immorality.

There are, however, still uses of language that reflect unconscious gender bias in society, and some of these are worth discussing.

The male-as-hero syndrome

What makes the man the leader, the one who decides and gets things done, at home, and in the wider world? According to recent modern studies, the answer lies in the myths and archetypes human beings have created for themselves down the centuries. Western culture has given us heroes like Prometheus, Hercules, Ulysses – not real men, but symbols of heroic masculinity for real men to aspire towards. (Superman and the magical Harry Potter are apparently the best our somewhat unheroic age has been able to come up with.)

Heroic female archetypes, on the other hand, simply don't exist. Women are pictured as the passive sex, waiting to be rescued by heroic men. While Ulysses wandered the world for 10 years, for instance, Penelope sat at home weaving and hoping for his return. Some writers have suggested that the Ulysses myth provides the archetypal images for the battles, feats and triumphs in the career journey of the present-day male executive.

In place of Ulysses, Xena has been proposed as a female archetype of leadership. Although she is a fictional product of the modern entertainment industry, she is depicted as the leader of a band of women who act as heroically as men while remaining quintessentially female in every way (like Lara Croft, tomb raider). Xena has acquired a cult following in parts of the United States, and is an icon for certain groups of young women in Britain. We can't tell whether Xena and Lara will evolve into archetypes embedded as firmly in the unconscious mind as Ulysses and other male heroes. At the moment, for most people, Andromeda still sits chained to her rock for years waiting for Perseus to come to slay the dragon and set her free. In Disneyland, where little children get their first exposure to fairy-tales, Cinderella still waits for her hero, warbling 'Some day my Prince will come'.

Seen as physically weaker than men, inferior in social status and economic power, wanting always to facilitate rather than manage and control, women do not conform to the expectations set up by the paradigm of heroic masculinity.

If they try to deny their own nature and adopt stereotypical male speech patterns, they are condemned as unfeminine harpies, aggressive and rude. If they resolutely persist in their own speech style, they're condemned as weak and helpless – not the thrusting go-getter who will win the glittering prizes.

To be fair to men, they are caught in a bind themselves: studies show that their manner, tone, and speech is warmer and more mitigated in non-competitive contexts, but full-on aggressive when having to defend or assert their position in the social or work hierarchy. They can't afford to be kind and helpful, in other words, because that would be sissy.

The male-as-the-norm-syndrome

In any book which deals with human beings in general, the nouns commonly used are *man*, *men*, and *mankind*, and the pronoun that naturally follows is therefore *he*. Women constitute half of the human race but don't even get a mention.

Attitudes in England and America have moved on since 1993, and only die-hards like Sir Patrick Moore (who claims that women have ruined television programming) persist in using the old sexist terms.

'*Man*', as Miller and Swift explain in *The Handbook of Nonsexist Writing* (1988), 'once was a truly generic word referring to all humans, but has gradually narrowed in meaning to become a word that refers to adult male human beings... (The Old English word for adult male was *waepman* and for adult woman, *wifman*.)' It's interesting that American slang has returned to this original usage in utterances like 'Hi, Julia, how're ya doin', man?'

Methods of avoiding sexist language

1 Use *humanity*, *human beings*, or simply *people* as the subject noun instead of *man* or *mankind*, then follow up with the plural pronoun *they*.

2 Use the double-pronoun construction *he or she*; e.g. 'If a student worries too much, he or she won't be able to think clearly.'

3 Use a plural subject noun that you can follow with non-sexist *they*: e.g. 'As students get closer to exams, they become increasingly edgy.' Even a singular subject noun is often followed by *they*: 'If you love someone, set them free' (Sting). People who object that following a singular noun with a plural pronoun is bad grammar will have to accept that if it was good enough for G.B. Shaw and George Eliot, it's good enough for them.

Miller and Swift point out that *gender-neutral* language has gained support from most major textbook publishers, professional and academic groups, and newspapers, and that many prestigious scholarly journals refuse to print articles unless they use gender-neutral language.

Many male writers have recognized the consequences of leaving women out of the language used to describe the most important areas of human life:

> ... that our language employs the words man and mankind as terms for the whole human race demonstrates that male dominance, the idea of masculine superiority, is programmed, institutional, and rooted at the deepest level of our historical experience.
>
> Richard Gilman, *Life* magazine

And yet, in spite of all these changes, many women feel that the dice are still loaded very much against them and in favour of men.

Man-talk – woman-talk

We like to chat about the dresses we will wear tonight
We chew the fat about our tresses and the neighbours' fight
Inconsequential things, men don't really care to know
Become essential things that girls all find so apropos…

We all meow about the ups and downs of all our friends
The who, the how, the why, we dish the dirt, it never ends
The weaker sex, the speaker sex you mortal males behold…
(*Girl Talk* – pop song made famous by Tony Bennett in 1965)

Discourse features

Frequency

There has long been a myth that women speak for longer and much more often than men, but a survey published in *Science* in September 2007 showed that this is not true. Men and women use roughly the same number of words daily. According to a report in *Scientific American*, 'Men showed a slightly wider variability in words uttered, and boasted both the most economical speaker (roughly 500 words daily) and the most verbose yapping at a whopping 47,000 words a day. But in the end, the sexes came out just about even in the daily averages: women at 16,215 words and men at 15,669.'

In public forums, however, things are different. Men really are the 'speaker sex'. In classrooms, in mixed group conversations, and in business meetings of both sexes, men tend to speak more often and at greater length than women. Teachers have been instructed to watch out for this and keep the balance as much as possible.

Linguistic style

Research has shown that men tend to speak in a forceful, direct manner reinforced by strong eye-contact and a loud, assertive tone of voice. They make emphatic statements, refuse to be interrupted, cross-question other speakers in an aggressive manner and generally behave in a way that seeks to enhance their individual status by dominating others. They ignore the conversational rules of turn-taking, yet often criticize women for overlapping (beginning to speak before a man has finished) because they interpret this as hogging the next turn. Other features of men's speech have been noted:

> … they include instrumentality (telling people what to do to solve problems); conversational dominance (for example holding the floor in meetings, diverting the conversation or interrupting others while they are talking); expressing themselves in assertive, absolute ways; not being highly responsive to others on a relationship level of communication; and communicating abstractly rather than at a personal level.
>
> S.S. Case, in *Women in Management: Current Research Issues*, ed. Davidson and Burke

Case considers that most of the latter orientation comes from the public and impersonal contexts in which men operate, such as business and management.

Women's style tends to be more gentle, indirect, and inclusive. Instead of competing, women encourage people to work together, using inclusive pronouns like *we, us, let's, shall we?*; modal verbs like *could, might,* and *may*; modifiers such as *perhaps* and *maybe*; tags like *isn't it* and *you know*, and tentative phrasings such as *I think perhaps we should/Do you think it would be sensible to*, and so on. They also make use of 'umms' to encourage speakers by showing they are listening.

Their style is collaborative, in other words, while that of the men is individualistic, and combative.

The linguistic double-bind

Ambitious women who are eager to get to the top find themselves caught in what has been described as a *femininity/competence bind*. If they adopt the direct command-oriented speech pattern of male managers they are condemned as rude, aggressive, and butch; if they perform as effectively as their male competitors but persist in their own speech patterns they are condemned as ineffectual and weak. The glass ceiling remains unbroken.

Because the nurturing, inclusive pattern of women's speech is found primarily in the domestic setting, men find it out of place at work and in public:

> A point that goes unstated in… much conversation analysis literature is that the rules and rituals on which mixed-sex interaction is based are derived from male communicative style. Female style is treated as 'other', as incorrect and in need of control.
>
> M. Barrett and J. Davidson, *Gender and Communication at Work*

Women are characteristically silenced by male put-downs when they speak in their natural style, as the following examples from *Gender and Communication at Work* reveal:

... a female manager in banking who modalizes* and uses inclusive strategies begins a proposal with 'I think maybe we should consider...' and is challenged by a man saying: 'Do you know or don't you?'

Another woman commences her recommendation in an academic meeting with 'Perhaps it would be a good idea if we thought about doing...' and is interrupted by a man who says 'Can you get to the point? Is it possible for you to do that?'

Another man, misled by a woman's finishing a sentence for him (a gesture meant to indicate interest and agreement), snaps 'You can't read my mind, can you? So don't tell me what I'm going to say.'

* uses modal constructions, as described on page 32

Instead of recognizing the value of women's tentative approach – that it gives others room to respond and put forward opinions – men like those above see it as a sign of uncertainty, deference, and lack of authority. These men cannot give women credit for involving others and for facilitating communication because to them, it is an abnegation of power. If you're powerful, you tell other people what to do.

Women who are treated in this way report being silenced and feeling diminished and humiliated. Even further, they internalize these negative assessments of their performance, criticizing themselves and other women for 'breaking the rules', and condemning women who engage in overlapping speech with men as 'aggressive', 'dreadful', and 'rude'.

Gender and communication in the Middle East

It's interesting to learn that under Islamic guidance a different set of conversational rules operates for both men and women in certain countries of the Middle East. According to B.D. Metcalfe:

The characteristics of a devout Muslim's identity are relevant both in the public and private domains. Above all, there is an emphasis on humility, benevolence and in maintaining balance and equilibrium in life, and thus in human interaction... Assertiveness, directive questioning, hedging and interruption tactics are therefore not culturally part of the language repertoire that would be linked with effective communication behaviours, for either men or women. Combative dialogue is not valued as communication style. Interpersonal exchanges that emphasise respect and recognize the value of others' opinions and nurture cooperativeness are encouraged. Participants in business meetings... would respect the authority of the chair and interruptions and staging would seem inappropriate and impolite.

B.D. Metcalfe, quoted in *Gender and Communication at Work*

Two conclusions seem to follow from this: one, that speech patterns really are social constructs (they wouldn't differ from society to society if they were not); two, that it might be a good idea to employ women for political and business negotiations in the Middle East, or failing that, at least to train men in a rather more feminine speech style.

Men and women on an equal footing? Only in fiction

'It's not just in politics that women's voices are inaudible, but in every other area of public life,' writes single mother and journalist Jane Shilling in *Times 2*, 4 May 2007. 'The Equal Opportunities Commission's racily titled annual report, *Sex and Power: Who Runs Britain?*, finds women in a tiny minority of those in top positions in politics, business, the public sector, the armed forces and even the supposedly female-friendly sector of media and culture.' Why, she wonders, do women seem to 'acquiesce in their own grotesque marginalisation?'

Rejecting the EOC's explanation for this – the 'absence of flexible working opportunities in senior roles' – she concludes that it is because, like Dorothea in George Eliot's novel *Middlemarch*, women spend their time in 'unhistoric acts' that benefit everyone in their lives but get little or no public recognition.

'The statistics tell their own story,' Shilling goes on, 'of passionate, idealistic natures exhausting themselves in the unproductive business of juggling work and domesticity, providing, with vast reserves of unacknowledged expertise and at huge personal cost, the ideal environment for countless [husbands] to make their names, consoling themselves meanwhile with those seductively diffuse diversions: the book club, the nice-glass-of-wine-and a-moan with friends, the wryly amusing blog.'

Activity

The BBC has recently caused dissent by proposing to drop Moira Stewart, aged 50, as one of its main TV newscasters. Write a letter to the Controller of the BBC, commenting on this action.

Gender and e-mailing

Unsurprisingly, perhaps, e-mails reveal similar differences in male/female communication patterns. The following findings are discussed in Barrett and Davidson's *Gender and Communication at Work*.

Emotional distance

Colley and Todd found that in a series of e-mails written between a mixed group of friends, the e-mails written by the women were in general warmer and more personal in tone than those that were written by men, and particularly so when the person they were addressing was male.

Etiquette

In their survey of e-mails written by a sample of male and female undergraduates, Jessmer and Anderson found that the women's were polite and grammatically correct; the men's impolite and ungrammatical.

Status and hierarchy

In a survey by Niki Panteli of e-mails sent between university departments, 70% of the male writers emphasized their status by adding their signatures and formal titles within the organization. None of the women did.

Written discourse features

E-mails sent by the women within the university were well-structured, lengthy, and thorough in their treatment of the subject under discussion. Only 10% of the male e-mails were long and well-structured, using paragraphs and lists. The rest were short, unstructured, to-the-point messages, more akin to oral than to written discourse because seeming more spontaneous.

Two conclusions were drawn from these different surveys:

- status within a hierarchy is signalled by the way e-mail messages are structured and expressed
- e-mail messaging is not a neutral medium in which women can communicate unhindered by gender roles.

Example A

Dear Karen

RE: INTERVIEW JOHN SMITH, ABC ORGANIZATION

Just a brief note to let you know that I have completed the tape passed to me by yourself, via Liz. I have put a print-out of the hard copy in your pigeonhole along with the disk and a back-up copy of the disk and the audio tape. Unfortunately, some of the words were very unclear so I have shown them throughout the document like this example [...] I hope this is okay for your purposes.

Thank you

Helen Routledge

Example B

I have just found out that the next two courses which Computer Services are running on PowerPoint are on 19 and 26 of August from 2-5pm. [Secretary A] will shortly have some booking forms.

(Mary – I've sent this to all academic staff on my standard mailing list. Can you copy to all admin/sec staff? Thanks.)

Professor John Hall
Dept of Beta Studies
Alpha University
Tel: (sec. Mary Shaw) fax:...

Activity

Consider the following.

1 Which e-mail is closer to written, which to spoken discourse?
2 Which is more personalized and friendly? Pick out the features that make it so.
3 Which is more remote and impersonal in tone? Pick out the features that make it so.
4 What gender differences do you find between the two e-mails? Relate some of the differences to the theories described above.
5 Beg examples of male and female e-mails sent within your school or college or a parent's workplace and analyse them for signs of differences of gender in such things as tone, attitude to receiver, structure, modes of address, signature, etc.

Women and the Internet

Women are popularly supposed to make less use of computers than men, yet more and more women are finding that the Internet enables them to function better in a still largely male-dominated world. They can save time and energy by shopping on-line instead of trailing round a lot of shops to find what they want. They can look up the products they want to buy and access all sorts of information about them before going into a store to look at them. This makes them more knowledgeable and empowers them in their dealings with assistants who might otherwise be tempted to talk down to or patronize them. Technology, in fact, may boost women's notoriously low self-esteem by helping them to take a step towards equality in the world outside the home.

Chat rooms and gender-speak

Single-gender chat rooms really flag up the differences in male and female communication. Women love them because they are places in which they can shake off male patronage and disparagement and feel free to swap stories and experiences with other women. The mood is communal, co-operative, friendly and warm.
Men's chat rooms are forums in which men feel free to josh and insult one another; competition is the name of the game. Sometimes the game gets out of hand, however unintentionally, as in a recent case when a man threatened suicide in a male chat room and was egged on to actually do it by shouts of 'Get on with it then'.

Activity

Visit one female and one male chat room on the Internet and write a report for the *Daily Mail* of the kind of linguistic styles you find there.

3 Language and Power

The nature of the power people hold – or wish to hold – in their relations to one another is reflected in the way they use language. This chapter will look at language and power in the following areas:

- social control
- political persuasion
- the language of newspapers
- the language of advertising.

Standard English as a means of social control

In the eighteenth century the Augustan writers encouraged people to use 'proper' English in the hope that civilized language would promote civilized behaviour. Some educationalists today still see a necessary connection between 'correct' – i.e. Standard – English and right behaviour: former MP Norman Tebbit, for example:

> The overthrow of grammar coincided with the acceptance of the equivalent of creative writing in social behaviour. As nice points of grammar were mockingly dismissed as pedantic and irrelevant, so was punctiliousness in such matters as honesty, responsibility, gratitude, apology and so on...

> If you allow standards to slip to the stage where good English is no better than bad English, where people turn up filthy at school... all these things tend to cause people to have no standards at all, and once you lose standards then there's no imperative to stay out of crime.

> Norman Tebbit, quoted in *The Cambridge History of English Language*

Others, like linguist Norman Fairclough in *Language and Power*, see such insistence on Standard English as oppressive: a means of sustaining the elite in their positions of power and keeping the uneducated in their more lowly place.

Speaking and writing are social acts, Fairclough argues, generated by the roles and positions in which people find themselves in society. Those at the bottom of the heap have more limited cultural and linguistic backgrounds than those further up the social scale, and will consequently be at a disadvantage in most interactions with them. Fairclough refers to such interactions as 'gatekeeping encounters': 'such as a job interview in which a "gatekeeper" who generally belongs to the societally dominant cultural grouping controls an encounter which determines whether someone gets a job, or gets access to some other valued objective.' In Britain today, the situation may often involve middle-class white 'gatekeepers' interviewing white working-class people and those from ethnic minorities. 'In such "gatekeeping" encounters,' Fairclough goes on, 'white middle-class gatekeepers are likely to constrain the discourse types which can be drawn upon to those of the dominant cultural grouping.' In other words, by speaking in the formal register natural to them, the gatekeepers assert their social superiority (a form of power) over the interviewees and make it difficult for them to respond effectively.

Fairclough claims that access to 'prestigious sorts of discourse' such as those of medicine and the law is unequal, leaving 'ordinary' people always in the position of clients.

The lower classes are also disadvantaged socially by their ignorance of formal rituals – even those as slight as the ways of answering printed invitations and introducing people to one another. Even middle-class people can be discomforted by those higher up the social scale: mocking laughter was aimed at Prince William's girlfriend's mother when she committed the solecisms of using *Pleased to meet you* instead of *How do you do?* and *toilet* for *lavatory*. (The irony is that *toilet* was originally a euphemism used by the same upper classes' ancestors for the now acceptable *lavatory*.)

Activity

Look up the discussion of the correct use of the following in *Fowler's Modern English Usage* or Eric Partridge's *Usage and Abusage: A Guide to Good English*:

- *between* or *among*
- *less* or *fewer*
- *like* or *as if*.

Write a letter to the *Times Educational Supplement* arguing the case for or against the inclusion of such grammatical rules in A level English specifications.

Language and hierarchy

It is easy to see how privilege perpetuates itself through the intimidating use of prestige language forms. The Queen may have modulated her vowel sounds to suit a more democratic age, but her 'o's are as rounded as those of Scandinavians speaking English, and the vowel sound in her pronunciation of words like 'back' is still much closer to that in 'beck' than that of most of her subjects.

Activity

Listen to a recording of a) the Queen, b) Tony Blair, and discuss the differences you find between the two modes of speech. If you are unfamiliar with the term 'Estuary English', look it up on the Internet and make some notes first.

Symbolic power: Language and ritual

The Queen has little actual power beyond that to open and dissolve Parliament, but her symbolic power over the minds of many of her subjects is great. The outward trappings of sovereignty – the crown and sceptre, the ermine cloaks and bejewelled robes, are matched by the rich and solemn language of ritual:

> Mr Speaker, the Queen commands this honourable House to attend her Majesty immediately in the House of Peers.

The Queen concludes her speech by saying:

> My Lords and Members of the House of Commons, I pray that the blessing of Almighty God may rest upon your councils.

This percolates down into the symbolic trappings and archaic linguistic rituals of the two Houses of Parliament, where MPs address one another as 'my honourable friend' or 'the honourable member for [name of constituency]'. Peers address one another as 'the noble Lord/ Lady'.

Critics of such practices claim that, like the public school system, they offend democracy by perpetuating class privilege. The fact that Clement Attlee, the first socialist prime minister with the power to abolish public schools, refused to do so, wanting his beloved Haileybury to carry on its 'great traditions', may seem to support the point.

Social control through political correctness

The political and social elites of the eighteenth century tried to use language as an instrument to control society. Their twenty-first-century counterparts are making similar efforts today by introducing a system of social control that has come to be called by its critics the 'cult of Political Correctness', or PC for short.

Justification of PC

PC starts from the belief that 'Certain people have their rights, opportunities, or freedoms restricted due to their categorization as members of a group with a derogatory stereotype' (Wikipedia).

Stick an insulting label on people, in other words – *Pakkis*, say, or *Kuffars*, or *Poofs* – and you deny their humanity by seeing them in terms of only that thing. As William James pointed out in 1902 (in *The Varieties of Religious Experience*):

> Probably a crab would be filled with a sense of personal outrage if it could hear us class it without ado or apology as a crustacean, and thus dispose of it. 'I am no such thing,' it would say: 'I am MYSELF, MYSELF alone.'

It is easy to mistreat what you have reduced to the status of a thing: Shakespeare shows the process in action in *The Tempest*, where the drunken Trinculo, no better than a savage himself, categorizes Caliban as a monster and 'could find it in his heart to kick him'. In the same way, it was easier for the Nazis to kill Jews once they had labelled them *vermin*, and to dispose efficiently of their corpses once they thought of them as *pieces*.

The coded language of PC

Recognizing this, a left-wing government, hand in hand with liberal thinkers in the worlds of education and the media, introduced a new, coded form of expression in which certain words can no longer be used. *Disabled* and *mentally retarded* were replaced by terms such as *differently abled* and *having learning difficulties*. (A person can't even be described as *suffering* from learning difficulties, since suffering implies weakness and victimhood and may give a derogatory impression of the man or woman concerned. The same applies to the different implications of *wheelchair-bound* and *wheelchair user*.)

Concerns about PC

1 If carried into law, it may become a form of state censorship, denying every citizen's right to free speech.

2 It is difficult to see how it can be fully effective even if legislation is passed. Macho types may think twice about patronizing women by calling them *girls*, for instance, but they can make the point just as easily by using *ladies* with a curl of the lip and a sarcastic tone. 'Ordinary' people can be remarkably inventive in their use of language: in the Falklands War, British troops called the unworldly islanders *Bennies*, after a rather dim character in a contemporary TV soap opera;

their commanders managed to stop them in the interest of public relations but couldn't do much about the 'innocent' replacement they came up with – the islanders had become *Stills* (i.e. *Still Bennies*).

Debate is currently raging in the media and on the Internet about the legitimacy of PCspeak. Where does free speech end and censorship begin? Are the coded euphemisms of PC a real step forward in human relations, or just a refusal to face facts? One caller to a recent Radio 5 Live phone-in seemed to think so: 'I've been *blind*, *partially sighted,* and *visually impaired* over the years, and now I'm *a person with no sight.* I don't care what people call me as long as they do it with respect. Respect is the key.'

Activity

Whatever your attitude to PC, no one can deny its impact on our language and our life today. Look at the two different ways of expressing the same idea below and you will almost certainly find that, thanks to the pervasive influence of PC, you would choose to use one rather than the other:

A When Ms Johnson was the chair(person)/ (woman), she insisted that everyone pay their/his or her dues.

B When Miss Johnson was the chairman, she insisted that everyone pay his dues.

1 What does your choice reveal about your attitudes to the following: feminism; grammar; conservatism (with a small 'c'); liberalism?

2 Write a paragraph in the style of a journalist in a popular newspaper, like Jeremy Clarkson or Rod Liddle or Richard Littlejohn, attacking PC for trying to impose constraints on what you write.

3 Write a paragraph in the persona of a left-wing female MP defending the use of PC language.

4 A 10-year-old boy recently sent an e-mail to another lad addressing him as *gay-boy*. Two policemen were sent to 'have a chat with' him. Argue the case for or against this action.

The language of politics

Advertisers use a variety of linguistic techniques to sell us consumer goods; politicians use the same techniques to sell us themselves. Writing about the Democratic candidate for the US presidency, Barack Obama, *Sunday Times* journalist Andrew Sullivan asserts: 'Obama's great appeal is that his identity and the content of his character **rebrands** America both to itself and to the world.' He could have written, 'shows America in a new light both to itself...' , but the metaphor of 'branding' clearly reveals acceptance that political candidates have to be as attractively packaged as consumer goods if they want to win votes.

So how do politicians market themselves and get us to buy? Largely by the use of the following linguistic techniques, loosely known as **rhetorical devices** and carefully calculated to work on our emotions.

1 **Alliteration and assonance**, because patterned speech impacts the ears more strongly and is easier to remember, e.g.

... in the years to come, wherever I am, whatever I do. I'm with you. Wishing you well. Wanting you to win.

I hated the 1980s not just for our irrelevance but for our revelling in our irrelevance.

2 **Metaphor and simile**, to make what is said more vivid, e.g.

> I feel the hand of history on our shoulder...

> I bear the scars on my back after two years in government.

> The challenge we face is not in our values. It is how we put them into practice in a world fast forwarding to the future at unprecedented speed.

3 **Rhetorical questions**, to break the monotony of a whole string of assertions, e.g.

> Britain is stronger, fairer, better than on the first of May 1997. So what now? So now in turn, we have to change again...

4 **Puns and word-play**, to add variety and a touch of humour. For example, responding to expectations of an about-turn in her policies against inflation, Prime Minister Margaret Thatcher declared:

> To those waiting with baited breath for that favourite media catch-phrase, the U-turn, I have only one thing to say: You turn if you want to. The lady's not for turning.

The obvious pun on *U-turn/ You turn* is followed by another piece of word-play – the deliberate echoing of the title of Christopher Fry's play 'The Lady's Not for Burning' in her punch-line.

5 **Triads**, the arrangement of nouns or phrases in groups of three, because this seems to have an in-built psychological appeal to audiences, lending force and conviction to what is being said, e.g.

> In the late twentieth century the world had changed, the aspirations of the people had changed; we had to change.

> We believe in tolerance and respect, in strong communities standing by and standing up for the weak, the sick, the helpless.

> I'm a progressive. The true believer believes in social justice, in solidarity, in help for those who not able to help themselves.

6 **Repetition**, to ram home a point and fix it in the memory, e.g.

> Ask me my three main priorities for government, and I will tell you: education, education, education.

> ... what won [the bid to host the Olympics] was London itself. A London with pride in its past, but with eyes fixed on the future. A London that said to the world: We're proud of our diversity; proud to stand before you on our merits; proud we are an open, dynamic, outward-going city full of life...

7 **Parallel phrasing**, to heighten attention and add conviction, e.g.

> When we campaign for justice in Africa, that is a progressive cause. When we push for peace in Palestine, it is a progressive cause. When we act against global warming, it is a progressive cause. And when we fight behind the standard of democracy in Afghanistan or Iraq or Kosovo or Sierra Leone, for me that too is a progressive cause.

Note how beginning the final sentence with *And* and inserting the phrase *for me that too* gives the sentence a falling intonation that clinches the argument with a note of finality.

These last three techniques can also have a compelling rhythmic effect that sways listeners' feelings and makes them acquiesce in what is being said.

8 Antithesis, which contrasts one word or phrase or clause directly with another, and in doing so has the effect of clinching an argument, e.g.

> The danger of government is fatigue; the benefit, experience.

> Conflict is not inevitable, but disarmament is.

> We believe in opportunity not for a privileged few but for all, whatever their start in life.

9 Allusions to literature, which strengthen and support what is being said by awaking echoes of earlier speeches in listeners' minds, e.g.

> Seventeen years of hurt. Never stopped us dreaming. Labour's coming home.
> (Allusion to World Cup song, 'Football's coming home'.)

> This country is a blessed nation. The British are special, the world knows it, in our innermost thoughts, we know it. This is the greatest nation on Earth. It has been an honour to serve it.
> (Tony Blair's speech announcing his resignation, 10 May 2007)

Examine John of Gaunt's speech from Shakespeare's *Richard II* (below) and ask yourself if this was in Tony Blair's speechwriter's mind:

> This happy breed of men, this little world,
> This precious stone set in the silver sea,
> Which serves it in the office of a wall,
> Or as a moat defensive to a house,
> Against the envy of less happier lands;
> This blessed plot, this earth, this realm, this England…

An alternative allusion might be to Sir Cecil Rhodes, who jingoistically asserted, 'I contend that we are the first race in the world and the more of the world we inhabit the better it is for the human race.'

> Whatever you do, I'm always with you. Head and heart.
> (Speech to Labour Party Conference, September 2006)

Compare Christ's words to his disciples after his death:

> Go ye therefore, and teach all nations… teaching them to observe all things whatsoever I have commanded you: and lo, I am with you alway, even unto the end of the world.

Rhetoric and grammar

Speeches may be written out and amended many times with great care, but they are still made effective by the speaking voice and show many of the characteristics of oral as opposed to written language. They are full of carefully calculated pauses, shown by the use of full stops that would be unnecessary and grammatically wrong in written discourse.

In the past famous speakers have used dramatic, highly symbolic expressions, as when Winston Churchill spoke of the 'lights going out all over Europe', or John F. Kennedy talked of 'the torch passing to a new generation of Americans', but in our much more hardened and cynical age most politicians use the language of every day to address us:

> I think most people who have dealt with me think I'm a pretty straight sort of guy and I am.

> When we made a decision about bidding for the Olympics, I'll be honest. I didn't think we could do it. But I also thought, come on, at least give it a try. And it was a risk. But we proved something important in taking it.

Like sports commentators, politicians often use what David Crystal in *Rediscover Grammar* calls minor sentences (ones that are missing a main verb or a subject or are otherwise incomplete in some way):

> Who would have thought that the Conservatives would still be debating which way to go after eight years in opposition? Or the Liberals, still debating which way to go after 80 years in opposition? The Tories without a leader. The Lib Dems too. Street fighters in local politics. Utterly unserious on the national stage.

Politicians are also fond of using the subjunctive mood when they wish to be seen as totally sincere and dedicated to a cause, probably because it helps to persuade us that they will lift us into a better world that does not yet exist but will be brought into being some time soon:

> Some day, some party will make this country at ease with globalization. <u>Let it be</u> this one. Some day, we will forge a new consensus on our public services. <u>Let it be us</u> who believe in them and let us do it now.

> Some day, some party will respond to the public's anger at the defeatism that has too often gripped our response to social disorder. <u>Let it be</u> the party that understands compassion as well as firmness is the only way a true community can be made.

> <u>Let ours be</u> the party, the one with the values of social justice, equality, fairness, that helps Britain turn a friendly face towards the future.

The **subjunctive mood** creates an atmosphere of uncertainty by using verbs like *may*, *might*, and *were* to talk about things that you doubt, or suppose, or fear, or wish will happen, e.g. It <u>*may*</u> come tomorrow; They <u>*might*</u> have sent it; I'd be careful if I <u>*were*</u> you. It's the opposite of the much more ordinary **indicative mood** that we use most of the time, which simply asserts facts: It <u>will</u> come tomorrow; They <u>have sent</u> it; I'm glad she <u>was</u> careful.

Because it creates this mood of doubt and uncertainty, politicians avoid the subjunctive mood at other times. Their job is to lead us, and leaders must not be seen to be in doubt about anything. Who would vote for or follow a leader who said: 'Look, this policy may work or it may not, but we think we'll give it a try'?

Activity

Comment on any rhetorical devices you notice in the following extracts from speeches.

A Look at Britain's cities. A decade ago in decline. Today – for all the problems that remain – thriving, waterfronts and canals renewed, business up, unemployment down and slowly, part by part, the regeneration of the inner city under way. Visit the centre of Birmingham. See Liverpool – European City of Culture for 2008. Or Manchester – site of the Commonwealth Games.

B There is only one government since the war that has cut unemployment, created 2 million more jobs, had eight years of growth without recession and halved interest rates from the previous government.

And cut waiting lists in hospitals, improved cancer and heart care, achieved the best ever school results, halved the number of failing schools, seen a five-fold increase in the best ones; achieved record numbers of police and cut crime.

Only one Chancellor to have delivered that economic record. This one. Only one Cabinet to have delivered these changes. This one.

Politics and spin

The following definition is from Wikipedia, the free encyclopedia:

In public relations, <u>spin</u> is a usually pejorative term signifying a heavily biased portrayal in one's own favour of an event or situation. While traditional public relations may also rely on creative presentation of the facts, 'spin' often, though not always, implies disingenuous, deceptive and/or highly manipulative tactics. Politicians are often accused of spin by their political opponents.

There has always been spin, and there have always been spin doctors to put it about. Shakespeare exposed the tricks of the trade 400 years ago by making Antony spin brilliantly in *Julius Caesar* and Coriolanus fall by refusing to do the same for himself in the play of that name.

In our own age, spin seems to have become a corrupting influence, causing the general public to become so cynical that many now refuse to believe a word that politicians utter, even when there is no evidence to suggest that they may not be telling the truth. The all-pervading presence of the media, hungry for sensational stories, is a major factor in politicians' need to portray themselves in the best light possible, and putting a spin on statistics, as discussed below, is one way of achieving it.

Spinning with statistics

[Only one government has] cut waiting lists in hospitals, improved cancer and heart care, achieved the best ever school results, halved the number of failing schools, seen a five-fold increase in the best ones; achieved record numbers of police and cut crime.

- -

Faced with these impressive claims few people stop to ask: how big were the cuts in crime and hospital waiting times? What criteria were used to judge school results? If the number of failing schools has been halved, why do 50% of children leave school unable to read and write to a good standard? Has all crime been cut or only certain minor kinds?

Spinning with grammar

Politicians can also put a spin on language itself in order to convey the message they want. When the government wanted to strengthen the dossier claiming that Saddam Hussein had weapons of mass destruction, its writers were asked to get rid of statements couched in the subjunctive mood and to put them in the indicative mood instead. *The Iraq military **may be** able to deploy chemical or biological weapons within 45 minutes of an order to do so* was therefore amended to: *The Iraq military **are** able to deploy chemical or biological weapons within 45 minutes of an order to do so*, turning a somewhat tentative statement into a positive assertion.

> **Activity**
>
> Read Mark Antony's speech over Caesar's murdered body in Act III Scene 2 of *Julius Caesar*, beginning at *Friends, Romans, countrymen*, and discuss the rhetorical techniques he uses to get his message across to the common people.

The influence of the press

The British read newspapers more avidly than any other nation in Europe, but do they read them to be told what they should think, or to have their existing opinions confirmed? The answer seems to be a bit of both. Newspapers may influence opinion by dramatizing events and hyping up their language, but people wouldn't buy them if they didn't have any appeal.

Readership is broadly divided along class lines: 'red-top' (i.e. most sensational) tabloids for the workers; the *Mail* and *Express* for the lower- and middle-middle classes, and the other newspapers, which were formerly broadsheets, for the rest.

In the comedy series *Yes, Minister*, writers Antony Jay and Jonathan Lynn neatly summed up the political affiliations of the different readerships:

Hacker: Don't tell me about the press. I know exactly who reads the papers: The *Daily Mirror* is read by people who think they run the country; the *Guardian* is read by people who think they ought to run the country; the *Times* is read by people who actually do run the country; the *Daily Mail* is read by the wives of the people who run the country; the *Financial Times* is read by people who own the country; the *Morning Star* is read by people who think the country ought to be run by another country; and the *Daily Telegraph* is read by people who think it is.

Sir Humphrey: Prime Minister, what about the people who read the *Sun*?

Bernard: *Sun* readers don't care who runs the country, as long as she's got big tits.

- -

However, generally speaking, therefore, newspapers can be said to influence readers' minds rather than control them; they may confirm and strengthen public opinion – even inflame it at times by the way they deliberately 'colour' the news – but with the exception of one particular area of specialized reporting – investigative journalism – this is probably as far as they can go.

However, when responsible journalists begin in-depth research into the political and/or financial doings of government or establishment figures, reputations and careers can be destroyed. The destruction of American President Richard Nixon by investigative journalists Bob Woodward and Carl Bernstein in 1972 is the classic example, but see also the case of the BBC's *Today* reporter Andrew Gilligan over the 'sexing-up' of the government dossier about the threat of Saddam Hussein's weapons of mass destruction (in May 2003). The then prime minister was not destroyed, but the reputation of his government was besmirched in many people's eyes.

The language of the media

As Allan Bell points out in *The Language of News Media*, 'communicators who work in the mass media are always in some sense trying to win audience approval'. Their intention may be to inform, persuade, provoke, or entertain, but unless they can attract their readers' or listeners' interest they are wasting their time.

The main method they use to attract this interest is what Bell calls 'audience design': speakers or writers call up a mental picture of the audience they want to impress, then tailor their material and style to suit. Audiences (the term is used loosely to include readers) have their expectations too; if they don't find a reflection of their own attitudes, values, and ideas in what they read, they will buy something else instead. Liverpool readers, for instance, refused to buy the *Sun* for months after it unfairly blackened the reputation of football fans caught up in the Hillsborough disaster.

Audience design in newspapers: Visual style

How then do newspapers present themselves to make the greatest impact on their readers?

Layout

Newspapers make their content attractive to readers by the way they arrange it on the page. As Ingrid Mardh points out (in *Headlines: On the Grammar of English Front-page Headlines*), the natural movement of the eye for Western readers is from top left to bottom right: items of the greatest interest are therefore usually, though not always, arranged in descending order from top left to bottom right. (The 'fallow corners' left empty by this technique are generally filled with pictures and/or less important, smaller headlines.)

Typography

Editors also grab our attention by the size and boldness of their headlines. As Bell remarks, 'Large headlines in striking black print are the written equivalent of an excited shout.' They are also reader-friendly in that they and the white space around them break down the body copy into smaller chunks. (The body copy is the technical term for the columns of writing below the headlines.) Nothing puts inexperienced readers off like long columns of close print: 'All that reading!' said one tabloid fan faced with a copy of the *Guardian*.

The greater the news value of a headline, the larger the type it is printed in: readers can judge its importance visually before they see what is being said. When something really important happens, the inevitable result is that headlines become so big they swallow up most of the front page, as the *Sun's* GOTCHA! did on the sinking of the Belgrano in the Falklands War. This is especially true of the tabloids, which in any case habitually give more space to their headlines than others, although Ingrid Mardh shows that the *Times* has doubled the space given over to headlines over the past 50 years.

Sub-headlines in smaller, heavy black type are similarly used to break up the body copy within an article. These often consist of one word hinting at what is to come in the next paragraph, e.g. *Attacker; Knife; Arrested.*

Activity

1 Compare and contrast the layout, style and content of the *Sun*, the *Daily Mail* and the *Times* and describe the kind of reader each of these papers aims to appeal to.

2 Do the same for one day's output of the five main television channels.

3 Read the following extracts from the sports pages. Which kind of paper might each extract be taken from?

A: Roger Federer's fifth win equals 'living legend'

By Mark Hodgkinson

Seated in the front row of the Royal Box yesterday was Bjorn Borg, so famously an emotional flat-liner. And so when Roger Federer put away a smash to win his fifth Wimbledon title in a row, so equalling the Swede's record, the Ice Man predictably allowed himself just a small smile. Federer, though, dropped on to his back on the Centre Court grass and began to blub.

The Swiss, a five-set winner over the brilliant Rafael Nadal after a superb final of controlled violence, simply had no hold over his emotions and his tear ducts. He cried as he worked himself to his feet, wept as he hugged the Spaniard at the net, and wiped away tears after sitting down on his chair, and then carried on sobbing. After what has seemed like the wettest Wimbledon in living memory, Federer gave the All England Club lawns yet another watering. 'It meant a lot to equal Bjorn's record,' Federer said.

B: Roger the Great

By Darren Lewis

BJORN BORG led the standing ovation on Wimbledon's Centre Court after Roger Federer had smashed the ball into an open court to celebrate emulating his own remarkable achievements.

The Swiss maestro had taken his fifth SW19 title in a row to join the Swedish legend who had been given a front row seat in the Royal Box to see if his record could be matched.

It was, against the fire and fury of Spaniard Rafael Nadal in one of the best Wimbledon finals for years – a roller-coaster of a contest that delivered everything it had promised and more.

In an arena bathed in sunshine, in stark contrast to the appalling weather that had torn this tournament apart over the previous two weeks, Federer brought the good times back with the fightback of a champion.

Audience design: The use of language in newspapers

Diction

Journalists make their material easier to read by using short, concrete, mainly Anglo-Saxon words wherever possible. There are three main reasons for this:

1 they take up less space, having fewer syllables

2 they can be immediately understood by a wide range of readers

3 they have a forceful quality that makes an immediate impact.

Thus words like *probe* are used for 'in-depth investigation', *slam* for 'criticize severely', *slash* for 'make sweeping or random cuts', *is set to* for 'is preparing to' and so on. Nicholas Bagnall, in *Newspaper Language*, calls words like these *buzzwords*, to convey the impression of urgent and exciting activity they create.

The red-top tabloids make further concessions to their readers by using colloquial language and outright slang in their reporting of serious social concerns, as in the article printed below.

Booze is 'Ruin of Britain'

HEAVY boozing is taking a whopping £3.3 billion toll on Britain.

Sozzled employees unable to work properly -- or who go sick -- cost INDUSTRY £2.8 billion.

Treating alcohol-related illnesses leaves the NHS with a £200 million hangover. Meanwhile the bill for CRIME and ROAD ACCIDENTS fuelled by drink is £257 million, Alcohol Concern revealed yesterday.

The *Sun*, 11 May 2000

- -

The tabloids go further than this in their lighter features, however, choosing a cheesy vocabulary of *snogging, canoodling* or *bonking* with *stunning blondes* or *vivacious redheads* in *secluded love-nests* where *sizzling sex-romps* take place. The result is a generally coarse, matey style and a knowing tone of voice.

Word-play

Headline writers also use rhetorical devices to catch our attention. Alliteration is common, especially in the red-tops:

MILE HIGH MANDY GETS RANDY ON BRANDY (The *Sun*)

So are puns and associated word-play:

TIME BAFTA TIME (*Sun* journalist reporting the Bafta awards)

IMPERFECT PASTS ARE THE BEST PRESENTS FOR PINTER (Theatre critic in the *Mail on Sunday*)

The *Times* and *Guardian* are happy to join in with headlines like *Time to Roam While The Fiddle Burns* (on the visit of a famous violinist to Italy) and *The Joys of Fourplay* (on new recordings by a famous chamber quartet).

Metaphor can also be found, though not always with any aesthetic intent: *HOP OFF, YOU FROGS* was an insult aimed at the French during a trade dispute.

The red-top tabloids have two further tricks up their sleeves to grab and hold readers' attention: sensationalism and the use of emotive clichés.

Sensationalism

The attempt here is to heighten already disturbing facts by the use of exaggeration. It is usually reserved for terrorists and sex-murderers, and runs the danger of going over the top. In the space of one article the following terms were used to describe the man accused: *psycho sex monster, lust-crazed, frenzied sex-fiend, caged, madman.*

Instead of being aroused, readers' emotions may be overwhelmed by the sheer weight of language hurled at them.

Emotive clichés

As Nicholas Bagnall points out, there is a ritualistic feel to the writing of the red-tops, where women, if young, are always *stunning* or *sizzling*, men are always *hunks*, the bereaved are always *tragic*, etc. Why? Because tabloid readers want stories that fit with their conceptions of what life is like, not ones that turn their ideas about the world upside down.

Clichés – statements that have been repeated so often that we take their truth for granted – are obviously part of this comforting ritual. The two most potent and frequently used are *brave* and *tiny*, as in *the brave parents followed the tiny coffin*. Other clichés Bagnall notices are *horrors, terror, mysteries, bitterness,* and *massive*.

Taken together, the buzzwords, the slang, and the clichés create a misguided impression of poor writing in the tabloids, yet their editorials often offer clearer and more cogent expressions of complex issues than writers in other newspapers can achieve. And all newspapers frequently resort to clichés in reporting the scenes of disasters and fires: *fire appliances, at the scene, battling, blaze, engulfed, threatened*, etc.

Personalization

Another technique used to stimulate interest is personalization. Conflict in the abstract hardly stirs the blood, but conflict between people does. Compare *Major differences of opinion over Europe were revealed in the Commons yesterday* with *Cameron clashes violently with Brown in Commons.*

Claire Lundgren Lerman, in *Language, Image, Media* (edited by Walton and Davis), suggests that 'sports and entertainment provide the thematic model' for news reporting of this kind: 'Political campaigns and issues of public policy are reduced to personality conflict, sporting contests, or battles. The focus is "who's winning?"' Not surprisingly, therefore, 'metaphors of warfare and to a lesser extent sport are prevalent', and even complex issues are presented in terms of conflict between two opposing sides.

Walton and Davis make much the same point:

> In practice, social descriptions are polarised and tend to operate with binary distinctions: for example, workers/ non-workers, dropouts; peaceful/ violent; organised/ disorganised; moderate/ extreme; democracy/ civil war, anarchy. This gives rise to the tendency to reduce a complex system of social relationships to simple opposites.

Connotation versus denotation

If political issues are presented in terms of conflict between two opposing sides, one aggressive (the workers), one passively resisting (the management), it is easy to see how accusations of subjective writing can be levelled at the journalists reporting them. When a journalist writes, for instance, *The mob swept across the car park, crushing Mr Blank against the fence*, he or she may simply be writing objectively what was seen (denotation); there may be no intention to vilify the 'mob' or present the person crushed as a victim (connotation). 'Mob' is simply a more exciting word than 'crowd', and more accurate, in that a mob's actions are more violent and unpredictable than those of the more ordinary crowd. It is not so much the language that is at fault here as the fact that the reporter has neither the time nor space to give an in-depth explanation of the reasons behind the 'mob's' behaviour.

On the other hand, reporters do have prejudices too, like the rest of us, and when these are awakened their writing may become overtly emotive: *The angry mob swept violently across the car park, crushing their helpless victim against the fence.* The adjectives *angry* and *helpless* and the adverb *violently* leave us in no doubt where the writer's sympathies lie.

Speech verbs also help to colour newspaper reports. *Say* and *tell* give a personal note; *announce, declare* and *refuse* are neutral, while *claim* is altogether more ambiguous in tone, and may be used to cast doubt on the truth of what is being said: *Mr Aitken claimed that his wife, and not he, had paid the bill in question.*

Verbs such as *threaten, insist*, and *denounce* show us events through the filter of the reporter's eyes; they create news action.

Walton and Davis (in *Language, Image, Media*) distinguish two main aspects of connotative/ subjective reporting: inclusion and exclusion.

- Inclusive reporting uses terms which 'linguistically express the consensus [of civilized society]', from which those who are perceived as hostile in some way are excluded. Examples are *the overwhelming majority, the people, ordinary citizens, the majority of decent people, right-thinking people*.

- Exclusive reporting can be signalled in at least three different ways.

    1 By the use of punctuation: the placing of inverted commas around the name of the excluded group, e.g. the '*Tamil Tigers*'.

    2 By the use of qualifiers: the placing of *self-styled* or *so-called* before the name of the excluded group.

    3 By the direct use of connotative terms carrying heavy implications of disgust: *criminals, killers, murderers, criminal psychopaths, left-wing extremists, urban terrorists, violent anarchists, political killers, Marxist revolutionaries*, etc.

In the same way, direct quotations in inverted commas allow journalists to report on controversial issues while preserving an impartial stance, as in:

Lecturer 'robbed of career' after she miscarried

Activity

1 Scan two different newspapers for nouns or verbs that signal conflict.
2 Find copies of Hansard for the years when Margaret Thatcher was prime minister and was battling with what she called 'the enemy within' (the miners), and examine the speeches reported there for the language of conflict. Analyse what this reveals of attitudes within society during the 1980s.

Stereotyping

Journalists often simplify complex social and political issues by presenting them in terms of stereotypes. Stereotypes are fixed ideas of individuals or groups that endow them with particular attributes, values, attitudes and ideas: radical feminists; a male chauvinist pig; the new man; New Labour; the far right. Once people have been slotted neatly into such stereotypes, they can be brought into conflict with one another without any of the niggling details or qualifications that might otherwise spoil the broad sweep of the story.

Activity

Read at least two newspapers, looking for articles about particular groups of people: political groupings, ethnic minorities, the unemployed, homosexuals, etc.

1 Examine the language used in relation to these for evidence of stereotyping.

2 Examine the language used in relation to these for evidence of prejudice on the writer's part.

Audience design: The grammar of newspaper reporting

All newspaper reports are written in good grammatical English. The tabloids make some concession to their readers, however:

1 by using shorter sentences with fewer dependent clauses

2 by using simple concrete nouns instead of abstract ones

3 by writing one-sentence paragraphs.

Sack Charlie

Gordon Brown will have plenty on his plate when he becomes PM.

But he must make time for one urgent priority – to sack Charlie Falconer as head of the new Justice Ministry.

This warbling clot has bumbled his way to high office without ever facing a voter.

Now he has shown how remote he is from real life.

Criminals who breach parole will be given a slap on the wrist with no more than 28 days behind bars.

This is a blatant attempt to conceal the crisis of our bulging prisons.

The *Sun*, 10 May 2007

Compression of appositional phrases

Journalists use this technique to save space and add pace to an article. Before the 1950s it was usual to place the name of the person in the news first – e.g. *Mrs Mary Message* – and the appositional phrase afterwards, e.g. *a widow of 30 Bow Terrace, London*.

Today, appositional phrases are largely replaced by modifiers which are placed before the names, resulting in the shorter, racier version below. The standard form of name apposition in many media is now as follows:

1or 2 pre-modifiers + Noun acting as title + First and last names

Notorious Tory	Rebel	Alan Clark
Former	Spice Girl	Geri Halliwell

Activity

It has been claimed that appositional phrases of this kind can function as pseudo-titles, conferring undeserved fame on people who simply happen to be in the news. How far do you agree?

Further compression can be seen in the writing of headlines, which are forced to break with conventional sentence structure for reasons of space. They use the kind of abbreviated writing we find in diaries, recipes, and advertisements.

Most headlines, therefore, consist of dependent clauses or phrases below the level of a sentence:

WORLD WEATHER

MORE HUMBUG THAN FUDGE

THE CAR YOU WIGGLE

THE HOME COMPUTERS ONLINE IN AN INSTANT

Block or economy language concentrates on words that carry the heaviest charge of meaning, leaving out the function words that carry little information – such as definite and indefinite articles (*the* and *a*) and finite forms of the verb to be, like *is* and *are*. The result is a kind of 'telegraphese' that can be understood only by reading the article beneath it. Perhaps this is the reason they are made ambiguous in the first place. Consider for example the headline EXPLOSION PLOT ALLEGED. Without a definite article we cannot tell whether the plot is fact or fiction; without finite verbs like *is*, *was*, or *has been*, the time-scale of events is totally vague.

The ambiguity deepens when heavily modified noun phrases are used as headlines:

HISTORY MAN TRIAL

HISTORY MAN TRIAL ACCUSATION

HISTORY MAN TRIAL ACCUSATION DENIAL, etc.

Several different interpretations are possible, and unless we have been following previous reports of the case, we can have no idea which is correct.

The language of advertising

As Vestergaard and Schroder point out in *The Language of Advertising*, advertising has certain things in common with the arts. Like novels, plays and films, like radio and television, advertising is a form of one-way communication with an anonymous audience. Like them, it creates ways of drawing that audience into what appears to be a two-way relationship.

Purpose

Advertisers have one purpose only: to make us buy one product over all its (usually very similar) competitors on the market.

Approach

Advertisers use a psychological approach – an implied promise to supply us with the things we want the most: sex (including attractiveness), status (including money), and power (including money). Most ads can be chased down to one of these three categories, however unlikely. Cleaning agents that practically work by themselves, for instance, promise less effort and greater leisure, the prerogatives of the wealthy upper class. As they readily admit, what advertisers really sell is hope.

Method

Like scriptwriters in the movies, advertisers construct fictional scenarios. According to Vestergaard and Schroder, a typical scenario depicts the audience as the subject or receiver of the action (which is some kind of problem that is troubling us), the product as the helper that solves the problem, and the object as some desirable quality.

Context

The success of any ad depends on the effectiveness of its verbal and non-verbal elements, and this in turn depends upon the advertiser's grasp of context. This includes:

- the specific features of the social situation in which the communicative interaction takes place
- the wider social, political and historical circumstances within which it is made meaningful.

Copy-writers must consider both the physical context (where the ad will appear, the spending power of the audience targeted) and the mental context (the degree to which the members of that audience share the copy-writers' knowledge of the wider cultural context). Ads featuring a cowboy would be unlikely to work in women's magazines, for example; the Carling ad showing the coming of football to England couldn't work without some knowledge of history. Recognition that what we're looking at is an ad is also an important part of context, since such knowledge shapes our perception of the material it contains.

Direct address advertising

The simplest form of advertising is both direct and impersonal. It avoids the second-person pronoun 'you', using deictic words like *here, this, now*, and imperatives like *look, see*, *watch*, referring to visible features of the product advertised. Direct address advertisements have two main participants: the addressor (the advertiser) and the addressee (the audience).

Direct address advertising can also take the personal approach and make a very explicit appeal to 'you', the audience. For example, car insurer RAC Direct Insurance used the persona of former football hard man turned actor Vinnie Jones in its advertisements. One print advertisement has this copy above a large close-up of a threatening-looking Jones:

> **70% of RAC Direct Insurance members pay less than £350.**
> **Don't make me tell you twice.**
> If you know what's good for you you'll call RAC Direct Insurance on…

- -

A less dramatic use of this direct address technique can be found in an advertisement for a watch, which uses the question-and-answer technique:

> Prefer wrapping your fingers round a joystick to a steering wheel? Then you'll love this watch.

Indirect address advertising

Indirect address ads introduce one or two secondary participants who act as vehicles for the advertiser's message. The simplest form of indirect address advertising has one speaker (usually a satisfied consumer or a supposed 'expert') who uses the first person 'I' or 'we' to create the impression of events happening in real life. The copy-writers' ability to handle register is vital here: it must be appropriate to the speaker's situation, social class, age, and sex, or it will sound like what it's trying to avoid – direct address copy.

The same difficulty presents itself in scenarios that introduce two secondary participants: how to make their dialogue sound convincing. The copy-writers' task is to dramatize a scene from ordinary domestic life – husband and wife, mother and child, householder and plumber, etc. – using ordinary language, and at the same time to praise the virtues of a product whose name can hardly be mentioned in case the whole thing sounds ridiculously artificial. The usual technique is to rely on colloquial language and slang, partly to make the participants sound convincing, and partly to make the audience relate easily to them.

Activity

Consider a TV advertisement for a cleaning product and discuss the accent and language the speakers are given to use in the light of the above, and the brand name of the cleaner.

Advertising stereotypes

The people portrayed in advertisements are stereotypes rather than individuals: women are always happy, well dressed and cheerful; they preside over homes that are orderly, clean and tidy, and even when they are glad to save on the cost of an item, they never seem pushed for cash. Husbands and other males are immaculately dressed and obviously middle class, unless brought in to advise on the right soap powder to use, when they can be either a scientific boffin in a stereotypical white coat or a salt-of-the-earth blue-collar worker. The great thing about stereotypes is that they contain a grain of truth and never offend the paying public – which is the last thing advertisers can afford to do.

A vein of British whimsy stretching back to *The Wind in the Willows* is tapped and up-dated in some advertisements, particularly those using cartoons or animations.

Activity

1 Find an example of:

  a monologue, and

  b dialogue in separate TV ads.

Examine each for its skill in handling language, and its effectiveness in promoting the product.

2 Find an advertisement using cartoons in a national newspaper, and discuss the appeal its visual and verbal elements make, or attempt to make, to consumers.

Verbal and visual interaction in advertising

Visual images may be the first things that catch the eye in advertisements, but for them to have their fullest effect, they need the help of words. It's sometimes difficult to tell what product an ad is promoting until the caption or slogan appears at the end. The relation between text and image is known as *anchorage*. The word anchors the image to the context.

Words are also needed to anchor an image in time. Most utterances indicate time by the use of the past or present tenses, but images by their nature are unable to do this. Vestergaard gives the example of the present tense used to anchor the image of a diamond in the text *A diamond is forever*.

The diction of advertising

Advertisers use certain emotive words more freely than others: adjectives like *new, good, better, best, free, fresh, great, delicious, full, wonderful, bright*; and evaluative ones like *sure, clean, special, crisp, fine, real, easy, extra, rich, safe, delicate, perfect, expert, glamorous, lovely*.

Extra force is added by turning some adjectives into compound ones: *undreamed-of, country-fresh, creamy-mild, shining-clean*, etc.

Since the advertiser's task is to make us act, most verbs are in the imperative mood. Certain verbs are repeated time and again; like those favoured by the tabloids, they are short, crisp and forceful:

make	set	give	have	see	get	come	go	know	keep	look
need	love	use	feel	like	take	start	taste	call	hurry	let

send for   use   ask for

Get is used far more often than *buy* for psychological reasons. *Buy* is a word that has one major meaning: the spending of money. It denotes what for most people is an unpleasant action. *Get* on the other hand is a word with wider and vaguer associations. It connotes acquiring, and makes the spending less obvious. Other verbs like *choose* are also ways of avoiding *buy*, as are *make _____ your way to start the day; give someone you love a _____ .*

Negated interrogatives are also common: *Isn't it time you* (did something or other), *Why not* (do something or other). These of course are just disguised imperatives.

Sometimes the nudge to buy is given in the form of advice: *If* (something or other is a problem) *you should try _____ .*

Finally, the least obviously directive is the apparently objective remark: *You'll find _____ at all good stores; You can use _____ in the kitchen or the bathroom.*

The grammar of advertising

Advertising language is grammatically simple. The use of an imperative without a subject is particularly common.

Advertising copy is written in disjunctive rather than discursive grammar, closer to the block style of headline writing than to conventional prose. Dependent clauses and phrases are used in their own right, without the support of a main clause, particularly in TV advertising:

> Introducing the outstanding toploader
> Toploader's new album out now

Sometimes the grammatical unit consists of a single word:

> Tesco. Every little helps

The shorter units of disjunctive grammar make a more immediate impact on idle listeners than discursive sentences, and fewer demands on their concentration.

In some ads they can also create the kind of brusquely masculine effect that goes with hard physical labour:

> The all new Transit
> Job done

Advertisers also break the rules of grammar with unconventional spelling. Sometimes the violation is used to enhance an effect, as in *Krisp*, where *k* gives an apparently harder edge to the sound than *c* could do, or in *creem*, where doubling the vowel may help to intensify a rhyme. Sometimes the changes in spelling seem to have no purpose other than to attract attention by looking different, as in *Whiskas Glocoat*. Playing games with the normal distribution of upper- and lower-case letters is another attention-seeking device.

The creative use of language in advertising

Since products vary very little from one another or from month to month, advertisers try to inject originality into the copy used to promote them. They use neologisms (newly coined words) like *peelability, temptational, outsparkle*, and phrases like *unzip a banana*.

They turn common sense and conventional meaning on their heads in coinings like *In the best circles washing machine is pronounced Parnell*.

They use figurative language also to subvert conventional sense in paradoxical phrases like:

> eating sunshine   smiling colour   purposeful shape

and assertions like:

> Flowers from Interflora speak from the heart

Copy-writers also give the kiss of life to old clichés:

> Are you a Cadbury's fruit and nut case?

Sometimes they use outright puns:

> When it rains, it pours! (Morton's salt)

Sometimes, however, originality appears in language of a terse and simple kind:

- *It is. Are you?* (The *Independent*)
- *I think, therefore IBM* (adapting the famous statement of Descartes).

The use of pattern in advertisements

If the judgement of the Advertising Hall of Fame's panel is anything to go by, the thing that really makes an ad stick in our minds, sometimes for years, is the repetition of linguistic patterns. Even the *Sun*, not normally interested in language studies, ran a full page on advertisements under the headline:

10 BEST SLOGANZ WE'VE EVER 'AD

– testimony to the significant part that advertising plays in most people's lives today.

Many of the most popular ads picked out by the panel work on devices borrowed from poetry: alliteration, assonance, metre, rhyme, and onomatopoeia.

- If you want to get ahead, get a hat
- Hello Tosh, gotta Toshiba
- Happiness is a cigar called Hamlet
- Don't be vague, ask for Haig
- My goodness, my Guinness
- Snap! Crackle! Pop!
- A newspaper, not a snoozepaper
- Ariston and on and on
- A Mars a day helps you work, rest and play

- -

See www.adslogans.co.uk for more on this topic.

Activity

1 Analyse the use of language in any five of the above advertising slogans.

2 Find five recent ads that use the same devices, and analyse their appeal.

Parallelism, arranging equivalent pieces of text close to one another to create a formal pattern, is another device used by advertisers:

It's new! It's crisper! It's lighter!
It's the new Ryvita!

Beginning a number of equivalent clauses with the name of the product achieves the same effect.

One ad stood out above all others in the popularity poll. Why? Because it contained just about every device in the list above. Here it is in full:

A million housewives every day
Pick up a tin of beans and say
Beanz
Meanz
Heinz.

Notice:

- the almost perfectly regular iambic metre in the first two lines
- the rhyme on *say* and *day*
- the internal rhyme or assonance of *Beanz, Meanz,* and *Heinz*
- the alliteration of the *p* in *Pick up* and the voiced consonant *z* at the end of the last three lines.

Notice also how the lines build up to a climax, allowing for three separate stresses on the three final monosyllables. No wonder once heard it could never be forgotten.

Activity

1 Consider the following ad from the point of view of a) metre, b) assonance.
   Mum rollette protects you best

2 Find an example of a recent ad that uses metrical patterning.

3 Assess the appeal of the Pepsi ad below. It may help to copy it out without any of the apostrophes. What kind of consumers do you think it targets?

Lipsmackin'thirstquenchin'
acetastin'motivatin'
goodbuzzin'cooltalkin'
highwalkin'fastlivin'evergivin'
coolfizzin'Pepsi

Pragmatics

Pragmatics is the branch of linguistics which studies the factors that govern our choice of language in social interaction and the effects of our choice on others.

David Crystal, *How Language Works*

In theory, we can say or write anything we like. In practice, we follow a large number of social rules (most of them unconsciously) that constrain the way we speak and write. There are norms of formality and politeness which we have intuitively assimilated, and which we follow when we are talking to people who are older, of the opposite sex, and so on.

When advertising began it was a simple process. In just two lines in a newspaper column, sellers would inform potential buyers what was on offer, and how much it cost:

Cherry Blossom boot polish
2/- a tin.

It was a take-it or leave-it sort of affair.

By 1937 they had taken a step towards persuading potential customers to buy:

A right Merry Christmas with no aches, no pains. R. Garnett Pickles of Kings Parade N3, sells St Clare linement for rheumatism, lumbago, neuritis and gout, for 2/- per small bottle. Remember to buy it for the muscle strain caused by Xmas shopping.

The punch-line, *Remember to buy it...*, is actually a directive, telling readers what to do. The advertisers soften the possible bossy effect, however, by making it sound like a memo on the usual shoppers' list of things to do, along with 'Remember to order the turkey', 'Remember to collect dry cleaning', etc.

Advertisers very quickly learned, in fact, the two central tenets of pragmatics:

1 The way we speak or write is governed by the nature of our audience, and the context in which we are addressing it. We can tell dogs and children what to do, for instance (as long as they're ours), but the constraints of formal politeness dictate that we can't do the same to people we don't know.

2 We often convey meaning obliquely by hinting at what we mean and leaving our listeners to fill in for themselves what we don't actually say. Parents often use this indirect method with small children. 'You don't really want to eat that now

that it's been on the floor, do you?', they say cajolingly, and sooner or later the child learns to interpret this oblique utterance as the directive: 'Don't do that!'

Illustrative example A

Cars of different colours are shown looping through the waves like dolphins, some with dolphin drivers and their families. The movement and the background music create an atmosphere of joyous excitement, matched by the laughing expressions of the dolphins in the cars. A sudden jump cut switches the scene to a car travelling gaily along a road beside the ocean, with a human family inside. A male voice then delivers the punch-line as we watch: *What _____ could do for you.*

Sample critique

The advertisers want to sell you a particular smallish family car. How do they persuade you to buy it in preference to other models in the same price range? By creating an appealing fantasy world for you to visit, carried there by the car. Since dolphins have a reputation as joyous creatures, travelling together in happy, affectionate family groups, much like us, the assumption that the ad is encouraging you to make is clear: choose the car that behaves like a dolphin, the car that dolphins would choose if they were human, and you will share their joyous lifestyle. They revel in the space and freedom of the ocean; you and your passengers will revel in the space and freedom of… in reality, a rather small metal box.

Nowhere in the ad are you told or advised to buy the car. Instead you are enticed unconsciously to collude with the assumptions the advertiser builds into the ad – that you want a happy family life and a free, action-packed lifestyle – and that buying this particular make of car will get them for you.

Illustrative example B

A whole-page glossy ad in the magazine *Source* shows a beautiful young woman pretending to snarl into the ferociously snarling face of a leopard. In the left foreground is a Panasonic plasma TV. The white on glossy black caption in large blocks across the top of the page reads: EXPERIENCE WHAT OTHERS CAN ONLY SEE. The advertising copy at the bottom of the page opposite the TV talks of its ability to *capture the wild,* give you the *thrill of the chase* and deliver a colour experience that gives you *the true intensity and depth of the jungle.*

Sample critique

The ostensible appeal is based on the sheer technical brilliance of the picture quality. Under the surface, however, lies another, unspoken assumption that the ad is working on – that you want to be one up on other people. Buy this superb piece of kit, it assures you (*experience what others can only see*) and you will be. The ad is therefore clearly pitched at the most competitive lovers of gadgetry (and beautiful women): men.

Illustrative example C

A two-page ad for L'Oreal's Elvive Protecting Conditioner for coloured hair. The left-hand page shows a beautiful woman with a cascade of long, lustrous, blonde hair. The facing page shows a crimson container of the product against a largely empty white background, with the phrases COLOUR PROTECT and PROTECTING CONDITIONER highlighted in white capitals against the red background. On the white space to the right of the container the phrase COLOUR PROTECT is repeated, this time highlighted in red. The concept of protection is highlighted five times in all in this advertisement, in the forms PROTECT, PROTECTING and PROTECTIVE, supported by the words TRUST and CARE in the slogan: *Millions of women trust the UK's No. 1 Colour Care Programme.* The whole ad is rounded off with the phrase that has become L'Oreal's trademark: *Because you're worth it.*

Sample critique

According to *Male, Female: The Evolution of Human Sex Differences* by David C. Geary, women's brains are programmed to nurture, protect, and build relationships with others. They also feel a strong need to be protected by someone they know they can trust. The appeal in this ad plays to those needs by emphasizing the words *protect, trust,* and *care.* Potential buyers can *trust* L'Oreal because it *cares* about their hair and wants to *protect* it. A warm feeling is generated, making women readers of the ad feel looked after and empathized with.

But the majority of women also feel guilty at spending money on themselves instead of on those they love. Knowing this, the ad's creators answer the unspoken question bugging the women's minds – 'How can I justify spending all this money on myself?' by assuring them 'you're worth it'.

Activity

Researchers have found that both men and women are motivated by an *achievement* impulse – it's just that they want to achieve rather different goals, and have different strategies for achieving them.

Consider these goals, listed below, then write the copy for an ad designed to appeal to:

a men

b women.

Masculine strategies in day-to-day life that evidence – and fulfil – the achievement impulse:

- status symbols that assert position
- one-upmanship
- politics and playing the game
- focus on the headline, not the detail
- the creation of hierarchies
- focus on hard, rather than soft, measures.

Feminine strategies in day-to-day life that evidence – and fulfil – the achievement impulse:

- working for the greater good
- improving physical surroundings
- self-enhancement
- searching for new answers
- anticipating pitfalls and laying off risk
- assuming responsibility for everything
- improving relationships.

4 Language and Technology

Technological innovation has had a strong influence on language use since the beginning of the twentieth century. Three of the most important developments are outlined below:

- the spread of Standard English through technology
- the increase in scientific and technological vocabulary
- the influence of electronic communication on language and expression.

The spread of Standard English through technology

Before cheap means of travel were invented, most people spoke with the accent and dialect of the region in which they were born; they had little chance to hear any other. Technology has been the key factor in breaking down these linguistic boundaries by introducing the country as a whole to the prestige dialect of the middle and upper classes – **Standard English**.

The arrival of railways (from 1825) and the car (from 1885) helped to bring different groups and classes into physical contact, but the spread of Standard English really got going through the introduction of the telephone (1876), the 'talkies' (feature films with sound, 1927), and most importantly, BBC radio (1922) and television (1936).

To begin with, both radio and television newsreaders and announcers spoke in flawless Standard English, delivered in the 'cut-glass', upper-class accent (**received pronunciation**) still to be found today in the utterances of people like the Queen and the art critic Brian Sewell. (They also had to wear evening dress – even if broadcasting invisibly on the radio.) Together, Standard English and received pronunciation (RP) became the speech model for anyone who wanted to get on in public life, and this is still what the majority of educated people prefer to use today. Some, like the former deputy prime minister John Prescott, stick defiantly to their regional accents to show their allegiance with 'the man-in-the-street', but most content themselves with retaining a short Midland and northern 'a' in words like *bath* and *laugh*, and otherwise conform to the conventional norm.

Activity

Listen to recordings of early BBC broadcasts and write a piece contrasting the following characteristics with those in use today:

- lexis
- accent and grammar
- modes of address
- presentation of programmes.

The impact of radio and television on language use

The impact of these two media has been mixed. On the one hand, both reinforce the position of Standard English by ensuring that all the most important information programmes – news bulletins and documentaries – are broadcast in that prestigious dialect. This is not simply the decision of the controllers of the BBC. When broadcasters with regional accents – Yorkshire, Scottish Highlands, Trinidadian – have been chosen as newscasters and continuity announcers, vigorous protests have been made by some sections of the listening public.

On the other hand, both radio and television have allowed 'ordinary' people to use the airwaves through quiz shows and phone-ins, broadcasting a wide range of local dialects and accents from Norfolk to Bristol to Glasgow.

The presenters of these shows are also chosen because they have, or choose to assume for the sake of the programmes, an accent that diverges from RP. Jonathan Ross speaks more or less Standard English, but brings his lisp and Estuary English glottal stops to his telling of near-the-knuckle jokes and the joshing of celebrities in his late-night programme. (Why wouldn't dirty jokes sound as funny if enunciated carefully in RP?) The Midlands accent of Adrian Chiles is considered suitable for a range of common-interest programmes from football to financial investment.

There is a clear hierarchy of social importance and authority here, reinforced by the careful pre-selection of contributors to radio phone-ins and television quiz shows. Anything too radical or disagreeable is screened out by a show's producers before it reaches the microphone or TV camera, and many callers, as a consequence, fall victim to political correctness before they have chance to speak. The Internet is left as the sole medium uncensored by public opinion or the social and political establishments.

Sport and grammar

Sports broadcasts are perhaps the ones with most claim to have affected the structure of the language:

- by replacing adverbs with adjectives: *I played brilliant[ly] to get this far; He's not perfect[ly positioned] on the red and he's not ideal[ly positioned] on the blue either*
- by using a non-standard past tense: *He done [did] it good [well]*
- by replacing the long-established preposition *by* with non-standard *to*, e.g. *Chelsea's defeat to Manchester United* rather than *Chelsea's defeat by Manchester United*. Thanks to the popularity of sport, this usage spread practically overnight and is now standard in all news bulletins.

Note

Other prepositions have also been replaced by *to* in the nation's affections. Respectable broadsheets like the *Times* commonly use formulations like *The secret to getting rich* and *The cure to baldness*, where a few years ago they would have written *secret of* and *cure for*. Purists have argued for years about the preposition that should follow the adjective *different*: should it be *to*, *from* or *than*? There's no doubt about the winner any more: *to* it is.

Activity

Make short recordings of the following pairs of programmes:

- Radio 5 Live Breakfast Show and Radio 5 Live's 10 am phone-in
- Radio 4 *Today* and Radio 4 *Any Questions*
- Any two programmes of your choice.

Analyse them under these headings:

- Target audience
- Presentational style: serious or humorous; personally involved or neutral; attacking and aggressive or gently questioning
- Language: accent (RP or regional); lexis (formal or informal); grammar (standard or non-standard); tone/ pitch/ volume (calm and well modulated or frenetic and strongly fluctuating)
- Structure: rambling and diffuse or having recognizable structure, e.g. introduction of main topic; 'placing' of main subject, i.e. why it is of interest or to whom; present status/condition of subject, perhaps with supporting evidence from interviewees; in-depth discussion/explanation of subject; narrative commentary; discussion of future developments in relation to subject, plus consequences.

The increase in scientific and technological vocabulary

The remarkable growth in scientific knowledge, particularly in the fields of physics and medicine, has led to a large increase in related vocabulary. *Cardiac arrest, cholesterol* and *chemotherapy* are examples of new words made known to almost everyone through TV programmes such as *Casualty* and *ER*.

Where Anglo-Saxon once created new words by combining old ones (see page 134), modern English coins new words for new things by combining formatives borrowed from French, Latin and Greek. The classic example is *television*, combining Greek *tele* ('at a distance') with *vision* (from Latin *viseo*, sight, from *videre*, to see.) *Emoticon* is another example, created from a combination of *emotion* and *icon* to describe the visual symbols that convey the writer's feelings in rapid-fire electronic communications such as e-mails. David Crystal gives an excellent account of *netspeak* (a positively Anglo-Saxon coinage, this) in his book *Language and the Internet*, 2001.

The invention of the computer has given new meanings to existing words such as *windows, virus, boot, hardware* and *program* (spelled American-style with one 'm' only). Computer technology has also created completely new terms and acronyms such as *DOS, ASCII, byte, RAM*, etc., known only to those in the IT field.

Creating new words

American writers are particularly prolific at word creation, and not just in the technical field. They turn nouns into verbs (newspaper boys *porch* the papers they deliver) and turn the names of particular brands of goods into generic nouns standing for whole categories: *escalator, cola, filo-fax*. Verbs are frequently combined with particles to create new nouns such as *take-off, face-off, check-up, rub-down*, etc., and sports journalists who have to get their reports across as quickly as possible have come up with adjective–verb formulations like *top-score* to replace the longer construction 'scored the highest number of runs'.

The influence of electronic communication on language and expression

Electronic communication differs from traditional letter and memo-writing in several ways.

- It is instantaneous (well, practically – you can e-mail someone thousands of miles away and receive a reply within minutes).

- It ignores formal writing conventions for the sake of speed: *Dear Blank* is replaced by *hi there*, or nothing at all.
- It uses coded abbreviations such as *imo* for the sake of speed and economy.
- It often uses emoticons to show how the writer feels about what is being said, e.g. %-((confused).
- It uses elliptical sentences or incomplete clauses for speed and economy, e.g. *party@8* (the party will start at 8 pm).
- It frequently uses non-standard spelling, deliberately or by mistake, e.g. *program* for *programme*, or other US instead of English versions.
- It flouts conventional punctuation by omitting apostrophes and using only lower-case letters: no capitals for names, titles or the beginnings of sentences.

Is electronic communication therefore a threat to what journalists call the 'gold standard' of written expression – Standard English?

Old-fashioned **prescriptivists** – those who want everyone to follow 'prescribed' grammatical rules – think it is, and dread the slovenly writing that they fear will result. **Descriptivists** like David Crystal, on the other hand (who seek to describe language as it is used), think that the freedom writers find on the unsupervised Internet can result only in more creative and inventive forms of expression. Language belongs to those who use it naturally and spontaneously to express what they think and feel, Crystal says in *Language and the Internet*, and since the Internet is getting more people to write than ever before, it can only be a good thing.

Those who can agree with neither find themselves between a rock and a hard place. On the one hand they can see the ingenuity and fun displayed in good e-mails and texts; on the other they see their limitations.

Activity

Construct an argument in favour of or in opposition to the opinion quoted from Crystal above.

The impact of electronic media

As Marshall McLuhan pointed out in 1962, 'the medium is the message'. The methods we use to communicate affect not only the way we speak and write, but also the way we think, and therefore act.

Before the invention of printing, for instance, knowledge was communicated largely by word of mouth; important events were committed to memory then transmitted to others in the form of stories and poems, often with the help of rhyme and metre (both great memory aids).

With the invention of the book, individuals were able to sit by themselves and read silently. Because they could read the words as often as they liked without the strain of memorizing them, they could focus their attention on them and develop the technique of critical analysis. Writing and reading became the mark of sophisticated intelligence, and speech began to take the back seat it has occupied more or less ever since.

Today, writing and reading in their turn are being affected by new technologies. People who might have felt bound by the formal rules of spelling and grammar when writing with pen and paper happily ignore them when writing e-mails and texting. Something in the abstract freedom of cyberspace seems to encourage a carelessness of style: misspellings, misplaced words and an absence of punctuation.

Under the headline *Is e-mail killing literacy?*, the education correspondent of the *Daily Mail* worries about the effects of the new medium.

> Aficionados of all things high tech and computerised claim that e-mailing should be regarded as more akin to talking, rather than writing.

> Just as we converse with each other in bursts of formal, unedited speech, they insist, the e-mail should be free and easy, unfettered by grammatical rules.

Such an argument is fair enough, she concedes, but not only is sloppy writing an insult to the receiver:

> … the danger is that, with e-mailing becoming more and more commonplace, within a generation people will no longer be able to write in any other way.

And a further problem will then follow:

> … if the e-mail culture continues to spread, bringing with it a deterioration of literary skills, there will not be anyone left to write the books that people want to read.

It's the medium itself that is to blame, she concludes:

> As speed is the prime attraction of the e-mailing process, the whole point is to whack it off into the ether as soon as possible. The time-consuming niceties of literary composition sit uneasily in our pace-obsessed era.

> Monica Porter, *Daily Mail*, 26 October 1999

Writing in answer to such concerns, Joe Joseph claims there is no going back:

> Our brains seem to have adapted so skilfully to this new laissez-faire approach that experiments show that as long as the first and last letter of a word are correctly in place, we can generally understand the sense of a message even if the sentence would look like gibberish to a lexicographer ('Idened, our birans seem to hvae apedtad so slkfilluy to tihs new lissaez-friae aorppach taht exrepeinmts…' – you see what I mean?).

> … So you could certainly offer to correct spelling and grammar on websites that vex you. But don't be surprised if the site-owners respond by offering to give u a bg salp in yuor fcae.

> 'Modern Morals', The *Times*, 24 January 2007

Some writers even claim that e-mailing has widened the range of expression we can use. *ROFL* ('rolling on the floor laughing'), for instance, once used only by teens, has been taken up on mumsnet.com as an onomatopoeic noun in sentences like *Let's go for it – it'll be a roffle*. In the same way, e-mailers who have got fed up with time-consuming emoticons are now beginning to turn them back into written expressions, e.g. *Sorry I can't come tomorrow, sad emoticon face*. E-mailing can encourage writers to be original, in other words.

Maybe it's just the ability to structure that educationalists need to worry about, if journalist Caitlin Moran is right: from a writer's point of view, she rejoices,

> the most enjoyable thing about e-mails is that structure and planning are completely unnecessary. You never really have to come to any stirring conclusion, joyous farewell paragraph or well-considered summing-up. You can just stop typing.

> Caitlin Moran, The *Times*, 23 April 2007

The writers of web-logs are hardly exploiting the richness of English vocabulary, however, according to research conducted for the Oxford English Corpus. The top 15 most frequently used words by writers on the web, as reported in July 2007, are: blogger, blog, shit, oh, yeah, stupid, post, ok, stuff, lovely, myself, update, nice, me and my.

Activity

1 Using your own experience, discuss how far you think e-mails are capable of destroying people's ability to write conventional English.

2 McLuhan initially thought that the invention of electronic media would bring us all into contact again: the world would become a 'global village'. Looking at how people use their mobile phones – in the street, on the train, etc. – and the way in which we watch television, how far do you think the electronic media have succeeded in re-uniting us into one community?

3 The following piece has been translated from e-mail format into conventional letter form. Translate it back into e-mail form, using all the usual abbreviations, such as numbers in place of words or letters, the @ sign for the letters *at*, the & sign for the letters *and* within words, etc.

My only one, thank you so much for your letter* of consolation. I don't know why, but things are clearer now. It feels as if a great weight has been lifted from me. Even as my father lies in St Andrews, fatally unwell… you know what I'm thinking? I think I'm falling in love with you, Clint. Yes, you, and no one else. You, Clint! You, you, you!

I'm mad for you, Clint. Come to me on your return. Only when you and I are one will I feel truly at peace.

Tenderly,

Kate

PS I venerate you. I light candles to you. I make a god of you.

* Use 'e' here as the abbreviation for e-mail.

Compare your electronic version with the conventional one. Do you get the same impression of the writer and her feelings in both versions, or does the conversion into e-mail language alter anything?

Finally, compare your e-mail with the original, written by Martin Amis, on page 71.

If e-mails mangle conventional English, texting goes some way towards replacing it with private codes and a systematized grammar of its own. Below are some of the codes and acronyms used by teens in on-line chat rooms when they want to conceal what they're talking about from parents who might be looking over their shoulders. They were compiled by the software company In Loco Parentis to mark Safer Internet Day on 8 February, 2007.

A/S/L (or simply ASL) = Age, sex, location

LOL = Laugh out loud

PIR = Parents in room

BF/GF = Boy/girlfriend

MorF = Male or female

POS = Parents over shoulder

BRB = Be right back

MOS = Mum over shoulder

G2G = Got to go

NMU = Not much, you?

PRW = Parents are watching

For the sake of speed and economy, single letters, numbers and graphic symbols such as * replace whole words or parts of words (syllables) with the same sound, e.g. *CUL8r* ('see you later'); *RUUp4It?* ('are you up for it?'); *URA** ('you are a star').

Since we can recognize most words when reduced to their most important consonants (see page 65), texting prunes them down to these: it also helps recognition by using capitals for initial consonants and lower case ones for the rest. For example: *Wnt 2 Prty 2nite?*

It also spells words phonetically, cutting out consonants that are never pronounced, like the *gh* in 'night', leaving us with abbreviations like *nite*. All this is eerily reminiscent of the old days of sending telegrams, which were also charged by the number of words and letters. Just as in texting, the art was to cram the most meaning into the fewest words; a message from a student on a gap year, for instance, might have started life as *Please send me £100 and some more clean clothes as quickly as possible to the Hotel Marrakesh, Istanbul, Your loving daughter Ellie* and end up in telegrammese as *Send £100 + clothes Hotel Marrakesh Istanbul ASAP, Ellie*. The trick is to use only the words that carry meaning, ignoring the bits and pieces of grammar that normally string them together. Using acronyms instead of well-known phrases, such as *ETA* for 'estimated time of arrival', is another way to save on words. Put the two together and you arrive at something like: *Wnt 2 Prty 2nite? ETA 8.30* ('Do you want to come to a party tonight at about half-past eight?')

Activity

Write advice for a friend who has just been given a mobile phone, under the heading *Texting for Beginners*. Set it out in the form of a table and use a bullet point to introduce each piece of advice you give.

The influence of texting on register and grammar

Since brevity rules in texting, it's reasonable to suppose that sending SMS messages will tend to simplify expression and cut down the range of vocabulary used. When there are several words to choose from, the one that can be replaced with a single letter will be chosen: for example, *meet you*, *call for you*, *pick you up* will be discarded in favour of *see you* (*CU*). Short words will be preferred to longer ones, and lexis will generally be Anglo-Saxon rather than Latinate.

Sentence structure may be similarly affected, with short, simple sentences predominating over ones that are longer and more complex; but in order to assess this, we shall have to compare some text 'sentences' with the more orthodox sentence structures of Standard English.

In Standard English, every sentence has a central structure called the **independent main clause** (imc). The imc consists simply of a subject (a noun or pronoun) and a verb, e.g. *I* (subject pronoun) *know* (verb). The imc is a complete sentence in itself, and because its structure is simple – one subject, one verb – it is known as a **simple sentence**.

Simple sentences can take the form of:

- statements, e.g. *I am going out.*
- questions, e.g. *Are you going out?*
- commands, e.g. *Go out.*
- exclamations, e.g. *Going out again!*

They are always self-sufficient, i.e. they always make sense on their own. (Don't take this too literally: none of the simple sentences above would mean anything to anyone outside the context they were spoken in, but they would make perfectly good sense to anyone taking part in the conversation.)

In real life, most simple sentences tend to be longer than this, of course. Many will also have an object (another noun or pronoun), e.g. *I am going with* **Harry**.

Still others will have a phrase that extends their meaning, e.g. *I am going with Harry* **in that new car of his**.

The simple sentence is obviously ideal for texting. Short, sharp and to the point, it gets the message across with the minimum of fuss and the maximum of force. (Too much force sometimes, unfortunately. In the wrong hands it has been used to bully people.) Brief as it is, however, texters have managed to pare it further down to the bone with the help of ellipsis (omission of words or phrases). By leaving out the subject they can cut straight to the meat of the message, contained in the verb, e.g. *CU 2nite.*

The compound sentence

Compound sentences are made up of simple sentences strung together by **co-ordinating conjunctions** such as *and*, *but*, *so*, and *then*. The idea is to make a series of short, staccato simple sentences run more smoothly and sound more pleasant, e.g. *I'll see you at eight. We'll go to Raj's party about nine.* becomes *I'll see you at eight* **and** *we'll go to Raj's party about nine.*

Since economy is more important to texters than a smoothly flowing style, compound sentences will be junked in favour of something shorter and less expensive, like *CU@8 Rs prty 9.*

The complex sentence

The complex sentence is so called because it adds at least one other clause to the independent main one, making its structure more complex, e.g. *I'll see you at eight* (imc) *if I can* (dependent clause).

This second clause is described as **dependent**, to indicate that it depends for its meaning on the imc it is attached to. It has exactly the same structure as the independent main clause, but because it is introduced by the **subordinating**

conjunction *if*, it cannot stand on its own two feet as the imc can. Compare *I'll see you at eight* with *if I can* and you'll see the difference.

There are a number of other subordinating conjunctions, e.g. *because*, *although*, *when*, *until*, *as if*, *unless*, and all introduce dependent clauses that in some way modify our perception of what is told to us in the main clause.

Why are complex sentences important? Because while simple sentences generally make unqualified statements and assertions, complex sentences allow us to say much more about the circumstances surrounding those statements. With their help a speaker/ writer can add the following kinds of information about events:

- **when** they happened: ***After*** *Harry went to the party, he forgot Louise.*
- **why** they happened: ***Because*** *he was a flirt, Sally ignored him.*
- **how** they happened: *Louise acted **as if** she didn't care.*
- **what concessions** are being made: *Sally ignored him, **although** secretly she was pleased.*
- **what limits** are being set: *Harry waited **until** his patience ran out.*
- **what constraints** are being imposed: ***Unless*** *Sally phoned him soon, he would go back to Louise.*

Punctuation in simple sentences

Punctuation seems somehow out of place in e-mails and text messages – it looks too heavy. Consider two statements like the following, for example:

Harry soon dumped Louise   He preferred Sally

Both are simple sentences containing a subject and a verb, and according to textbook rules of punctuation, only two correct punctuation marks can be used between them: a full stop (also called a period) to separate them, e.g. *Harry soon dumped Louise. He preferred Sally.* or a semi-colon to join them, e.g. *Harry soon dumped Louise; he preferred Sally.* (They can of course be joined by a co-ordinating conjunction like *and* or *because*, but that is not the point at issue here.)

Neither the full stop nor the semi-colon seems to suit the emotional context here: both give an impression of stability and common sense at odds with both the short time-span of the relationship and the fickle nature of Harry. Some writers, even ones as famous as Iris Murdoch, get round the problem by simply using a comma to emphasize the careless speed of the affair: *Harry soon dumped Louise, he preferred Sally.*

This is frowned upon by purists, however, since commas are normally used to separate incomplete clauses or phrases from ones that are complete in themselves. Use them to separate two complete ones, as in the case above, and you signal your ignorance of what a sentence is. (Writers like Iris Murdoch can get away with it because they've passed all their exams. You haven't, yet – better stick to the rules.)

For the writers of texts and e-mails, the preferred solution is often an unconventional dash, leaving the readers' imaginations to fill the gap it creates: *Harry soon dumped Louise – he preferred Sally.*

This solution again is strictly speaking incorrect, and in formal writing would be held against you. It might be safer to avoid the problem entirely by using one of the following methods:

- using short simple sentences in situations calling for a common-sense, practical approach

- using a simple sentence plus a phrase, e.g. *Preferring Sally, Harry soon dumped Louise.*
- using a complex sentence, e.g. *Because he preferred Sally, Harry soon dumped Louise.*

Punctuation in complex sentences

Complex sentences, you will remember, consist of an independent main clause or simple sentence and one or more dependent minor clauses that flesh out its meaning. For example:

After he dumped Louise [minor clause depending on the imc]

Harry waited several days [imc]

before ringing Sally [phrase dependent on the imc]

because he felt [minor clause depending on the imc]

a bit of a brute. [phrase dependent on the preceding minor clause]

If the relationship between imcs and dependent clauses is clear, as in the above example, punctuation is again a matter of style. The sentence above is quite clear as it is:

After he dumped Louise Harry waited several days before ringing Sally because he felt a bit of a brute.

Nothing much is gained by adding commas to the sentence like this:

After he dumped Louise, Harry waited several days before ringing Sally, because he felt a bit of a brute.

They're not wrong; it's just a question of taste.

On the whole, it's probably best to avoid unnecessary commas. They should never be used for either of the following reasons:

- to allow the reader time to take a breath (speakers might need a chance to take a breath, but readers don't!)
- because you've written several lines without using one: they're not meant to act as decorations!

The real purpose of commas, apart from the stylistic use described above, is to mark a clause or phrase off from another clause or phrase that it doesn't belong to. Fail to use a comma in a sentence like the one below, and your readers may be misled:

If a pregnant woman smokes her baby may be harmed.

They may read *smokes her baby* as one unit of sense before realizing they should be kept apart. Put in the comma and there is no risk of misunderstanding:

If a pregnant woman smokes, her baby may be harmed.

Apparently the most simple punctuation mark, the comma is actually the trickiest of all to handle, and you should treat it with care.

Activity

In the light of what has been said above, write an article of about 300–400 words speculating on the possible effects of texting on students' writing. You should consider lexis, sentence structure and punctuation, and illustrate what you say in the light of your own experience.

E-mail text for activity on page 66

my only 1: thank u so much 4 your e of consol8ion. i don't no y, but things r clearer now. it feels as if a gr8 w8 has been lifted from me. even as my father lies in st &rew's, f8ally unwell… u no wat i'm thinking? i think i'm falling in love with u, clint, yes, u, and no 1 else. u, clint, u,u,u!

i'm mad 4 u, clint. come 2 me on your return. only when u & i are 1 will i feel truly@ peace.

10derly, k8

ps: i vener8 u. i lite c&les to u. i make a god of u.

Martin Amis, *Yellow Dog*

5 Writing to Inform and Instruct

Guidelines for creating texts

'I'm looking at a sheet of blank paper. How do I start?'

You're not alone. All over the country professional writers are sitting at their desks, wondering the same thing. One even wrote a radio sit-com on the subject recently – neatly using the difficulty of getting started to get out of the difficulty of getting started. Since inspiration rarely strikes out of a clear blue sky, the best thing is to look at some practical suggestions and see if any of them work for you.

You have four over-arching categories to work in:

- writing to inform
- writing to instruct
- writing to persuade
- writing to entertain.

The kind of texts you might produce in these categories are suggested below:

Information texts (discussed in this chapter)	Entertaining/persuasive texts (see Chapter 6)
instruction leaflets	accounts of personal experience
information leaflets	newspaper/magazine articles
newspaper articles	short stories
biographies	
sit-com scripts	

In any of these categories, the more practical your purpose is the more factual and plain you need to make your style. Conversely, when you want to advise or encourage or enlighten or persuade your readers the more varied and colourful (and possibly emotive) your style needs to be.

Choosing your material

If you've got just one main interest, the problem is solved: you can write about that. If you're really passionate about something, your enthusiasm is bound to rub off on your audience. If you've got several genuine interests, try to work out which you can get the most mileage from. You don't want to write 500 words and then find you've nothing else to say. One way of checking this is to ask yourself the questions below about your potential subject area. These questions won't all spark off ideas, but one or two might.

- **Social questions:** Is it well-known? Does it play an important part in social life? Is it popular?
- **Economic questions:** Is it expensive? Does it need subsidizing? Do the political parties disagree about its funding?

- **Scientific questions:** Is there scientific evidence or support for your subject? Is there a link with ecology or the environment?
- **Religious questions:** Does religion have anything to say about your subject? Is there a link with morality?
- **Historical questions:** How was your subject regarded in the past? What difference do you see today?
- **Aesthetic questions:** Have there been any films, plays, books, paintings, etc. of your subject?

You need to think hard about these possible connections – they can help you to produce really wide-ranging and substantial pieces on subjects as diverse as 'The Importance of Sport', 'The Addictive Personality', 'Does God Exist?'.

Alternatively, if you are struggling to find a topic, go through the feature pages of the *Times*, the *Independent*, the *Daily Telegraph* and the *Guardian* and make a list of the subjects discussed. (The features pages deal with topics of general interest – avoid the sections that deal with sport, politics, finance and international news unless you intend to write about something in one of these areas.) If the same subject or topic crops up in two or more papers, you've got a lead on something of public interest that you might be able to write about from your own individual angle.

If all else fails, ask ten people of your own age (five male, five female) and ten people over the age of 45 (five male, five female) what they would most like to read a magazine or newspaper article or short story about. (Since teenagers apparently always come up with the same two answers – 'sex' and 'drugs', you may have to listen politely and then ask them for the next most appealing topic.)

Defining your purpose

Ask yourself what you want each of your two pieces of writing to do for your audience: entertain, inform, persuade, or instruct them? Or a combination of two or more of these aims? It's vital to know before you begin because, like your choice of audience, it will influence your style. It's best to avoid jokes, slang, and exotic images, for instance, if you're setting out simply to instruct.

Deciding on your target audience

Begin by asking yourself what kind of audience you're going to write for – what age group, sex, class, education level, interests, newspaper readership – because this is what will determine the kind of vocabulary and sentence structure you will use. (Remember, for example, that people who have not achieved a high educational level may struggle with abstract nouns. One person applying for housing benefit was asked about 'length of residence' and replied 'About 50 feet'.)

Choosing your genre

Your brief is to show the examiners that you can write in two broadly different styles: one clear, precise, and objective; the other imaginative and entertaining. You therefore need to choose two contrasting genres and produce two texts amounting to 1500–2500 words in total.

'How do I know which genres to choose?' you may ask.

Choose by asking yourself what format would suit each subject best. Suppose you decided to write about a pair of aspirational (i.e. 'pushy') parents, disappointed because their only child doesn't live up to their expectations in looks and personality, or in intelligence. You could treat it as a short story; a fictional child's biography; a discursive essay on the do's and don'ts of parenting; an instruction booklet; the text for a lecture on how to bring up children; or a persuasive piece pleading the case for children being allowed to develop without undue pressure from parental expectations. It's up to you.

Register and style

This will obviously vary according to your purpose and intended audience. As a rule of thumb, you will need to keep your vocabulary and your sentence structure at the informal end of the scale when writing to entertain, and at the more formal for more serious purposes like instruction and persuasion.

The rest of this chapter deals with writing to inform and instruct, and how to put together effective commentaries on this type of writing. See Chapter 6 for writing to entertain and persuade.

Writing to instruct

Because its purpose is strictly limited – to enable someone to do something they have never done before – writing instructions is easy to do and easy to describe.

Approach and manner: This should be impersonal and matter-of-fact. Avoid addressing your readers as 'you'; your purpose is not to build a relationship with them, just to explain what to do.

Structure: Arrange each step in the procedure in chronological order. For example, start with a list of the equipment and/or materials needed, describe any necessary preparations, and go on from there to step 1 and all the other steps.

Lexis: Use simple, precise vocabulary, avoiding abstract nouns, slang, or colloquialisms.

Grammar: Avoid personal pronouns, e.g. 'I' and 'you'; these belong to more friendly, conversational styles of writing.

Use only the kind of adjectives that relate to physical attributes such as weight, size, colour, and so on: a *sharp* knife; *heavy* material; *level* ground; a *three-person* tent, etc.

Use only verbs that are **directive** (i.e. that tell someone what to do) and **dynamic** (i.e. involve action of some kind), e.g. *collect* the things you will need; *check* that your torch is working; *smear* the honey on to the tree trunk, etc.

Sentence structure: Make this as short and concise as possible so that each point is easy for readers to take in.

Graphology: Lay out your instructions on the page so that each step in the procedure has a line to itself; this will help readers who have looked away from your instructions to find their place again quickly. For extra clarity, preface each line with a number or a bullet point.

You can also lay out information in columns as in the example on the next page – instructions offered to first-time campers.

DO	DON'T
Gain permission from the landowner	Buy too big a tent
Pitch your tent on level ground	Buy too much equipment
Dispose of rubbish thoughtfully	Make noise late at night
Only light fires in designated areas	Let children kick a ball round the tents
Check the weather forecast	Forget the tin-opener – or the corkscrew
Avoid busy periods	
Be considerate to other campers	
Keep dogs under control	

Turning instructions into advice

Instructions give commands in a detached, impersonal manner; advice suggests what you might want to do, and says it in a more friendly, personal way. The odd direct command may creep in once in a while, but usually if the writer feels readers need to be told what to do, he or she does it by using modal verbs like *should*, *ought*, *need* and so on. Verbs like these suggest that there are good reasons why readers should do what the advice says: they're required to do so by considerations of commonsense and received opinion.

See the example below.

> One of the keys to successful camping is choosing the right tent. You need room in your tent for more than just sleeping, so if you want to accommodate two people, for example, choose a three-person tent.
>
> The shape of the tent is also important. Will it be a dome (large dome tents can be unstable), tunnel, cabin, frame tent (these can be heavy and take longer to erect), or a hybrid of dome and tunnel?
>
> Tents can be made of traditional cotton canvas, or nylon or polyester, which are lighter materials but not breathable and can lead to hot interiors. Ventilation in tents is important, so check out the size of the doors and windows.
>
> When choosing a suitable place to erect a tent, campers should look for a flat, well-drained spot. Hilly or bumpy sites are uncomfortable. Do not pitch your tent under a tree, because tree roots can make the ground hard and rough. It will be more difficult to hammer in the tent pegs. Trees can also be struck by lightning.
>
> Priorities vary when choosing a camp site. Is the site easily accessible? Does it cater for families with young children or people with special needs? Do dogs have to be kept on leads? Some sites have specially designated dog walks.

Points to note

Paragraph 1: Uses personal pronouns, creating a friendly tone. Use of the minor conditional clause *if you want to accommodate two people... choose a three-person tent* allows readers freedom of choice in a way that a purely instructional style would not, e.g. *To accommodate two people, buy a three-person tent.*

Paragraph 2: The text engages readers' interest by asking them questions; it also helps them to make their own choices by informing them of the different types of tent available and their individual characteristics.

Paragraphs 3 and 4: Note the use of the modal verb in *campers should look for*, in place of the blunter 'look for'; note also that when the text does use directive verbs – e.g. *check out the size of the doors and windows, Do not pitch your tent under a tree* – the writer is careful to explain why. This is something the writer of pure instructions doesn't have time to do.

Activity

Using the above list of points to guide you, turn the list of Do's and Dont's on the previous page into a magazine article advising first-time campers how to get the most out of their experience.

Writing to inform

There are two main kinds of informative writing: in the first, writers are impersonal authority figures who know more than their readers and are concerned only with transmitting this knowledge to them. Writers of this kind are found in such subject fields as law, medicine, science and technology, and though what they write about (their **content**) may differ, their styles are much the same.

Characteristics of purely informative writing

Manner and tone: The manner is detached, the tone impersonal; the writer takes no prisoners but gets straight down to the subject:

> The genetic code relates the sequence of nucleotides in a DNA molecule with the amino acids whose nature and order of assembly into a protein they specify. An amino acid is specified by a triplet of nucleotides.

Lexis: This will contain many subject-specific, technical words (see the example above), most of which will derive from Latin, or Greek through Latin; many will be esoteric – i.e. known only to those who specialize in this subject field.

Sentence structure: This will vary, but will contain more complex than simple sentences. This is especially true in the case of legal writing, which can have sentences nearly a page in length.

Grammar: Writers in these specialized fields like to use **impersonal pronouns** and verbs in the **passive voice**; this allows them to create abstract constructions such as *It has been found/discovered/noted/recognized that…* instead of the more usual *Scientists have found that…* (see *An amino acid is specified by a triplet of nucleotides* above). The idea seems to be to get people out of the way in order to concentrate on the facts under discussion; writers also commonly use **stative verbs** (verbs that describe a state of affairs rather than an action) in this kind of factual writing, because they are talking about inanimate objects which are capable only of existing in one state or another.

It is unlikely that you will choose to produce this kind of writing yourself, though you may be asked to categorize and comment on it. The sort of texts you may choose to write will have more in common with the second kind of informative writing, discussed below.

Characteristics of general informative writing

At its simplest, informative writing of this kind does just what it says on the tin – offers information. Consider the information leaflet or flyer below:

THURSDAY JULY 14th

AT 7.30 pm

LIFE IN VICTORIAN LONDON

LECTURER: THOMAS TALLIS MA (Oxon)

Tickets: Adults £10.00; Concessions £6.50

Manner: Completely impersonal; the writer makes no attempt to make contact with the anonymous audience, for example by asking 'Anybody out there interested in Victorian London?'.

Style: The text is a bare announcement of factual information: spare and colourless.

Lexis: Only relevant words are used, and they convey only facts; with the exception of the figures indicating date and price, all the words are nouns, i.e. the names of the things that need to be mentioned; adjectives and adverbs to create colour are totally absent.

Sentence structure: There are no complete sentences; the writer is using ellipsis – the technique of deliberately leaving out parts of a sentence and relying on readers to supply it for themselves:

> [**On**] Thursday July 14th at 7.30 pm [**a lecture will be given/there will be a lecture**] by Thomas Tallis MA [**on**] Life in Victorian England. Tickets [**will cost**] £10 for Adults and £6.50 for Concessions.

Structure/organization: The writer has set out the text in the most logical order, with day of the week and date coming first so that readers can check whether they're free to attend. (It's irritating to get interested in something only to find you can't go.) Cost, on the other hand, logically comes last, because if you're sufficiently interested you'll want to attend the lecture, regardless.

Graphology: The information in this example would normally be arranged so that it took up a good part of the centre of the leaflet (about two thirds, say); this is because if you 'island' your print by surrounding it with wide margins you highlight it and make it look more important (tabloid newspapers make the most of a little news by using this trick); even in the small space allowed in this textbook, it's easy to see how the bold black print is set off by a white background (pastel colours would also work), and how the most important words – *Life in Victorian England* – are emphasized by being presented in larger print than the others.

A longer leaflet or brochure, in contrast, would give the lecturer the chance to introduce and outline the talk; there is an immediate softening of tone and the slightest hint of persuasion:

LIFE IN VICTORIAN LONDON   **Thursday 14 July**

Tutor: Thomas Tallis MA (Oxon), lecturer for the Asquith Portrait Gallery

After considering the phenomenal growth of the capital in the 19th century, we look at how London coped via its new forms of transport, new roads and bridges, new buildings and even its (all too necessary) new sewage system. We contrast the life of the upper classes with that of the poor of Dickens's London. We examine the work of those early photographers who recorded the lives of the workers of London in 1875 and asked them how they lived. We particularly study the photographs of John Thomson. This produces a unique insight into how ordinary people thought and felt. We end by considering the festivals and celebrations of Victorian London and make a special study of the Crystal Palace, taking its story up to the present day.

Manner: The manner is still formal and the tone impersonal, but the writer uses the inclusive pronoun 'we' to indicate that he wants his audience to be active participants in the proceedings rather than just passive listeners – that he intends in fact to be a friendly guide rather than a remote authority figure.

Lexis: The writer uses ordinary, middle-of-the-road vocabulary, without Latinate abstractions at one end of the scale or colloquialisms at the other, to suit the majority of his audience.

Sentence construction: The sentences tend to be short and straightforward, again aiming to ensure that the content is easily understood by everyone in the audience. If the first sentence is rather long, its length comes from the piling up of nouns (*new roads/ bridges/ buildings/ and sewage system*) to get as many facts into a small space as possible, rather than from any complexity of construction. Two sentences are simple one-clause statements: *We contrast the life of the upper classes with that of the poor of Dickens's London… We particularly study the photographs of John Thomson*. The final sentence is **compound**, consisting of two simple clauses joined together by the conjunction *and*.

The writer's purpose here is still mainly to inform, and verbs are therefore in the indicative or declarative mood throughout; there are no directives, such as *Come and hear how the poor of London lived and felt*.

Grammar: The writer's grammar is conventionally correct, as we would expect; two grammatical ploys are used to engage readers' interest and suggest that the lecture will be fun: 1) the inclusive pronoun 'We', in phrases like *we look, we study*, suggesting that the audience will be expected to work with the lecturer, and 2) the use of the present tense to describe the action, rather than the more usual future, to make readers imagine it's all happening here and now, and they're part of it: ***This produces** a unique insight into how ordinary people thought and felt*.

Structure/organization: The writer outlines the beginning, middle and end of the lecture clearly in very few words: the use of the participle phrase ***After considering** the phenomenal growth… we look at how London coped* informs readers that the lecture begins with the city's growth, then goes on to its reconstruction; the introduction of the word *classes* shows that the middle of the lecture is devoted to London's inhabitants, and the last part to how the capital flaunted its new wealth: ***We end** by considering the festivals and celebrations of Victorian London*.

Information/publicity leaflets

When we move away from more serious subjects into the world of entertainment, the mood softens further, and the tone becomes more persuasive. The leaflets still give information, but they do it in such a way that they influence and shape people's thoughts about it at the same time. For example, a rather formal-looking leaflet publicizing the Savill Garden starts with the dynamic directive **Head for** the *Hidden Gardens...*, and follows it with an emotive adjective or two: *to find plants that* **explode** *into colour...*

In the same way, theatrical flyers will give potential audiences the dates and times of an upcoming production, but will also 'puff' the show to draw them in with headings like these:

FOR TWO WEEKS ONLY!   PRIOR TO THE WEST END

The message is: 'Get there quick – it's not on for long.' 'Go now – it'll be cheaper and you'll be one up on your friends.'

'THIS SHOW WILL ENCHANT EVERYONE' * * * *

INDEPENDENT

'A GREAT BIG HIT!' * * * * *

DAILY MAIL

The message is: 'Better go – you don't want to miss out on something everyone's talking about!'

Information and inducements go hand in hand in leaflets put out by tourist boards and institutions like English Heritage or the Royal Society for the Protection of Birds. Look how the writer of a National Trust booklet hooks parents dreading the long school holidays with a catchy header and a terrific periodic second sentence:

Discover 1000s of unforgettable family days out

The long summer holidays just won't seem long enough with our calendar of fantastic family activities in your area. From chasing butterflies in the fresh air, dressing up as knights and painting faces as *Jungle Book* characters to discovering what's living in the ponds and tucking into delicious treats in one of our tea-rooms, there is something for every family to enjoy together whether you're indoors or out.

Activity

Explain how the structure of the above sentence creates the impression of endless activity and choice.

Having captured readers' attention, the writer goes on to bombard them with the following.

Directives: *Get all dressed up at Bodiam Castle.*

Direct questions: *How many cabbage whites and red admirals will you spot?*

Invitations: *Bring the whole family for a bright and colourful walk.*

Financial concessions in larger print, one for parents, one for kids: *3 months' family membership for free; Kids! Start your Hidden Nature adventure here with your free Nature Passport.*

Word-play to add appeal in sentences like: *Pick up a pond dipping net and try your hand at discovering what creepy crawlies and insects are living in the lake.* Kids love patterned sound like the repeated 'p's and 'c's and 'l's here.

Layout and graphology: The layout of publicity material like this adds enormously to its appeal; the two main pages have three coloured rectangles set against a basic white background, two green, one blue; each rectangle contains a description of one of the activities mentioned in the periodic sentence at the head of the page, plus a snapshot of children engaged in actually doing it; the different size and colour of the captions within the rectangles and in the white space between them also add interest and visual appeal.

Activity

1 Read through the critiques given above and make a list of all the techniques to (a) inform and (b) engage readers that are mentioned. You will then have some guidelines to follow if and when you choose to produce similar texts of your own.

2 Follow the steps below to create an extended publicity leaflet giving information to tourists who might want to visit your particular region, county, or home town (or all three – it will depend upon how much there is to say about each). These steps describe the process using a sheet of paper, but you could of course create the leaflet on screen instead.

   a Take a sheet of A3 paper; fold it once lengthways, then once across to give you four small pages.

   b Allow each page margins of white space: a 5cm margin across the top, a 2cm margin at each side, and a 1cm margin across the bottom. (The white space at the top is where you will write your header in coloured lettering, e.g. *Discover 100s of unforgettable...*)

   c On the main body of the page draw three rectangular boxes measuring roughly 12 cm wide by 5 cm deep, leaving thin strips of white space between them. Ideally, the boxes would have a background colour to make them stand out against the white background and look more appealing. You can of course alter the size and arrangement of the boxes to suit yourself. You could even get rid of them altogether and use photographs of different buildings, landscapes and local scenes with printed comments about them underneath, above, or to the side. The idea is just to create some eye-appeal.

   d Use each of the boxes to give information about a different feature of the area or place you're describing, e.g. history (prehistoric remains, ruined castles, architectural treasures); landscape (beaches, lakes, hills); local culture (galleries, museums, folklore, customs, crafts, foods, traditional pubs, gourmet restaurants); sporting activities (local teams, golf courses, sports facilities); famous people (writers, soldiers, politicians, performers); famous gardens, festivals, shows, exhibitions and events; and anything else you can think of.

(continued)

If this approach seems too formal for the tone you want to achieve, you could write in the persona of a tourist who has visited all these places, using 'holiday photographs' to illustrate the leaflet, and writing in your own hand (or your computer's version of handwriting) to friends and family about your experiences.

Another idea is to use the letters of the alphabet to introduce the different aspects of life in your chosen locality: e.g. *A is for Animals, and where better to see them in a natural setting than in the wide open spaces of Whipstead Safari Park...*

e   Give information in small print at the bottom of the last page about ways of travelling to your chosen locality by bus, train, and road, and indicate the range of accommodation available. Make up a few website addresses for readers to access for further information.

f   Give some thought to graphology as well as layout: use stencils to produce different sizes and styles of lettering, and use 'handwriting' styles where it seems appropriate to get a more friendly, personal effect. Differently coloured lettering also creates variety.

Writing biographies

If you are producing biographical material, your writing almost structures itself: every life has a beginning, middle, and end, and it's easiest and probably best to follow this pattern. If, however, the man or woman you are writing about lived a life full of drama and died in unexpected or even tragic circumstances, you could involve your readers by giving a vivid picture of the death and leading them back through the various circumstances and events that brought it about. But if your subject is your grandfather or some other less famous figure, it's better stick to the first pattern. Either way, it's up to you to provide the facts. Books, the Newspaper Archives at Collingdale, and the Internet should provide you with plenty of these.

Background

Begin with an account of the subject's family background as far back as his or her grandparents, since the influences that shaped your subject's parents will also have played a role in shaping him or her. (Look at the royal family, for example, or Gordon Brown, for illustrations of how the upbringing of one generation impacts on the development of the next.)

Next, you could talk about the geography and economics of the village/ town/ city/ region in which your subject grew up. What social class was he or she born into? What was his or her reaction to this social and economic background? Did your subject stay loyal to these influences or attempt to escape them as soon as possible?

Personal development

Discuss your subject's educational background: What kind of school? What talents and interests shown? What kind of relationships with staff and fellow students? Popularity? Any further education, e.g. university? If so, in what subject, at what level? Again, discuss interests, activities, and any lasting friendships/ contacts made at university. If your subject went straight into work or work-related training, give details.

Experiences in middle life

Having got your subject launched into the big wide world, spend the middle of your biography discussing his or her successes and failures in relation to:

- career, work and any public matters
- personal life, e.g. marriage, children, family, friends.

Later life

Discuss the closing stages of life and eventual death.

Evaluation

Discuss your subject's life as a whole: was it a happy and successful life? Did your subject make other people's lives happier or better in some way? Was your subject ultimately responsible for what happened to him or her, or did the circumstances of life make him or her to some extent a victim? Do you like your subject as a human being, or not?

Activity

Decide on a person whose life you would like to write, then research the facts you will need to use, following the guidelines above.

Writing a commentary

When you have finished each piece of work you will need to write a commentary (of about 500 words) on it, exploring the writing process and assessing the success of the finished piece. This will be easier if you plan ahead for the writing of the commentary, and keep detailed notes at each stage of the work you do while you are creating your text.

At the beginning of the process you will have chosen the subjects for your two pieces of original writing, and the kinds of audience you'll be writing them for, bearing in mind that your two pieces need to show different skills. For each piece, the audience could be a wide cross-section of the population (old and young, male and female, educated and less well educated, rich and poor); or teenagers and young adults; or children, and so on. These two things – subject and audience – will influence every other part of the writing process: the manner and tone you adopt, the kind of lexis and sentence structure you use, etc.

You will also be clear about your reason and/or purpose for writing at this stage, too, because this is tied up with your choice of subject and audience.

So begin your commentary by explaining why you chose your particular subject, and why you thought it was important to write about it for your particular audience.

Choice of subject

You might begin with something like this:

> After a lot of thought, I decided to write about [*insert either the title of your piece here, e.g.* The Dangers of Cannabis, *or the title of your subject field, e.g.* The Use of Drugs in Contemporary Society.]

Audience and purpose

Go on to explain who you were writing for and why.

> It seemed to me that the people most likely to use cannabis – those between the ages of 15 and 35, mostly male – see it as harmless pleasure, not as bad for them as nicotine or alcohol, and I wanted to give them enough information about it to enable them to decide whether to give it up for the sake of their mental and physical health.

Genre

You also need to explain your choice of genre, as any subject lends itself to different kinds of treatment.

> I could have shown the dangers of using cannabis in a number of different genres: a short story in which the main character starts by smoking cannabis to control stress and anxiety and ends up a physical wreck through losing control of his car; a fictional biography in which a cannabis user's promising career is bought to an end by paranoid schizophrenia; an imaginary personal account by a former user, describing in vivid detail how and why he came to give it up.

> In the end, I decided against all of these because they could just be shrugged off as fiction: 'Things like that only happen in stories, not to people like me.' A magazine article seemed a better bet because although I could use some emotional language to move readers' feelings, I could try to influence their minds with some reasoned argument based on cold fact, too.

Style models

The examiners want to know about the texts you used as style models, so they can judge how successful you've been in adapting your style. If you have been reading around to learn how informative or persuasive writing is done, you might say something like this (see Chapter 6 page 104 for a discussion of these technical terms):

> I decided to use the introduction–thesis–antithesis–conclusion structure for my article, putting forward any evidence that cannabis is beneficial first, to avoid being thought prejudiced, then following it with evidence of the opposite kind. Since I'm writing an article aiming to inform and advise, I want my readers to be free to make up their own minds on the drug. I have read several articles by journalists like Michael Gove that use this structure.

> If I'd wanted to persuade and convince, I could have gone in really strongly with a slashing attack on it and a conclusion that it should be classified with hard drugs: the introduction–thesis–conclusion model. I've read lots of articles by writers like Rod Liddle and Richard Littlejohn that argue aggressively like this.

Having got the preliminaries out of the way, you then need to get down to details and discuss the style of your writing. In the case of the article about drugs, you would be writing for young people without any in-depth knowledge of the subject, and would adapt your style to suit.

Below are some examples that may help you in writing your commentary for the examiners to read.

Manner and tone

If you tell people of my age what to do, it makes them want to do the opposite, so I aimed for a friendly, conversational manner and used modal verbs and verbs in the subjunctive mood rather than imperatives, e.g. 'Perhaps we *should do* a bit of research for ourselves…'; 'It *might be* better to listen to what scientists have to say in the latest reports…'; 'We *ought* at least to think about…'; I also used inclusive pronouns, e.g. *you*, *we*, *our*, and contracted words like 'cannot' and 'you will' to 'can't' and 'you'll' to help soften the tone.

Lexis

I wasn't able to avoid some technical vocabulary, because it's used in official reports on cannabis, so I used specialized terms like 'paranoia', 'schizophrenia', and 'psychotic disorders' when necessary, then explained what they mean in my own words, e.g. 'Most users will admit that they sometimes have mild fits of paranoia. This makes them imagine they're being persecuted, so they shrink away from other people – even their best mates – and end up alone and frightened.' I had to do the same for the slang terms used by cannabis users in case some people might not be familiar with them, e.g. spliff, joint, weed, grass, skunk, etc.

Changes made in the first draft

When I'd printed off my first draft I looked at the writing to see if I could upgrade the style in some way.

Sentence structure

I managed to liven up some ordinary sentences by turning them into balanced and periodic ones. For instance, I turned the sentence,

'Some cannabis users claim that cannabis is less harmful than tobacco, but doctors are not convinced because the claim hasn't been fully proved yet.'

into the sentence,

'Users claim that cannabis is less harmful than tobacco; doctors say the claim has not been fully proved.'

I think the disagreement comes out more strongly through the neat contrast between the two halves of the sentence, with users set directly against doctors.

I also changed the sentence,

'Common side-effects of smoking "dope" are short-term memory loss, shortened concentration span, and the slowing down of reflexes.'

to one with a periodic structure because it seemed to make the point more forcefully:

'Short-term memory loss, shortened concentration span, the slowing down of reflexes – all are common side-effects of smoking "dope".'

Grammar

I also changed the impersonal tone of one very formal sentence by replacing the third-person pronoun 'they' with the second person 'you', to make the danger seem more real and close to my readers. The first version was:

'Most users will admit that they sometimes have mild fits of paranoia. This makes them imagine they're being persecuted, so they shrink away from other people – even their best mates – and end up alone and frightened.'

I changed this to:

'If you're like most cannabis users, smoking it will sometimes give you fits of mild paranoia – the feeling that you're being persecuted. You'll feel like hiding away from other people, even your best mates, and end up frightened and alone.'

Keeping records of your research

You must list all the substantial articles and books you have read or consulted to gather material for your writing, giving the names of author, title, publisher and date.

There are two reasons for this:

- to avoid charges of plagiarism: if the examiners suspect you have used substantial chunks of somebody else's writing they will access your sources to check
- if your work were to be published, your publisher would need to ask any writers you have quoted for permission to use their work in your article.

You can use a sentence or two from the writer you're quoting without permission, but only as long as you make a clear reference to him or her, e.g. 'As Rosalie Pacula explains in her book, *Cannabis Use and Dependence…*'

Longer extracts must be fully attributed – you must give the name of the author, the title, publisher and date.

You need to provide a list of your source materials. You could present it as in this example.

The materials I read when researching my projected article are listed below.

Books:

Cannabis Use and Dependence, Rosalie Liccardo Pacula, Cambridge University Press, 2003 (I did not read the whole of this book, just Section 3: 'The psychological effects of chronic cannabis use'.)

The press:

A report by Nigel Hawkes, Health Editor of the *Times* newspaper, of a paper published in *The Lancet* in July 2007, on the risks of psychotic illness associated with cannabis smoking; the *Times*, Friday 27 July 2007

Article entitled 'Evidence of "reefer madness" is not new' by Dr Thomas Stuttaford in the *Times*, Friday 27 July 2007

Internet websites: bbc.co.uk Science and Nature 'Hot Topics' – Cannabis website.

Adaptations of the source material

The examiners want you to explain any ways in which you had to adapt your source materials to suit your writing. Continuing with the cannabis example, you could write along the following lines:

All the sources I accessed for my information on cannabis were written in a very impersonal style using very learned, scholarly lexis. They were full of specialized scientific phraseology using many abstract Latinate nouns, not easy for general readers to understand. The sentence structure was also quite hard to cope with, being lengthy and full of different clauses. The first sentence of the Stuttaford article I read is a good example of this very formal style:

'The meta analysis of research into cannabis smoking and psychosis may at last convince some politicians and doctors who have persisted in promoting a libertarian approach to the use of cannabis to change their mind.'

This is very heavy reading for someone in their teens, like me, and so I realized that the best thing to do would be to make notes on all the important facts – the names of the dangerous ingredients in cannabis, the dangerous psychological states it can give rise to, etc., and then write it all up from scratch in a more personal style, using much less technical vocabulary.

Reflections on the finished piece

This should be quite straightforward. Just look over all the things you've said you were trying to do, and assess how well you've achieved them, concentrating especially on your tone and style.

You may feel too close to your work to be able to see what it's like, so the more feedback you can receive, the better. Ask a friend, an older sibling, or a teacher in another subject to tell you how it strikes them. Invite them to be honest with their criticism, and see whether you agree. Use their comments to inform your final assessment of the piece, and say what you would do differently next time to reflect all that you have learned.

6 Writing to Entertain and Persuade

Chapter 5 discussed the processes you may go through in choosing a genre, subject, audience and so on for your writing, and went on to discuss writing to inform and instruct. This chapter is concerned with the types of writing that aim to entertain and/or persuade a reader.

Writing to entertain: Fiction

Creating characters

Whether you want to write a short story, a script for a sit-com episode, a scene in a three-act play, or the opening chapter of a novel, you need to start by thinking about characters you would be interested in writing about.

You may need three main characters, say, and perhaps three or four minor ones to interact with and comment on what the main ones are doing. It's fine for these characters to be stereotypes – i.e. to have only one obvious personality trait – because you're not going to have chance to make them well-rounded by showing them in a lot of different situations. In any case, many of Alan Bennett's and Alan Ayckbourn's characters are stereotypes, and it doesn't stop them from being funny or moving or tragic, or all three at once. But you must be interested in revealing whatever it is that drives your characters – shyness, vanity, greed, snobbery, competitiveness, the longing to be married or divorced – because if you're not, you won't be able to make them interesting to anybody else.

Conflicting characters

It's often claimed that drama is based on conflict, but so are the mini-dramas we know as soap operas and sit-coms, and so, often, is the short story.

In sit-coms it is particularly obvious; practically all are based on a love-hate relationship between two main characters. Others can get involved to some extent – think of *Absolutely Fabulous*, where Edina has Patsy for support in her battle with Saffy, but the real conflict is between the twosome. In *Ab Fab* it's mother and daughter; in *Only Fools and Horses* it's between brothers; in *Steptoe & Son*, it's father and son; in *Keeping Up Appearances*, a respectable housewife and yobbish brother, and so on.

Secondly, the two protagonists have to be engaged in a struggle for control over something – usually the freedom to be themselves and to do what they like without interference from the other. The struggle needs to be something the audience can immediately relate to, or at least recognize as part of everyday life; so, not surprisingly, most sit-coms are located in the bosom of the family. (It is a surrogate family in the case of *The Vicar of Dibley*, perhaps, where the character played by Dawn French finds herself mothering the whole dysfunctional parish.) Feuding neighbours can also provide rich pickings for sit-com writers – think of *One Foot in the Grave* and *The Good Life*.

Finding a plot

When you've got your characters, you need a story-line (the old-fashioned term for this is **plot**), whether you're writing a short-story or a sit-com episode or a playlet. The kind of characters you've created will drive the action – your shy characters will have to be given the chance to show that they're shy, your snobbish ones that they're snobbish, your aggressive ones that they're bullies – but you have to give thought to how you're going to structure that action.

Since conflict has a big appeal for audiences, a good idea is to give your main characters something to fight over. Since Britain is still a very class-conscious society, this could involve one-upmanship of some kind or other – characters pretending to be wealthier or better educated or from a 'higher' social background than they really are and getting into an embarrassing situation; children being embarrassed by parents wanting to be cool – that sort of thing. If you can give the conflict an unexpected slant, so much the better. What made *Ab Fab* so funny was that it reversed our usual experience of life: the mother was the out-of-control 'adolescent' and the teenager was the earnestly sensible adult.

Doing the twist

In both the short-story, the playlet, and the sit-com episode, the easiest and most common structure is a linear plot with a final twist. The story-line pictures the main character(s) setting out to do some particular thing only to find that they achieve something very different, either through the mysterious workings of fate or the actions of other people (the plot of Shakespeare's *Macbeth*, among thousands of others, is basically like this.) Our hero and/or heroine, for instance, might decide to impress the boss by giving an elaborate dinner party for him or her, only to find everything going disastrously wrong for some reason – an uninvited guest, the wrong choice of menu, the host getting drunk and telling the boss some home truths, etc. There are hundreds of ways to create this twist. Perhaps a character's longed-for wish (for money, fame, success, or escape) comes true, bringing only disappointment or disillusion; perhaps a character experiences an 'epiphany' (a moment of intense insight and self-knowledge) that changes his or her life for ever; perhaps unexpected depths are suddenly revealed in an ordinary-seeming character. The possibilities are as many as your imagination is capable of.

Somerset Maugham supplies us with the perfect (and extremely short) example of the short-story with a twist. The speaker is Death.

The Appointment in Samarra

There was a merchant in Baghdad who sent his servant to market to buy provisions and in a little while the servant came back, white and trembling, and said, 'Master, just now when I was in the marketplace I was jostled by a woman in the crowd and when I turned I saw it was Death that jostled me. She looked at me and made a threatening gesture; now, lend me your horse, and I will ride away from this city and avoid my fate. I will go to Samarra and there Death will not find me.'

The merchant lent him his horse, and the servant mounted it, and he dug his spurs in its flanks and as fast as the horse could gallop he went. Then the merchant went down to the marketplace and he saw me standing in the crowd and he came to me and said, 'Why did you make a threatening gesture to my servant when you saw him this morning?'

'That was not a threatening gesture,' I said, 'it was only a start of surprise. I was astonished to see him in Baghdad, for I had an appointment with him tonight in Samarra.'

- -

If this seems too neat and tidy to you, you can always go one step further and make a double twist. Having made your ambitious but indiscreet dinner-party host tell the boss exactly what he thinks of her, for instance, you might then decide to make the boss promote him for honesty rather than sack him for cheek. That's the beauty of writing fiction – you're in charge of life for once.

Narrating the story: First or third person?

There are several different ways of telling a story. The usual way is to simply describe the characters and what they do and say from a detached point of view, writing in the third person. Your opening sentence might be something like:

> Martha had to wait at least an hour before Mary turned up, but this was something she was used to by now.

The advantage of this method is that you're just an impersonal observer, a camcorder recording what is said and done in front of your lens for the benefit of your readers. You don't have to comment or explain: you just record what happens, leaving your audience free to see what they will.

Alternatively, you could use the first person direct method, in which case your opening might be:

> I had to wait at least an hour before Mary turned up, but this was something I was used to by now.

Using this method, you turn yourself into one of the actors in the story, describing things as you see them, and manipulating your readers to look at everything from your own point of view.

A different approach is to use the first person indirect method:

> Martha told me she had to wait at least an hour before Mary turned up, but that this was something she'd grown used to.

The readers would still be presented with a scenario coloured by your ideas and feelings, and you'd have to explain how you came to know Martha and what your place in the story was.

One other possible way is to use a variation of the first method: you still tell the story as an observer, recording what your main character does and says, but you make that main character reveal what the other characters are like by quoting what they say. For example:

> Martha had to wait at least an hour before Mary turned up, but this was something she was used to by now. ('I can't bear standing in queues for hours on end surrounded by common people', Mary had said to her.)

Dialogue

You've got your characters and your story-line. Now you need to make them talk, because if you, as narrator of the story, spend a lot of time just describing what they're like, they won't come alive.

The hardest thing to learn when you're writing the script for a sit-com or play is that you must make the characters reveal themselves through what *they* say. Make a character say *Que?* all the time and he will soon sound as bewildered as Manuel in *Fawlty Towers* (Shakespeare used the same technique to create the character of Hamlet, though the Prince's question was *Why?* rather than *What?*).

If you want to create a working-class character, you must make him talk like one, and perhaps address people as *sunshine* or *mate* or *chum*; give him some non-standard grammar and pronunciation (*What you expect me to do wiv them tiles, then?*), and some colloquialisms (*bloke, bird, booze, fags,* etc). Characters who use ordinary Standard English in his company will then automatically sound middle class. (*The Two Ronnies* were brilliant at this sort of thing.)

On a more subtle level, try to give your characters the kind of speech patterns that match their personalities and attitudes. If Edina automatically calls everybody *sweetie darling* it's to reveal that she doesn't care about anybody but herself – she can't even remember their names. Like Patsy's habitual *Super smashing thanks a lot* response to a kindness, it's totally insincere. In other words, the kind of things characters say should rise naturally out of who they are. That's when we find them convincing.

So, for example, if you want to create a character who is upper class, languid, self-confident, and in his own eyes superior to lesser beings, make him speak something like this (you should imagine that he's been asked whether he's read the latest Harry Potter yet):

> **Adrian:** *(Stifling a yawn)* Sorry. Don't do lit meant for the kiddies. Tedious, rather, I find.

If you see him as the dogmatic type who likes to lay down the law for less intelligent beings, he might speak like this:

> **Adrian:** Absolutely not. No. Useful for making working-class oiks read, I suppose. Complete tosh for those of us with a brain.

Using idiolect in dialogue

Most people have what is called an idiolect – a way of speaking that is peculiar to them in some way. So the easiest way to bring characters to life is to make them use different speech patterns. Someone who lacks self-esteem and therefore confidence will speak in a tentative way: they'll probably say *I'm not sure* a lot, and ask questions like *don't you think?* and *isn't it?* at the end of sentences because they're too unsure to assert something strongly as a fact. People like this will probably use a lot of modal verbs, particularly *would*, in phrases like *I wouldn't want to get in the way*. Self-confident people, on the other hand, assert things all the time: *I'm not waiting a minute longer; The man's a complete bore; This food's disgusting,* etc. Confident women also tend to exclaim a lot, secure in the knowledge that listeners will find what they say interesting: *I can't bear the Tube!* If they use modal verbs, they use the ones that put other people under an obligation to do (or not do) something: *It would be better to take a taxi; Must you smoke those foul cigarettes?* Confident people are never unsure. *Absolutely!* and *Certainly not!* is rather more their style.

Technical points about dialogue

Put the actual words your characters speak inside inverted commas – unless you're setting your script out in play format as with Adrian's speeches quoted above, when you can put the characters' names followed by a colon in front of their actual words.

It's best to use single inverted commas to mark speech, and then if the character who's speaking quotes another person, you can mark that with double ones, like this:

Alex described what happened next: 'When Ali finished the book he turned to me and said "That was brilliant – I'm sorry it's over." I had to admit I'd never read it.'

Always start a new line for a new speaker. This helps your readers to sort out who's speaking when you don't use their names.

Try to avoid the constant repetition of *So-and-so said, So-and-so replied, etc.* Two ways of doing this are:

- use a descriptive phrase to introduce what the character is going to say, e.g.

  Adrian looked distinctly annoyed. 'I say…'

- name the character being spoken to, to indicate that he or she is expected to speak next, e.g.

  'Not quite up to Oxford standards, Alex, do you think?'

Writing features articles for newspapers or magazines

The main thing to remember here is not to approach your topic in too business-like and direct a manner. You're not trying to lecture or instruct, but to entertain and possibly add a little information on the side.

Subject matter

The features editors of newspapers and magazines are always looking for new material, so if writers find a topic or a personal experience of sufficiently wide interest, editors might well be ready to consider it.

Style

Features articles are intended to entertain a wide range of readers, so should be written in a relaxed, friendly, personal tone and a relatively informal style. You should therefore use the following.

- **Inclusive modes of address and inclusive pronouns:** Use phrases such as *people like us*; *all sensible men and women*; *as we all know*; *you and I*; *our better judgement*, etc.

- **A mix of sentence lengths and structures:** Some sentences can be incomplete, and none should be too long.

- **Largely conventional but not Latinate lexis:** Avoid both colloquialisms and abstract nouns.

- **Analogies or images to add humour or interest:** Look at the examples below from the openings of two magazine articles. Both give an entertaining account of personal feelings and experience.

A I do realize that to celebrate the joys of taking holidays in a travel magazine is on a par with presenting the case for the Arctic Monkeys in NME. But I can't help it. I have, belatedly, taken up holidays.

B The honeymoon is over. Good grief. My adorable new wire-haired dachshund puppy, Gertie, has degenerated into the hound from hell. Ten inches long, fluffy, waggy-tailed, cuddly, she looks as if butter wouldn't melt; but her fiendish fangs have ripped my loose covers and her tiny paws have clawed the paintwork and dug up my delphiniums…

Both extracts illustrate a personal tone and friendly manner, inviting readers to share the writer's experience through the use of the personal pronouns *I* and *my*.

Both use a mix of sentence lengths; Extract A uses an analogy (presenting the case for the Arctic Monkeys in NME), B a metaphor (the *hound from hell* with *fiendish fangs*).

Both button-hole the reader immediately with their impression of the speaking voice. B is particularly riveting with its suggestions of a honeymoon gone wrong. (Other people's disasters are always fascinating.)

From this opening, the writer of A could go on to discuss a lifetime's experience of holidays, or write discursively on holidays in general: their purpose (a sun-tan? getting to know new people, new cultures? learning about art, architecture, history?); their range (from the tropics to the Antarctic, from the rainforests to the deserts); their cost (are the most expensive always the best?) and so on.

The writer of B also has a choice: to continue describing the experiences connected with the new pet (visits to the vet, trouble with friends, the general upheaval of daily routines), or to develop the piece into an exploration of the relationship between humans and animals in wider terms: who controls or owns whom? Should we keep pets at all? and so on.

Discursive writing

Discursive writing comes somewhere between the magazine article and the more academic and tightly structured argumentative essay. It allows you to write round a subject from more or less any angle that you think might be interesting, without necessarily coming to a definite conclusion.

Suppose you've decided to write an article entitled 'Ghosts'.

Introduction

To get your readers' attention, give them some startling accounts to think about: a man on a country walk who suddenly felt himself grow cold with fear and distress and later found that he had been walking across the site of a bloody battlefield; a man who saw a cohort of Roman soldiers *from the knees up* marching across the cellar of his house, built on top of a Roman road that would have been considerably lower in the 5th century AD; the numerous pallid figures in old-fashioned dress that haunt the corridors of stately homes and manor houses, and so on. The Internet will give you plenty of such material.

Setting your material in perspective

Having gained readers' interest in your spooky material, you might then step back from it and set it in some kind of perspective. What causes some people to have such experiences? Are they all slightly mad, or is there something in the human brain, some intuitive sixth sense, that can register phenomena beyond the reach of physical sight, sound, touch and smell?

Expanding on your material

You might then go on to widen the scope of your material by bringing in different kinds of experience of the paranormal. If the brain really does have powers we know little about, this would explain what gives patients out-of-body experiences under anaesthetic, or enables members of 'primitive' tribes to communicate telepathically across miles of empty terrain. Again, illustrate from the experiences of people who have given accounts of such things.

You could then give the other side of the story by admitting that scientists can find no hard evidence for such phenomena; they put it down to the brain playing tricks in the case of out-of-body experiences, or to trickery by so-called mediums when the living appear to be contacted by the spirits of the dead.

You might then proceed to sit on the fence by wondering why, in our rational, scientific age, we remain so fascinated by stories and films about the world of the supernatural: the living dead, mummies that come back to life, vampires that die and are reborn and all the other monstrous beings that haunt the human imagination. Even serious authors write about and film such things, witness Henry James's *The Turn of the Screw*, Susan Hill's long-running play *The Woman in Black* (in its twentieth year on the London stage), films like *The Blair Witch Project*, *The Sixth Sense*, and so on.

Conclusion

You might conclude that the case is still open, but give a hint as to your own ideas on the subject.

Developing your style

The following are suggestions for making your writing lively and giving it appeal.

Lexis

1 Use abstract nouns sparingly, unless you want to make a point about a character by putting them in his or her mouth. You may want to be satirical and portray someone as being pompous, e.g.

> 'Did you say you wanted a poached egg, dear?'

> 'I believe I expressed a degree of affirmation to that effect, my love.'

You may be creating a character whose natural mode of expression is to speak rather formally, using a fair sprinkling of abstract terms – someone in business or politics or education, for example. On the other hand, if your intention is to create a less educated, working-class character, use more colloquial words and phrases, or dialect if it's appropriate.

2 Use active rather than passive verbs; make people *do* things: *The Dursleys were bullying Harry badly at this stage* is livelier than *Harry was being bullied badly by the Dursleys at this stage*.

3 Use personal pronouns to achieve a friendly, persuasive approach to your readers. You can give the impression of talking to them by speaking to them in the first person singular (using 'I'), addressing them as 'you', and including them in what you say by using the pronoun 'we' and referring to 'people like us'. You won't persuade anyone of anything by talking down to them.

If you're writing dialogue, remember that women use more personal pronouns than men, presumably because they talk more about people and feelings, while men tend to make more use of the impersonal third-person pronoun 'it', and of nouns, presumably because they think in terms of systems and processes:

She: I need to talk to you about Ellie and David, dear. Have you got a moment?

He: It's ten to nine, Diana, and the train leaves at a quarter past. Can't it wait?

4 Use adjectives to describe the exact quality of a sense impression or an emotional experience: e.g. an *electric* shade of blue, a *velvety* texture, an *intense* feeling. The journalist Simon Barnes is famous for the extravagance of the adjectives he uses: *glorious, enthralling, dizziest, unquenchable, bold*, and *tumultuous* are just some of the ones he used to describe the quality of Roger Federer's tennis in the Wimbledon final. Sometimes simply lining them up in a row can create a vivid effect, e.g. (after heavy rain) *We are soaked, sodden, drenched and clammy*.

5 Use verbs that convey a vivid sense of action, e.g. 'Serena *ripped* her opponent's game apart'; 'Tigers are *slithering* towards extinction'; 'Rainforests *shrink* as cities *swell*'. Even when there is no physical action – perhaps especially when there is no physical action – verbs need to be strong enough to make an impact. Even the act of sitting down can be made into a pretty active affair; you can make somebody *sag, drop, flop, sink* or *collapse* into a chair, then *loll* or *slouch* or *droop* in quite a positive sort of way.

Forceful verbs like these make a livelier effect than using more ordinary ones and trying to liven them up with adverbs, e.g. 'He sat down *wearily*'. Never be afraid to use a thesaurus or crossword dictionary when you're stuck for a good word. You'll be surprised how many options they give you that you hadn't thought about.

6 If you want to persuade or urge your readers to do something, use verbs in the subjunctive mood. *Let work begin*, said Gordon Brown on the day he finally became prime minister. Other examples might be *Let us try to make a difference*; *If we were all to do our best, things would become enormously better*.

Modal verbs also describe things that you hope for but are not entirely sure will happen: use them if you want to talk about **intention** ('I *will* stop smoking'); **obligation** ('All parents *ought to/ should* stop smoking for their children's sake', 'You *must* do some work or you'll never pass'), or **prediction** ('We *will* win if we train hard enough').

You could also use a modal verb if you're writing a short story or a biography and want to give your readers a glimpse of what is going to happen in the future, e.g. 'If you had told the teenage Piaf that she *would* one day become an icon for the whole of France, she *would* have laughed in disbelief'; 'A failure in his maiden speech, he *would go on* to be one of the best orators the House had ever known'.

7 Use adverbs to add shades of meaning to neutral verbs, e.g. 'She told him *firmly* that he was mistaken.' 'He sprinkled the powder *daintily* into the wound.' Adverbs can also be used to intensify the effect of adjectives, e.g. 'He was *absolutely* delighted.' 'She was *very* cross.' It's best not to use intensifiers like these too often, though, as they can end up weakening the force of your writing instead of increasing it; see point 5 above about using forceful verbs instead.

Sentence structure

To quote the old song, 'It ain't what you say, it's the way that you say it. That's what gets results.' Write a sentence one way, and nobody takes much notice. Write it another, and they do. Below are some patterns you can follow, both to keep your writing lively and to get your meaning across in the most striking way.

Broadly speaking, as we saw on page 68, sentences are either **simple**, **compound** or **complex**. The simple sentence is called simple because it has just one clause (e.g. *I spend money like water. I always look good.*). The compound sentence has two or more clauses joined together with conjunctions: *I spend money like water* **but** *I always look good*. The **complex sentence** is so called because it contains both a simple sentence or main clause, and a minor sentence or dependent clause, e.g. *Although I spend money like water* (dependent clause), *I always look good* (simple sentence/ main clause).

Good writers can get excellent effects using compound sentences: combinations of simple sentences joined together by conjunctions. In the example below, for instance, look how they are used to give the impression of increasing pressure and growing tension:

> The rainforests continue to come down and the seas are full of lethal crap and the cities swell and the greenhouse gases gather as we demand more room and more wealth and people.
>
> Ben Macintyre, The *Times*, 7 July 2007

Note how the piling of one clause on top of another here gives the impression of uncontrolled frenetic action, and how the absence of commas between the clauses increases the impression of unstoppable speed.

Matthew Parris uses the opposite approach to get a different, more dramatic effect, breaking down what he has to say into short, sharp sentences that echo perhaps the minimalist style of rap and street slang: *Evil is cool. Evil is wicked. Evil sells DVDs and airport thrillers.*

He wants the media to stop using the word 'evil' in connection with terrorism, because in our twisted age, evil is seen as more attractive than good. He goes on to mix these short sentences with longer structures that will be discussed below:

> Evil is a gang you might want to be in if you were a clever boy in a cultural mess with a chip on your shoulder. We're not talking anything as clever as Evil here: we're talking Weird, we're talking Crackpot, we're talking Sad. The idea of using a Jeep to make a terminal explode was, in the latest lingo, a bit gay. We're talking Failure.
>
> Matthew Parris, The *Times*, 7 July 2007

Activity

Write a note considering Parris's use of capital letters on words such as 'Evil' in this extract.

Types of complex sentence

According to grammar books, there are three main types of complex sentence: the **loose**, the **balanced**, and the **periodic**.

The **loose sentence** gets its name from the fact that its various clauses are combined in rather a random fashion, without any attempt to make a particular impression on the reader:

> If I spend money like water / it's because I only feel confident / when I know I look good.

This is the sentence form you will probably use most of the time. On the other hand, when you want to achieve certain effects through your style, you should consider the two further types discussed below.

In the **balanced sentence**, the clause in the first half of the sentence is echoed or balanced by a very similar one in the second half. The ideas in each clause can oppose each other, as in the following examples:

> Harry Potter is drearily obsessed with birthrights, social privilege and the perpetuation of the status quo; Bart Simpson exists solely to interrogate, and in some cases, demolish these obsolete ideas.

> Harry Potter is an old-fashioned prig; Bart Simpson is a cool dude.

Alternatively, the second one can expand on or illustrate what is said in the first:

> Philip Pullman does not believe in a benevolent God; human beings have to find their own path to salvation.

> Success in exams isn't all that matters; nous and hard work count even more.

The balanced sentence is a good pattern to follow if you want to present a reasoned argument. The symmetrical neatness of the matching clauses gives readers the impression of unhurried calm and intellectual control. Remember, this was the favourite form of all those eighteenth-century writers who valued reason and commonsense above turbulent emotion.

In the **periodic sentence**, the writer's most important statement is held back until the end, using suspense to add force to what is being said. For instance, criticizing the way in which male MPs paid more attention to Jacqui Smith's cleavage than to her speech on terrorism in the Commons, *Times* journalist Sarah Vine wrote:

> From Theresa May's shoes to Ann Widdecombe's hair, it's always the same: the slightest whiff of a 'female' angle and all interest in their profession goes out of the window...

> Put it this way: if the stock market crashed, no one would be debating the tightness of Alistair Darling's trousers.

> Sarah Vine, *The Times*, 5 July 2007

This is obviously a good sentence pattern to follow when you want to make a dramatic impact, and give your point as much emphasis as you can.

Activity

Go back to the Matthew Parris extract on page 97 and see whether you can identify all the different sentence types used in it.

Rhetorical devices

Imagery

Do use images if you can think of any original ones, preferably based on real life. Metaphors like *a sky the colour of a fading bruise* or *the colour of mushroom soup* are good because we recognize them from experience. Gerald Durrell's memoir, *My Family and Other Animals*, and Laurie Lee's *Cider with Rosie* are full of wonderful images to inspire you. (Don't steal any of them, though, because every examiner in the land will have read both.)

On the other hand, some writers manage to give wonderfully vivid descriptions without using an image at all, simply by choosing exactly the right words:

> I took my first look at my son. Little Jimmy was brick red in colour and his face had a bloated, dissipated look. As I hung over him he twisted his tiny fists under his chin and appeared to be undergoing some mighty internal struggle. His face swelled and darkened as he contorted his features then from deep among the puffy flesh his eyes fixed me with a baleful glare and he stuck his tongue out of the corner of his mouth.
>
> James Herriot, *Vets Might Fly*

When Herriot does use imagery, however, it does its job so exactly that it's as good as watching a film:

> He strode over to the tray, selected a needle and caught hold of the free end of the catgut protruding from the jar. With a scything sweep of his arm he pulled forth an enormous coil of gut, setting the bobbin inside the jar whirring wildly like a salmon reel with a big fish on the line. He returned to the horse, stumbling slightly as the gut caught round his ankles, and began to stitch.
>
> James Herriot, *It Shouldn't Happen to a Vet*

The skill for the writer, it seems, lies in really looking at things and allowing images to suggest themselves if they will.

Activity

Comment on the quality of the verbs and the phrase *with a scything sweep of his arm* in the extract above.

Irony

This is the technique of luring your readers into thinking you approve of something, perhaps waiting until they've had chance to agree with you, then springing it on them that in fact you don't approve – just the opposite, in fact. Well used, this is a very effective device for making your readers think, and possibly turning their ideas upside down:

> I'm afraid we are often too hard on our children. For instance, we expect them to study all day to pass exams, then complain if they indulge in a little harmless binge-drinking to relax; we nag them into going to bed as early as 3 am, then criticize them for wanting to stay there; we say we want them to have a great party then throw a hissy fit if the house gets trashed. Worst of all, we tell them to 'grow up, for God's sake', then refuse to let them go on holiday alone – even though it's only to some perfectly respectable place like Polzeal on the Cornish coast. For heaven's sake, there'll be five hundred other kids on the beach every night, so they can't possibly come to any harm. I ask you, is this the attitude of reasonable parents??

Writing to persuade

When you think about it, persuasion is actually a disguised form of instruction. You are trying to get other people to do, or think, or believe, what you believe is valuable, right, and good; something that may not have occurred to them before, or which they are not yet ready to accept. You can't simply tell them what to do – that would be dictatorship – so you have two main methods of persuasion: the **polemical**, which is direct and forceful, and what we might call the **gently persuasive**. Both use evidence and some sort of reasoned argument to make their case, but the one attacks, hoping to compel agreement through sheer force of argument, and the other gently urges and suggests.

Polemical writing

A Criminal Absence of Will

Another shooting in the early hours of yesterday in North London adds to the grisly toll of gangland gun violence over the past fortnight.

There has been particular revulsion at the youth of some of these murder victims – two of them only 15, and one 16 years old, and the humdrum settings of their killings, with one gunned down at an ice rink, one at home and another in his own bedroom.

The shocking situation has elicited the predictable signs of political panic. The Prime Minister says Something Must Be Done. He calls a summit of ministers and community leaders. He floats the possibility of lowering the age limit of gun crime prosecutions from 21 to 17, and giving more powers to the police.

These are all knee-jerk reactions. The problem is not too few laws or not enough police powers. It is that the laws we already have are being actively undermined by a culture that is sliding towards social anarchy…

As last week's devastating UNICEF report observed, Britain is at the very bottom of the league of western nations when it comes to children's well-being – and the root cause of that is nothing other than the disintegration of the family.

In such shattered family backgrounds, the young person's peer group becomes all important; the gang becomes his surrogate family and the gang leader his replacement father. This is a particular problem for the black community, where fatherlessness is endemic and drug culture entrenched.

This fundamental breakdown in social control is then compounded by just about every agency that deals with young people.

The schools deliver a broken educational system, with the most vulnerable children left illiterate and innumerate; with the same 'child-centred' dogma destroying all boundaries and discipline; and with special schools catering for the most disturbed children, shut down in the benighted cause of 'social inclusion'…

Worst of all is the total shambles of drugs policy, which has led directly to the epidemic of drugs on our streets, the rise in drug use and the ever younger age of both users and dealers.

This appalling situation is the direct result of the grip of the drug legalisation lobby on the Government, police, and fashionable society, the downgrading of cannabis and the subsequent explosion of hard drugs as the bottom fell out of the flooded cannabis market.

When they look at the recent carnage on the streets [of our major cities], all those people who promoted this chain of events should hang their heads in shame. This blood is on their hands.

On top of all this is the profound racism of a society which, while demonising as 'racist' anyone who dares discuss black crime, actually ignores the growing mayhem within black communities – because of the shameful and unstated belief that while it's only black people who are committing violence against other black people, there's no reason for anyone else to bother about it.

Such an attitude is as short-sighted as it is terrible. It is terrible because the lives of black people are as valuable as those of anyone else.

It is terrible because this racism leads directly to the killing and abandonment of human beings under the camouflage of progressive attitudes.

It is terrible because it is mainly white drug users who are being supplied by these black gangs. And it is short-sighted because the mayhem is spreading well beyond the black population.

Across the Atlantic, they've already been there and done all that… and come out the other side.

Communities previously written off as shattered beyond repair have turned themselves around…

This was achieved by black pastors leaving their church pulpits to patrol the streets and pull in their errant young for correction, drug treatment and other measures… In Britain, encouragingly, a growing number of pastors from black churches are trying to do the same thing. The problem is the absence of appropriate support for them…

The belief that authority is a dirty word means there is no recognition of the crucial fact that the more shattered a child's background, the more urgent is his need for the strongest possible boundaries and clear sanctions if they are transgressed.

Those who do grasp this achieve stunning results. In East London, the Eastside Young Leaders' Academy transforms black boys from jail fodder into model pupils.

It does this through the tough love of uncompromising discipline…

So the problem is not hopeless. It can be turned around by a tough-minded, no-nonsense attitude to personal and social responsibility. What is hopeless is the moral muddle of a society whose antipathy to authority has reached such a pitch that tough discipline is said to infringe a child's 'human rights'.

A society which believes that locking up large numbers of young criminals is worse than allowing them to continue to terrorise the streets. A society which places freedom of expression higher than stopping gangsta rap messages promoting violence, murder and bigotry as 'cool'.

A society whose rich, white cocaine habit is serviced by a sordid and violent black drug economy, the truth of whose existence that same white society is at pains to sanitise and censor. Such a society produces dead children.

It need not be so. All that is needed is the will to change. It is the absence of that will that is truly criminal.

Melanie Phillips, *Daily Mail*, 19 February 2007

- -

Manner: This is detached and impersonal; the writer plunges straight into the subject in a short introductory paragraph without addressing readers in any way: *Another shooting in the early hours of yesterday in North London adds to the grisly toll of gangland gun violence over the past fortnight.*

Lexis: This is formal and educated: there are a number of Latinate abstract nouns in phrases such as *social **anarchy**, social **inclusion**, uncompromising **discipline**, and **antipathy** to **authority***, and a number of adjectives derived from Latin roots: ***predictable**, **illiterate**, **innumerate**, **surrogate***; at the same time, much of the vocabulary is highly emotive: the opening sentence contains the highly charged adjective *grisly*, and other emotive nouns include *revulsion*, *disintegration*, and *carnage*; adjectives are similarly highly charged: *shocking*, *devastating*, *disturbed*, *benighted*, *sordid*, *terrible* and *violent*; the choice of verbs adds to the impression of a situation out of control: *laws* are being ***undermined**, culture* is ***sliding** towards social anarchy.*

Sentence construction: The writer varies the length and structure of her sentences to suit what she wants to get across: when she is setting out the situation, her sentences are short and crisp: in paragraph 3, for instance, she uses a succession of short, crisp sentences to give the impression of actions done in haste: *The Prime Minister says Something Must Be Done. He calls a summit of ministers and community leaders. He floats the possibility of lowering the age limit of gun crime prosecutions from 21 to 17, and giving more powers to the police.* She then kicks these suggestions into touch with another crisp, authoritative sentence: *These are all knee-jerk reactions.*

She uses antithesis to make a forceful contrast between the 'wrong' idea of the problem and the right one: *The problem is not too few laws or not enough police powers. It is that the laws we already have are being undermined...* Also note the use of minor sentences towards the end: *A society which...*

Grammar: The article is written in perfectly correct Standard English; the only individual touch is the writer's habit of using both single and compound nouns as adjectives, e.g. *the shambles of drugs policy*; *knee-jerk reactions.*

Spelling: The use of initial capitals on the PM's words in *Something Must Be Done* (paragraph 3) is designed to mock the empty pomposity of official announcements; it may also be a satirical reference to King Edward VIII's similar remark in the 1930s about the impoverished working classes of his day; nothing was done then, either.

Rhetorical devices: In places the article reads like the transcript of a speech, particularly when the writer uses repetition to drive home her points: *Such an attitude is as short-sighted as it is terrible*, she declares, then picks up the key words *short-sighted* and *terrible* and drives them home in four repeated sentences:

> It is terrible because the lives of black people are as valuable as those of anyone else. It is terrible because this racism leads directly to the killing and abandonment of human beings under the camouflage of progressive attitudes. It is terrible because it is mainly white drug users who are being supplied by these black gangs. And it is short-sighted because the mayhem is spreading well beyond the black population.

The writer also uses the orator's trick of speaking in **triads**, or 'threes':

> The schools deliver a broken educational system, with the most vulnerable children left illiterate and innumerate (1); with the same 'child-centred' dogma destroying all boundaries and discipline (2); and with special schools catering for the most disturbed children shut down in the benighted cause of 'social inclusion' (3).

> ... the total shambles of drug policy, which has led directly to the epidemic of drugs on our streets (1,) the rise in drug use (2) and the ever younger age of both users and dealers (3).

She also uses a very emotive metaphor, saying that the politicians and educators and social workers who have allowed these benighted children to die are as guilty of their deaths as if they had murdered them with their own hands: *This blood is on their hands.*

Prosodic effects: The reader can sense the dramatic pauses between each statement, and the way the voice rises at the end of the first three sentences of the fourteenth and fifteenth paragraphs, only to fall with withering force on the final words of the fourth, *well beyond the black population*; she uses the same speech-maker's technique again in the two penultimate paragraphs, where the word *society* is picked up and repeated four times in the following four sentences – *a society which, a society which, a society whose, such a society* – (compare Martin Luther

King's famous 'I have a dream' speech). Readers can sense the contempt in the writer's 'voice' as she contrasts the connotations of the word *society* – the things we associate with it such as mutual respect, concern for one another's well-being – with the selfish behaviour of those who are supposedly in charge of it.

You don't have to accept the writer's thesis to recognize that this is a piece of very skilfully written, extremely forceful journalism.

Techniques of gently persuasive writing

Manner: This should be friendly, informal and conversational, as if the writer is talking to people he or she knows. Inclusive pronouns rather than impersonal ones will help to achieve this, as will the use of words like *perhaps*, which polemical writers would never use because they suggest room for doubt or disagreement.

Lexis: The writer will use vocabulary drawn from the common pool, conventionally polite, without abstract Latin nouns on the one hand or colloquialisms and slang on the other; since their purpose is to persuade, writers will use words with emotive connotations, e.g. *sorry* (in the sense of 'to be pitied'), *monstrous, callousness.*

Sentence structure: Writers will use a mix of ordinary loose and simple sentences on the whole; when they want to contrast one idea strongly with another, however, they may use a balanced construction. In the same way, if they want to create an impression of 'muchness' – of a lot of things being given, for instance, or a lot of things being done, they may well use a periodic sentence.

Grammar: This will be conventionally correct, though writers may use contractions such as *you'll* and *can't* to help create an informal style.

Punctuation: This is usually conventional; if writers want to add a note of drama, however, or call readers' attention to something surprising or ridiculous, they may use a dash rather than a more conventional colon or full stop.

Rhetorical devices: Writers may use repetition to emphasize a point; they may also use exclamatory sentences (you can recognize these by the exclamation mark at the end) to represent a shocked tone of voice, which in turn represents an attitude of shock-horror, or amazement, or some other startled state of mind.

Prosodic features: Writers may use the speech-maker's device of writing in **triads**: mentioning three rather than two or four items in a row, e.g. *She loved clothes, she loved parties, she loved men*; for some unknown reason, the rhythmic effect of uttering and writing things in threes like this makes a strong impression on audiences.

Activity

All the features mentioned above can be found in the writing below. Use them to write a critique of the piece.

It is said that the novelist Evelyn Waugh, asked which he would choose to rescue from his burning house, his children or his books, opted to save the books. Children, he pointed out, were easier to replace than first editions.

Parents everywhere will shudder at such callousness. To care more for a book than a child! Monstrous! Would we put anything in the world before the needs of our children? Never!

We are devoted parents. We chauffeur them wherever they need to go to protect them against traffic and stranger-danger; we buy them mobile phones to keep us in constant touch; we fill their bedrooms with electronic toys to keep them happy and busy at home: all we want in the world is to make them happy. And yet, and yet, apparently we don't. Our children, recent surveys reveal, are the most depressed and anxious in Europe.

Various reasons are suggested for this sorry state of childish misery: too much junk food, too much exposure to sex and violence on TV and in the cinema, too much of their own way given by over-indulgent parents. Some or all of these may indeed contribute to the malaise, but if institutions as diverse as the Royal Society for the Prevention of Accidents and the National Association for Mental Health (Mind) are to be believed, the underlying cause is deeper and more basic: what children in western societies are really suffering from is a lack of contact with the natural world.

Parents, teachers, governors, and politicians all conspire to shield their precious charges from the dangers of the great outdoors: they might fall in slippery mud and break a limb, get stung by nettles, be bitten by adders, fall in rivers and be drowned. And so they stay indoors – and risk obesity and repetitive strain injury from constant tapping on computer keyboards instead.

Research shows that contact with nature is good for children in all sorts of ways. Exploring unfamiliar natural environments teaches them that there's another world outside their own, and learning how to cope with it builds self-confidence and self-esteem. Simply being in contact with Mind's 'green therapy' relieves stress, and can even instil calm in otherwise hyperactive children.

Knowing this, oughtn't we to acknowledge our mistakes? Shielding children from the natural world does not made them happy; giving them more contact with it does. Rather than keeping them in, then, let us think of possible ways to get them out. Sowing seeds in a window-box and watching them grow; making a small pond in a half-barrel for frogs and water-beetles; smearing a mixture of fruit juice and honey on a tree trunk and looking at it with you by torch-light to see what moths and beetles have come to call – this is all it takes to awaken the sense of wonder that hooks children's interest for life.

We might even come to recognize what contact with nature can do for us, as well as for our children. Relieving their levels of stress and anxiety will automatically relieve ours, too, but there may be another spin-off also. Walking through woods and fields with our children, watching birds and animals, trying to identify flowers – these are experiences that will stay with us for the rest of our lives and bond us together in a way that nothing else can do.

Writing a thesis

This is in some ways the least demanding genre of writing to undertake, simply because it is so easy to structure. Let's begin with some definitions:

Thesis: 'A proposition to be maintained or proved' (Concise Oxford Dictionary).

Antithesis: A case or argument put forward in opposition to the thesis.

Synthesis: A case or argument that combines points made in both the thesis and antithesis.

Putting forward a case

If you want to make out a case in favour of political correctness, say, you could use the following structure.

- **Introduction:** Define the terms of your thesis, i.e. *political correctness is the term used to describe the avoidance of expressions that exclude or marginalize people who are disadvantaged or discriminated against in our society.* Explain how it evolved, i.e. *in response to the growth of liberal ideas in a multi-ethnic, multi-cultural society.*
- **Thesis:** The way in which language is used can greatly affect people's behaviour: *PC language promotes good behaviour and makes people happy.* Discuss and give evidence.
- **Conclusion:** This might be: *British society is kinder and happier now as a result of PC.*

The case against

If on the other hand you felt that there was a case to be made against the automatic use of PC, you could counter your thesis with an antithesis.

- **Thesis:** The way in which language is used can greatly affect people's behaviour: *PC language promotes good behaviour and makes people happy.* Discuss and give evidence.
- **Antithesis:** *Being forced to use PC makes many people unhappy because they feel their freedom of speech is being taken away.* You would then have to alter your conclusion.
- **Conclusion:** *Many people resent PC as a form of censorship, and British society is less happy and harmonious as a result.*

Synthesis

There is one further option for those who can always see both sides of an argument: to claim that both sides have equal weight and to advocate a compromise position by adding a synthesis.

- **Thesis:** The way in which language is used can greatly affect people's behaviour: *PC language promotes good behaviour and therefore makes people happy.* Discuss and give evidence.
- **Antithesis:** *Being forced to use PC makes many people unhappy because they feel their freedom of speech is being taken away.*
- **Synthesis:** *Most people are ready to agree that we should be careful not to cause unnecessary distress to people who are disadvantaged in some way; what they balk at is the exaggerated concern that finds offence in ordinary words where no offence was intended: in* black *moods or* black-hearted*; in phrases like* we all have our cross to bear*; in the noun* crusade *used as a metaphor for any serious campaign; and in the attempt by the RSPB to ban the use of the term* cock *for a male bird in case it should cause distress to a member of the public. If the powers that be could agree to curb these more extreme manifestations of sensitivity, it seems likely that the matter would resolve itself without further dissent.*

Writing a commentary

See Chapter 5 pages 83–87 for general pointers about writing a commentary. For entertaining and persuasive pieces of writing, it may be particularly important to write about the style models you have used.

Style models

The examiners will want to know the kind of reading you did to help you produce your own text, so that they judge how successful you've been in achieving what you set out to do. You'll need to give the names of the writers you read, and details of the kinds of newspaper or magazine articles and books. For example, for a personal viewpoint essay you need to write something along the following lines:

> Since I wanted to write an article that would interest a lot of general readers, I accessed the websites of the *Times*, the *Guardian*, the *Telegraph*, the *Independent* and the *Daily Mail* to find the names of their regular columnists. I then visited their individual websites and read examples of their recent work. Afterwards, I did the same for the Sunday papers.

> I decided that the style I really wanted to model my piece on was Jeremy Clarkson's. He's never boring because he says directly what he thinks and doesn't care about political correctness, which he hates. In fact, he deliberately sets out to be outrageous, just to shake conventionally minded people out of their complacent attitudes.

> When I read the newspaper article below, I asked myself what Jeremy Clarkson would have thought about the ideas contained in it, and wrote an article modelled on his style.

Viewpoint

Have you met my beautiful friend?

Why would a woman choose a prettier friend?

MARIANNE MACDONALD

explains

It's August. You could do with a holiday. Preferably a week without your beloved best friends' children, who treat the pool as a crèche, waste your SPF15 on their imaginary friends, and disturb your lie-in with screams for ice-cream.

So who do you call? a) Lucy: your blonde, skinny, sexy best friend, who knows how to have fun and attracts a crowd of young men wherever she goes. But last time you went on holiday with her, you found yourself in a taxi with a man who referred to you as 'Lucy's mate'. b) Abigail: your loyal, pretty, darts-playing friend from childhood days. Abigail's also, well, curvier than you. You haven't been on holiday with her for years, but last time you went out with her, you attracted all the attention and went home feeling like a million dollars.

Though you might think that Abigail is a safer bet, new research claims that Lucy would in fact be a wiser decision. According to researchers from Harvard Medical School, those with fat friends are more likely to put on weight themselves. Stick with Lucy and you can bask in her reflected dazzle, as well as ensuring that you're less likely to come back a dress size larger.

But hanging out with a girlfriend who is noticeably better looking than you comes with its own hazards, say experts…

The *Times*, 27 July 2007

Adapting style models

It is important to describe how you adapted your style models to produce the effects you needed. You might want to write something like this (continuing the example above):

How I adapted my style models

The first thing I had to change was the whole manner and approach. MacDonald is writing exclusively for women – note the inclusive pronoun 'you' in the question she asks her readers: 'So who do you call?' and her assumption that they share the same problems and attitudes as herself. Clarkson would start from a much more aggressively sexist, 'blokey' viewpoint, such as this:

No wonder women are multi-taskers. They spend so much time gazing at the inside of their pretty little heads that they'd never get anything else done if they weren't.

A change of writing style was also needed. MacDonald writes rather tentatively. Clarkson writes in a much more dogmatic manner. She asks a question and then, rather than answering it herself, offers us differing opinions from the fields of psychology and literature. When Clarkson asks a question it's only so that he can assert the answer himself, as an expert in the field of life-experience and common-sense:

I'll tell you why an ordinary-looking woman goes on holiday with a babe – it's because that way she'll at least get to look at some blokes.

Where MacDonald uses conventionally polite vocabulary like 'attractive', 'dazzling', and the rather clichéd 'princess' and 'prince', I had to downgrade it to something slangier, like 'a real looker', and a 'dog'.

Stylistic devices used in the text

To entertain his readers, Clarkson goes off on exaggerated flights of fancy, so I had to do the same. To describe a beautiful woman he would say something like:

… someone whose face made you want to leap over a line of ten parked cars, sing the Alleluia chorus three times then fall to your knees in gratitude to God for having made you a man.

I also used imagery in the Clarkson style, drawing it from one of his favourite subjects, the motor car:

Women are a lot like cars. Some are unfailingly reliable, have lots of room in the boot, give you loads of mileage for your money and look so boring they make you want to die. Others break down regularly, need a lot of expensive servicing, make you extend your mortgage every time you fill the tank, and have lines that bring tears to your eyes. So which will you buy? No contest, compadre.

This same article could be used as the starting point for a short story, a scene or episode in a sit-com, soap opera or play, or a discursive essay on friendship. If you chose one of the first three options, you might say something like this.

Style models

I chose a collection of short stories by Angus Wilson to model my own story on, because they show so well how to use the twist mechanism to surprise readers. He also often surprises his main character at the climax of the story by giving them an epiphany – a moment when they suddenly realize something they'd never been aware of before.

Source materials

The inspiration for my story came from a newspaper article discussing the reason why attractive women often have plainer friends. I thought this gave an interesting insight into human relationships, and could be structured with a twist and an epiphany as one or even both of the main characters realized what lay behind their apparent friendship.

Creating characters

The first thing I had to do was turn a piece of analytical writing about real-life relationships into a piece of fiction. I had to create two main characters, one more attractive and popular than the other, giving them names and constructing lives and jobs and families for them.

Devising a story-line

I then had to consider the story-line. I would need to create several situations in which the attractive one 'uses' her plainer friend – e.g. getting her to share the costs of a holiday then ignoring her most of the time – then an epiphany scene in which the plainer one catches on and sees her 'friend' and herself in new light, then a climactic scene in which the friendship is ended.

I could keep to the ending described in the newspaper article and have the plain Jane snapped up by a man on the same ordinary level as herself, leaving the siren to grow old alone. I could reverse it and have her chosen over her attractive friend by a 'prince' who sees her finer qualities (something that happens in fiction perhaps more often than in fact). I could make the 'prince' initially choose the more attractive girl, only to be disappointed by her shallowness and turn in the end to her more ordinary friend. Or less worthily, perhaps, I could turn the whole thing on its head and make the 'prince' perfectly happy to marry the attractive girl for her looks alone, willing and able to pay servants to do what she can't or won't do herself. If I did this, I could let the prince tell the story from his own point of view, which would make a change. In the end, that's what I decided to do.

Significant changes made during the writing process

Only you can know what changes you may have felt necessary to make in the writing of your text. But if you have made significant changes, you could introduce them along these lines:

Changes to lexis: When I looked over my first draft with my English tutor, she asked me if I was satisfied with the dialogue I had given my main characters. She thought the vocabulary was a bit too formal for ordinary conversation, and also the sentences were much longer and more like the ones you read in a book than the ones you hear most people speak. So I changed some of the more technical language I'd made my plain character use to something more simple, as follows:

'I think associating with you is harmful to my psychological well-being, Martha. It's damaging my self-esteem and making me feel very insecure.'

I changed this to:

'I don't think being friends with you is very good for me, Martha. You make me feel second-class, somehow. Your friends don't help, either. They just ignore me when you're around.'

Or it might be the way you handled the plot that you questioned after receiving feedback. Your reader may have felt that you treated the splitting up realistically, but then rushed the ending by saying something like: *Soon after the split, Jane married and started a family. Martha refused to settle for anything less than perfection and ended up alone.*

It may have been suggested to you that one way round the problem would be to use the flashback technique, and so you decided to reconstruct your story completely.

> I decided to start with a conversation between Jane and the man she's recently become engaged to, in which Jane tells him about her friendship with Martha, and he points out that Martha is constantly undermining her self-confidence and giving nothing in return.
>
> I then moved to a middle section in which Jane thinks about what Finn has suggested, and recalls several past scenes in which Martha has made fun of her or ignored her in front of other people. I make her gradually realize the truth, and feel let down and hurt – but also sorry for Martha, who has to do other people down in order to feel good about herself.
>
> I then wrote the climax of the story – the scene in which Jane tells Martha that she doesn't want to see her any more. I made Martha angry and unclear about Jane's reasons for deserting her, while Jane stays calm and understanding.
>
> I then went back to the beginning of the story to let Jane tell Finn what has happened, and to have them agree to get married.
>
> When I showed the new draft to my tutor, she thought it read much better and seemed more professional than the first one.

Whatever needs improvement in your text, just describe it along these lines in your commentary, then explain what steps you took to put it right and quote from your work to illustrate it.

If you've been writing persuasively for a general audience, check whether you've made your manner and tone sufficiently friendly and inclusive, and if you haven't, explain in your commentary how you amended it. For example:

> My tutor remarked that my manner and tone seemed too formal for writing that was trying to persuade in a friendly fashion. She advised me to think how advertisers seduce readers into buying their stuff with slogans like 'Because you're worth it!' and 'People who value quality buy [whatever].' So I went back to the drawing-board and altered a sentence like 'Every parent wants what's best for their children' to 'Like all parents, you want what's best for your children.' I also put in some rhetorical questions to make my readers feel they were being talked to instead of lectured at, changing the sentence, 'There are several ways to deal with a case like this' to 'What to do in a case like this?'
>
> To avoid a dogmatic tone, I followed this with a verb in the hypothetical subjunctive mood: '*It might be* a good idea to…', suggesting a possible course of action rather than giving them a directive to follow.
>
> Another way I tried to achieve a better tone was by using inclusive pronouns and pronoun phrases such as 'As intelligent people, we know…', 'Thoughtful people like you', 'People like us…' etc.

If on the other hand, you've been writing fiction and having trouble with writing convincing dialogue, you could say something like:

> My tutor told me my dialogue sounded stilted and I needed to make my characters speak in shorter sentences. When people talk to each other they often give one-word answers, and they also ask each other questions instead of just saying things. That's why I altered the bit of dialogue quoted below:

'I'll leave ringing up about the tickets to you, Martha, because you're so good at that sort of thing,' Mary said.

'I'm not going to get them, because it's your turn,' Martha replied crossly. 'Anyway, I'm not even going, so don't get one for me.'

I changed this to:

'Will you ring up about the tickets, Martha? You're so good at it,' said Mary, oozing false charm.

I ought to be, thought Martha bitterly. I've had plenty of practice.

'Get them yourself,' she said crossly. 'But don't get one for me – I shan't be going.'

Reflections on the finished text

When you have produced your finished piece, whether it's meant to entertain or to persuade, run through all the aspects that make up such a text, and discuss how well you think you have dealt with them. For example, if your purpose was to persuade, you might say something like this:

> **Purpose and audience:** My intention was to produce a text that would persuade a wide cross-section of readers to think that/ agree that… I think I have succeeded in offering reasons in a gently persuasive tone rather than telling my audience what to do.

If you have written a discursive text, or one putting forward a particular case or argument, you might want to say at this point that you have taken care to mention opinions that differ from yours, in order to leave readers free to make up their own minds.

> **Style:** I have tried to write in a lively style, using a basically English rather than Latinate lexicon, so as not to bore readers with no special knowledge of my topic. In the same way, I have tried to vary the length and structure of my sentences rather than use a sequence of short, jerky, simple ones, or strings of short simple sentences joined together by conjunctions like 'and', 'but', 'so' and 'then'. Some of my sentences have a loose, some a balanced, and some a periodic structure. To strengthen the point about how many things parents need to be good at, I wrote 'Settling temper tantrums, calming fears, teaching manners, showing love – parents are expected to take all these, and more, in their stride.'

If on the other hand, your purpose was to entertain, and you have written a story, a sit-com or some other form of drama, you will obviously need to talk about story-line, characterization, lexis, dialogue, and any prosodic effects you've tried to achieve.

> I have tried to give my story a linear structure, introducing the characters and their relationship, showing the one-sided nature of the friendship, and escalating the action to a climax where the relationship explodes in anger on one side and disappointment on the other.

> I think I have succeeded in making one character seem dominant and selfish, and the other much more gentle and tentative in her manner. I tried to do this by giving the dominant character shorter sentences and more dynamic verbs; she uses a lot of directives and assertions – 'Get my coat for me, dear, would you?', 'You're so uptight, Martha!', etc. I made Martha use a lot of modal verbs in contrast, to show how lacking in self-confidence she is: 'I wouldn't want to get in your way'; 'I'm sure Tony wouldn't want to look after me all evening', etc.

Writing a scene in which two people quarrel was very difficult. I had to find emotional vocabulary that conveyed anger without being too crude, e.g. 'thoughtless', 'selfish', 'egotistical', 'self-centred', 'rude'; and I had to give some sentences a rising intonation to get across the idea of the character getting more and more angry (a prosodic effect), e.g. 'You're rude^, you're selfish^, you don't give a toss about any^body's feelings but your own^ and I've had enough of you^ to last me the rest^ of my life!'

Feedback

Some of the changes you introduced during the course of your work were probably made on the basis of feedback from your English Language tutor. You may like to obtain feedback on your finished piece from other people, preferably those who have not read it before. Their comments may be helpful in writing your final reflection on the finished work, and give you further ideas for what you would do differently next time.

7 Language Acquisition

Theories of language acquisition

Chomsky's Innatist theory

According to Noam Chomsky, children learn language easily because the brain is pre-programmed – wired up for language acquisition in the womb. In some mysterious and unspecified way, all human babies, simply by virtue of being human, 'know' what kind of a system language is, and 'understand' the universal principles on which it operates – all unconsciously, of course. All they have to do when exposed to their own particular language, therefore, is discover how these universal principles operate in it. They don't have to learn that strings of sound can be combined into words, for instance; only what particular sequences of sound are the ones used in their society.

Support for Chomsky came from Dan Isaac Slobin, who pointed out that both anatomically, through the specialized development of our oral and respiratory systems, and neurologically, through the direct linking of these organs to Broca's and Wernicke's areas of the brain, human beings are 'specifically adapted to produce and process temporal sequences of distinct speech sounds' – i.e. talk. (Chimps and monkeys are not so adapted: chimps lack the necessary vocal equipment, and the equivalent areas of the monkey brain are used to control the workings of the hands, feet and tail.)

Skinner's Behavourist theory

Chomsky's theory was evolved in opposition to B.F. Skinner, who claimed that children learn to speak in the same way as they learn anything else: by reinforcement from the environment. (In the case of language learning, 'the environment' presumably includes the parents.) Children are born with a general learning potential which is shaped, in the case of language, by positive and negative feedback (rewards and punishment from their parents). Positive feedback for the child's simple early responses is given for a short time, then dropped in favour of increasingly sophisticated responses, until eventually the child's language comes to match that of its parents.

Difficulties were found in both these theories. If Skinner is right and response to the environment is the key, how do children born into impoverished surroundings acquire language as easily as more fortunate ones? How do children with learning difficulties learn language at all? Parental reinforcement didn't seem to be the key factor either, since observation shows that:

- most parents correct for politeness and truthfulness of content, rather than for grammar
- parental corrections of grammar don't work in any case: children have to learn at their own pace.

Children can't be hurried into applying a rule until they've reached the stage where they're ready to do so. Witness the frustrations of the parent below (who might have been better occupied in assuring the child that she was liked).

Child: Nobody don't like me.

Mother: No, say 'nobody likes me'.

Child: Nobody don't like me.

Mother: *(After eight more tries)* No, now listen carefully, say 'nobody likes me'.

Child: Oh! Nobody don't likes me.

Quoted by David McNeil in *The Genesis of Language*, eds. Frank Smith and George A. Miller

From content to process

Chomsky's theory was much more acceptable, but had one major stumbling block: if rules are built in, how are we to account for children applying a rule, then forgetting it, then applying it again at different stages of language development? No one questioned the existence of some kind of innate capacity for language, but no one was clear what the nature of it was.

Since then, direct and intensive study of children learning language in natural settings has suggested that the innate capacity is nothing more mysterious than a specialized ability of the brain to work out the rules of the language it is exposed to. Dan I. Slobin contrasts this 'process approach' with the 'content' approach of Chomsky.

It seems to me that the child is born not with a set of linguistic categories but with some sort of process mechanism – a set of procedures and inference rules, if you will – that he uses to process linguistic data. These mechanisms are such that, applying them to the input data, the child ends up with something which is a member of the class of human languages. The linguistic universals, then, are the result of an innate cognitive competence rather than the content of such a competence.

Dan I. Slobin, in *The Genesis of Language*

- -

In other words, children are born with an ability to understand the processes involved in making language work, and can apply these processes to the examples of language they hear around them.

The Interactionist theory

The latest theories about language acquisition accept children's innate capacity for inference, but link it to their interaction with their physical and social environment. As Genishi and Dyson point out in *Language Assessment in the Early Years*, 'every instance of language the child encounters is contextualized – that is, it occurs in some real situation for some real communicative purpose'. By listening to adult talk, children learn that language can help them to do a number of useful things. It can be:

- instrumental: a means of getting them what they want or need
- regulatory: a means of controlling their own and other people's behaviour
- interactional: a means of socializing with other people
- expressive: a means of asserting their individuality and making their feelings understood
- heuristic: a means of learning things through Why? What? Who? and Where? questions

- representational: a means of conveying things about themselves to other people
- creative: a means of having fun by playing with words and making up stories.

Children learn to speak because they:

1 listen to the sentences adults speak

2 discern regular patterns in the language they hear

3 deduce the rules governing language use from these patterns

4 use these rules in the construction of new, totally original sentences of their own

5 compare their structures with those of adults and revise any that reveal themselves to be wrong until

6 their speech matches that of the adults in their particular speech community.

Children, in other words, are now seen to be 'hypothesis makers, testers, and revisers', working always within an interactive environment.

How babies learn to talk

Getting to grips with sounds

Babies begin to communicate with their mothers by crying as soon as they enter the world. During the first nine months they learn to vary the pitch and tone of their crying to tell their carers how they feel and what they need. (They also communicate by smiling back when their mothers smile at them; it looks like a game, but it has an important bonding effect.) Mothers quickly learn to distinguish a hunger cry from one caused by pain or the need for comfort and are quick to soothe, which is why these early sounds are technically described as **functional** (working towards a goal), and **regulatory** (aimed at controlling parents' behaviour).

According to Michael McTear in *Children's Conversation*, babies also begin in the first weeks of life to learn about rhythm: they have been seen to make subtle little movements of their arms and legs in time with the rhythms of their mothers' voices. The technical term for this is **synchronicity**.

It's in this early stage that babies begin making the little murmuring sounds known as **vegetative noises**; they also smack their lips together as if trying to pronounce the **plosive consonants** 'p' and 'b', made by expelling little puffs of air.

A little later, they progress to making lower-pitched and more musical sounds resembling the vowel 'u' and the consonants 'k' and 'g'. Later still, they start to string these sounds together into sequences like *kuu* and *guu*, giving rise to the descriptive term, **cooing**. Friction sounds like *fff* and a trilled *r* come next as babies experiment with lip and tongue positions, and at about six months of age they begin to **babble**, uttering long sequences of repeated sounds like *bababab, dadadada*. This fools many parents into thinking babies have said their first word, but they haven't. Instead, they play around with sound by switching consonants and vowels from one syllable to the next: *ada, maba*, etc. 'S' and 'sh' sounds are also heard at this stage, and babies are almost ready to start to speak.

Almost, but not quite. The **melody** and **rhythm** that make adult speech sound natural are still missing. Babies stop to breathe when they have to, not when the sense of an utterance demands, and until these skills are mastered, the first real words will not be heard.

Getting to grips with prosodics

By the time they're about 16 months of age, babies are able to recognize the rhythms of their own language and to control their breathing well enough to imitate them in what are known as **proto-words**: words that sound just like real words but don't yet have any actual meaning. The intonation patterns of questions, exclamations, commands, greetings and namings can all be heard in the child's speech, even though it is all quite meaningless. Only when the child learns to associate meaning with the sounds he or she is making will true speech emerge.

Getting to grips with grammar

Between 12 and 18 months, babies utter their first real words, in which sound and meaning are combined. At first, one-word utterances are the norm: *teddy*, *gone*, *more*, and so on. Some utterances, like *allgone* and *ready-steady-go*, may look different, but to the child they're single words. Most of these single-word utterances are common nouns and simple verbs. If a preposition like 'in' is heard, said very loudly, it is being used in place of a verb: *in* may mean *Put it in*.

The various intonation patterns learned earlier come in very handy for children now. They soon learn that if they utter a single word with the right intonation, it will do almost as well as a proper sentence. For example, *Biccy* said with a rising intonation will stand in for 'Can I have a biscuit?'. Uttered with a falling tone in answer to the question 'What do you want?', it represents the declarative sentence, 'I want a biscuit'. In the same way, the single-word utterance *Dadda* can do duty for many sentences that the child is not yet able to construct, as in the following example given by McTear in *Children's Conversation*:

'Is that daddy?' (Interrogative)

'It's daddy.' (Declarative)

'Pick me up, daddy.' (Imperative)

Children can also explore question-and-answer sequences on their own. David Crystal (in *Listen to Your Child*) gives the example of a child who murmured *allgone* to himself on a rising tone before deliberately dropping his cup of drink on to the floor and then saying *allgone* with a satisfied falling tone.

At about 18 months, children progress to two-word utterances like *coat off*, *kiss teddy*, *look car*. They haven't yet grasped how to use the little structure words that hold speech together and make it flow, so their speech sounds jerky and abrupt. Without a grasp of the relative pronoun, for example, all the child can do is utter the single words *bus* and *house* to act as clues to what he's trying so hard to say: *[Stephen] who lives in the house that has a toy bus inside.* Never think that grammar is unimportant. Mothers of young children don't!

Soon, however, they learn that words have to work with other words, and prepositions and pronouns begin to appear. *Teddy* becomes **my** *teddy*; *want biccy* becomes **me** *want biccy* (grammatically wrong, but on the right lines); location is signalled by phrases like *in there*, *on head*.

Children have trouble separating possessive pronouns from personal ones at first, leading to mistakes like these (quoted in McTear):

This is hims car.   I can see shes bed.

Mys want to come in.   My finished now.

They also have trouble in sorting out the object case (*me*, *him*, *her*, *them*) from the subject case (*I*, *he*, *she*, *they*).

Object case instead of subject:

Me want it.

Him did it.

Her gave me one.

Thems all gone now.

Subject case instead of object:

Let she do it.

I gonna push they over.

Inconsistent use:

She like that, her do.

Second year advances

By now, children are capable of distinguishing between the person doing an action (the **subject**) and the person or thing that is receiving it (the **object**), e.g. *Man kick ball.*

They also begin to use **adverbs** to indicate:

when the action takes place – *Man kick ball* **now**

how the action is carried out – *Man kick ball* **hard**

where the action takes place – *Man kick ball* **there**

Their formerly brusque two-word utterances start to expand into something more like sentences.

It's in the second year too that children start using question words like 'What?' and 'Where?'. Before this they'd had to rely on rising intonation to ask questions. These question words are used on their own till about 18 months of age, then are combined with other words into two-word utterances like *Where that? Where car? What that? What doing?* The other question words – 'Why', 'How', and 'Who' – emerge a little later, and 'When' is last of all. Children have trouble getting to grips with 'When', presumably because time is a more abstract concept. They often mistake it for 'Where' in questions like *When did he go?*

Third year advances

By the time they're three, children are using longer and more varied sentences:

Two-year-old	Three-year-old
Where daddy going?	Where will you put my presents in the morning?
Man kick ball.	The man is kicking that ball.
Push car.	Push the car in the garage now.

Three-year-olds can:

- use the definite and indefinite articles, *the* and *a*, and simple adjectives like *big* and *black*
- add inflexions to the endings of adjectives – e.g. *bigger*, *biggest*
- give verbs the different endings for the present and past tense: *The man kicks the ball*; *The man kicked the ball.* (They still make mistakes, of course. Having

worked out that the ending *-ed* is the way to make the past tense, they then apply it to irregular verbs also, coming out with forms like *wented, hurted, bited* and *thinked*.)

- use the word *and* to make lists of things, e.g. here is Lucy deciding which toys to take to bed with her: *And I want teddy, and that teddy, and my dolly, and Mr Happy, and that one, and…*

- use the word *and* to join sentences together: *I got a car and I got a gun and I got a game and we have a party and he gived me a big kiss and I was very tired* (quoted by McTear in *Children's Conversation*)

- use the auxiliary verbs *do, can, have,* and *will. Have* is particularly useful to them, because once they have mastered its different tenses, they can at last talk about **time**. Two-year-olds can't manage this: *daddy gone* might mean either *daddy's just gone* or *daddy went last night*. Three-and-a-half- to four-year-olds can make the time-scale clear by using the auxiliary to form the appropriate tense: *Daddy went* (ordinary past) or *Daddy has gone* (past perfect). Similarly, two-year-olds who can only say *Teddy sitting* can't distinguish between present and past until they've learned to use *is* as an auxiliary verb, as in *Teddy is/was sitting*.

Typical mistakes to be found at this time include using the uninflected form of the verb *to be* instead of the inflected *is*, e.g. *Teddy be sitting*. But by the end of their third year, children can use most parts of speech more or less correctly, with appropriate intonation and stress.

Later advances

Before the age of four-and-a-half, most children can use only simple sentences joined together by conjunctions like *and, but,* and *then*. After four-and-a-half, most can create **complex sentences**, joining dependent clauses on to main ones with conjunctions such as *if, what, when, because, that, where, before, after,* and *while*. They may still make a few mistakes, of course: mixing different constructions, perhaps, e.g. *quite a very difficult one*, or using the wrong prepositions, e.g. *I'm bored at shopping*. But on the whole they have become good speakers.

So good are they in fact that only one thing now distinguishes their speech from that of adults: its lack of fluency. It doesn't flow smoothly because they aren't yet accustomed to using the little connecting words and phrases that smooth the transition from one sentence to another: words such as *well, for instance, like, say, instead, anyhow, at least, maybe, perhaps, probably, anyway, actually, unfortunately, for example, believe it or not, you know, I mean, I'm afraid, also, of course, well anyhow, at any rate, however, really,* and so on. One survey found that even as late as 12 years of age, children used far fewer of these words than adults, and the words they did use were still simple: *now, then, so, anyway, though,* and *really*.

The distinguishing marker, then, between adult and childish speech is the ability to form sentences into smoothly flowing, natural-sounding sequences with the help of a wide range of linking words.

Getting to grips with conversation

How do children master such a complex skill as speech in five short years? Through the in-put of their primary carers. Mothers teach their children how to speak by talking to them as if they already can. Consider the following examples provided by McTear in *Children's Conversation*:

Ann:	*(blowing noises)*
Mother:	That's a bit rude.
Ann:	mouth
Mother:	Mouth, that's right.
Ann:	face
Mother:	Face, yes, mouth is in your face. What else have you got in your face?
Ann:	face *(closing eyes)*
Mother:	You're making a face, aren't you?

By treating the baby's one-word utterances as if they were contributions to a conversation, her mother is introducing her to the practice of turn-taking, and to question and response sequences.

Mothers also use initiation and response sequences with babies who are too young to speak:

Mother: *(making to remove bottle)* Are you finished? Yes? *(removing bottle)* Well, was that nice?

Even when the baby can't respond, the mother acts as if he has done, supplying the 'yes' of a possible answer so that when the baby *is* later able to speak, he'll know what to say. She plays his part in the conversation for him, in other words. Parents also help by taking part in what McTear calls summons-and-answer sequences. In the following example given by McTear, the child attempts to attract her father's attention by saying his name, *Daddy*. (Names are known as **vocatives**.) He then shows her how conversation works by supplying for her the structures she can't yet make for herself:

Child: daddy

Father: What?

Child: daddy

Father: What've you done? Broken a toy? Eh? Little scamp. *(Child laughs)*

Initiating conversation

Thanks to this early input, children as young as two are able to converse with each other, although at a very simple level. They can initiate conversations and respond to simple topics, as McTear's examples show:

A

Child 1: my car

Child 2: car go fast

Child 1: good car

B

Child 1: a flower broken

Child 2: many flowers broken

The main conversational ploy here is repetition, which is hardly surprising since children of this age have very little grammar and a lexis of only 100 words.

Early conversations like these are described as **closed**, because they don't go anywhere. Two-years-olds aren't yet able to pick up on what another person has said and say something related to it in return, so the conversation simply stops. To start it again would involve one of the two speakers opening up (**initiating**) another topic – difficult for children so young and with so little experience of the world.

The move towards conversation proper comes when children grasp the idea of reciprocity, that is, that they're expected to:

- respond when someone speaks to them
- make sure that that response will allow the other speaker to say something further in return.

This process is known as **turn-taking**. Look at the following transcript of a conversation showing conventional turn-taking. Short pauses are marked as (.); longer pauses are marked with the time in seconds, e.g. (1.0).

A: what do you think of football?

B: well (.) I don't mind the game but I think the players get far too much money, don't you?

A: yes (1.0) I know what you mean (.) but is it any worse than the fat cats in the City?

B: well they do do the economy some good (2.0) so they say anyway

By the time they're four, most children are getting to be quite good conversationalists. They know how to initiate conversations with attention-getters like *hey* or *do you know what*, questions, or statements:

Heather: and then you know what

Siobhan: what

Heather: they all standed up

They also know how to re-initiate when the first initiation fails; they use repetitions, attention-getting words, people's names (vocatives), and the technique of gazing directly at the other person:

Heather: then why do you not look for them? (5.0) Siobhan (1.0) Siobhan (*louder, leaning over to gaze at Siobhan*)

Siobhan: I'm too busy to talk

Heather: you are not (7.0) you aren't, Siobhan

Siobhan: yes I am

(Quoted by McTear in *Children's Conversation*)

By the time they're three or four children have also worked out where to place vocatives in a request in order to get the best response from their conversational partner. They place the vocative first when they're trying to attract the person's attention: *Katie, can I have your dolly?*; they place it last when they're really having to work hard to squeeze out a response: *Can I, Katie?*

They also know how to use rephrasing. When the first request is unanswered they change the form of the words to force an answer:

Can I have some sweets daddy? (4.0) You said you give me some sweets, daddy

They also use rephrasing in order to make what they're talking about clearer, e.g. by changing a pronoun to a noun:

She's not making it go forward daddy

She's not making it go forward daddy

She's not putting the bus forward daddy

They know how to make requests. McTear shows that children have definite strategies for making and answering requests; when a request in the form of an instruction gets no response, the speaker rephrases it more politely, disguised as a question:

Heather: Siobhan don't forget to bring your bikini round to my house (3.0) will you bring your bikini round to my house?

Siobhan: umhmm

When the request is answered with a firm 'no', children resort to what adults would probably describe as bribery: *I'll be your best friend if you do.* Sometimes the bribe can be a physical goody: when Siobhan refuses to change lunch boxes with Heather, Heather points out that she'll have the bigger one of the two if she does.

They know how to make 'repairs', i.e. to correct themselves when they've failed to give their listener all the necessary information, or when they've got a name or a fact wrong: *I gived it to Henry (.) um Emma's brother.*

They know how to use **anaphoric pronouns** instead of repeating the same noun:

A: I see bus

B: me see it

A: you see it

Checklist of children's conversational strategies

Remember that ages are approximate and results vary with the individual child.

Age	Conversational strategies
2–3 years	Repetition
3 years	Use of **anaphoric pronouns** to avoid simple repetition of preceding nouns.
	Use of **conjunctions** to connect sentences, e.g. *and, too, also, then, so, because, but, though, if* (these are given in the order in which children learn to use them)
3–5 years	Use of the adverb *well* for several purposes: to attract attention; to indicate that what has just been said isn't quite right; to mean 'yes but', as in *Well, I wanted a drink.* It is not used as adults use it, to play for time or signal indecision.
	Use of *now* and *right* for the first time as **discourse markers**, i.e. words that are meaningless in themselves but help to get children smoothly from one place to another in a conversation, rather like conjunctions. (In adult speech they may serve to prepare listeners for some sort of change of subject, or help to focus their attention on what comes next.) Both adults and children may also use them as attention-getters.
5 years	Use of *you know* also appears; McTear suggests that it may be used to soften statements that could otherwise sound superior, e.g. *You can colour it in, you know*, though this would presumably depend on the tone of the utterance.

Describing children's speech patterns

It is useful to remember formulations such as the following for describing children's speech:

The child expresses [possession, plurals, negation, questions, etc.] through the pattern [...].

At this stage the child is using elements like [...], [...] and [...], that were not present at earlier stages.

The word 'elements', as used in the above sentence, is an all-purpose term that can be used for any word in an utterance.

Checklist of features to look for

1 The child expresses himself or herself through telegrammatic or block language, with one- or two-word utterances: *teddy, me, dolly*; *want down, want dinner*.

2 The child omits to use verb phrases, e.g. [I] *want down*.

3 The child omits the personal pronoun *I*: [I] *want down*; [I] *want* [my] *dinner*.

4 The child reverses the normal subject–verb order: *cake eat* for *eat cake*.

5 The child shows that he or she is not yet able to handle auxiliary verbs by expressing the continuous present tense through the use of the participle only; he or she leaves out the auxiliary verb 'to be' that helps to form it: *I* [am] *sitting here*; *I* [am] *eating cake*.

6 The child expresses negation with a simple *no* or *not*: *no sit there/ not sit there*; he or she could be attempting any one of the following constructions, but the utterance lacks auxiliaries to make the exact intention clear:

- a direct command: [Do] *not sit there*

- an indirect command: [You are] *not* [to] *sit there*

- an assertion: [I am] *not* [going to] *sit there.*

7 The child expresses possession with the appropriate 'apostrophe s' marker: *Daddy's chair.*

8 The child expresses plurals by using the 's' inflection: *two cars.*

9 The child expresses interrogatives by reversing the normal subject–verb order: *Why can't Tim play?* instead of using the normal subject–verb order for a statement: *Why Tim can't play?*

10 The child uses the appropriate endings for irregular verbs: *I caught the ball*, not *I catched it.*

11 The child applies the -ed ending of regular verbs to irregular forms: *I seed the car; We goed swimming.*

12 The child uses modal auxiliaries to express:

- obligation (*you must, you should, you ought*)

- permission (*you can, you may*)

- prohibition (*you can't, you mustn't*)

- necessity (*you must*)

- possibility (*you can*, *you may*, *you could*)
- ability (*you can*, *you could*)

13 The child uses the special set of indeterminate pronouns that adults use in sentences expressing negation (*anything*, *anyone*, *any*): *I haven't got any money.*

Activity

Below are extracts in chronological order from the conversation of speakers of various ages, taken from David Crystal, *Listen to Your Child*.

Point out the features that make their speech characteristic of their different age groups.

3 months

Michael: *(loud crying)*

Mother: Oh my word! What a noise! What a noise! *(Picks up Michael)*

Michael: *(sobs)*

Mother: Oh dear, dear, dear! Didn't anybody come to see you? Let's have a look at you. *(Looks inside nappy)* No, you're all right there, aren't you?

Michael: *(spluttering noises)*

Mother: Well, what is it, then? Are you hungry, is that it? Is it a long time since dinner-time?

Michael: *(gurgles and smiles)*

18 months

Child *(at breakfast table)*: Bun. Butter. Jelly. Cakie. Jam.

21 months

Child *(coming in from garden)*: Daddy-knee.

Mother: What's that, darling? What about daddy's knee?

Child: Fall-down daddy.

Mother: Did he? Where did he fall down?

Child: In-garden fall-down.

Mother: Daddy's fallen down in the garden! Poor daddy. Is he all right?

Child: Daddy-knee sore.

Mother: Daddy's fallen over and his knee's sore? I'd better come and see, hadn't I?

28 months

Child: Me want – Look! Balls. You like those balls?

Mother: Yes.

Child: Ball. Kick. Kick. Daddy kick.

Mother: That's right, you have to kick it, don't you?

Child: Mmm. Um. Um. Kick hard. Only kick hard... Our play that. On floor. Our play that on floor. Now. Our play that. On floor. Our play that on floor. Now. Our play that. On floor. No that. Now.

Mother: All right.

Child: Mummy, come on floor me.

(*continued*)

3 years

Child: Hester be fast asleep, mummy.

Mother: She was tired.

Child: And why did her have two sweets, mummy?

Mother: Because you each had two, that's why. She had the same as you. Ooh dear, now what?

Child: Daddy didn't give me two in the end.

Mother: Yes, he did.

Child: He didn't.

Mother: He did.

Child: Look, he given one to – two to Hester, and two to us.

Mother: Yes, that's right.

Child: Why did he give?

Mother: Because there were six sweets. That's two each.

4 years 7 months

Susie: Oh, look, a crab. We seen – we were been to the seaside.

Baby-sitter: Have you?

Susie: We saw cr–fishes and crabs. And we saw a jelly-fish, and we had to bury it. And we – we did holding crabs, and we – we holded him in by the spade.

Baby-sitter: Did you?

Susie: Yes, to kill them, so they won't bite our feet.

Baby-sitter: Oh.

Susie: If you stand on them, they hurt you, won't they?

Baby-sitter: They would do. They'd pinch you.

Susie: You'd have to – and we put them under the sand, where the sea was. And they were going to the sea. And we saw some shells. And we picked them up, and we heard the sea in them. And we saw a crab on a lid. And we saw lots of crabs on the sea-side. And I picked the fishes up – no, the shells, and the feathers from the birds. And I saw a pig.

5 years 6 months

Dad: What do you want to play, then?

Lucy: I'll be the waitress and you have to eat in my shop. You come in, and sit down, and I can come and see you.

(Dad acts his part obediently. Lucy walks over, clutching an imaginary notebook and pencil.)

Lucy: Good afternoon.

Dad: Good afternoon.

Lucy: What do you want to eat?

Dad: Ooh, I'd like some cornflakes, and some sausages, please.

Lucy: We haven't got any sausages.

Dad: Oh dear. Well, let me see... Have you got any steak?

Lucy: Yes. We got steak.

Dad: I'll have some steak, then.

Lucy: O.K. 'Bye.

Writing skills

Children's brains are programmed to speak, but not to write, and fluent speakers take far longer to become properly fluent writers. When writing about things that have happened to them personally, even eleven-year-olds write in much the same style as children of seven speak: in short, declarative sentences strung together with *and*, *so*, and *and then*. Witness the following examples:

A Today it's my birthday and I had a spiaragrath and a airfix Bumper Books and I played with my spiaragrath and when daddy brought me to school hes going back and his going to play with my spiaragrath and today Gary is coming to tea and we will play subuiteo and football and with my spiaragrath and we might have a game at table soccer and Gary will have to go at about 8 o'clock and I will go and help him cary his things then I will go home and go to bed.

David, aged 7

B Dear Mrs Smith,

My monster is late because I did not finish it in English and I only had a cuple of lines to do and I finished it off in geography so my house tutor mister mordred taw it up and I had to take it home and do it. I hope you like it from Stephen Tolley yours faithily.

Stephen, aged 11

Quoted in Jones and Mulford, *Children Using Language*

- -

The most obvious feature of the writing in **Extract A** is its monotonous and repetitive style. The paragraph is a string of concrete nouns and simple sentences strung together with the help of the commonest conjunction, 'and'. If David had been able to use the anaphoric pronoun 'it' instead of repeating his noun 'spiaragrath' three times, it would have sounded much better.

His handling of past tenses is also shaky in the sentence beginning *when daddy brought me to school*. David is obviously writing this at school and has been there for some time, so the sentence should read 'After daddy brought me to school he was going back to play....' David isn't capable of such a sophisticated construction yet.

Spelling here (apart from the 'spiaragrath' and 'subuiteo') is very accurate, with only one error in 'cary' for 'carry', but David doesn't yet appreciate the part that punctuation plays in making sentences clear: he doesn't even use commas to mark sentence ends, and the apostrophe for omission is unknown to him as yet in phrases like 'he's going'. He does show a touch of more sophisticated writing, however, in using the modal verb 'might' as well as the simple future tense, 'will'.

The writer of **Extract B** uses short, blunt declarative statements and describes what happened in chronological order, just as David did above. His sentence handling begins more promisingly with a complex sentence (the simple sentence *My monster is late* linked by *because* to the dependent clause *I did not finish it*), but soon deteriorates into a string of simple sentences joined by 'and' and 'so'.

Punctuation is still minimal, with only one full stop in five sentences; there are no commas to mark off his teacher's name from the words that surround it (*my house tutor mister mordred taw it up* instead of 'my house tutor, mister mordred, taw it up'); no capital letters for 'House Tutor' or 'Mr Mordred', and no customary space left between the body of the letter and the signature.

Spelling errors occur: 'cuple' for 'couple', 'taw' for 'tore', 'faithily' for 'faithfully'.

Notice that the writers of both these pieces describe the events:

- in the order in which they occurred
- in short, blunt, declarative statements.

In A there is no logical connection between the events, and only the continuous use of 'and' binds them together into some sort of whole. Older, more sophisticated writers might single out one event as more important or interesting than the others and deal with it first, going back to describe earlier ones later on. They might also put in the kind of asides and linking phrases that would express their feelings about the events – *I had to go in to get my tea then, unfortunately.* This writer is writing simply as he speaks, and all the things that might make the accounts more interesting if they were heard rather than read – changes of intonation, stress, and rhythm – are of course missing.

When asked to write about things outside themselves, nine- and eleven-year-olds use fewer conjunctions. This makes the writing sound more controlled, but at the same time rather monotonous and clipped:

A On Thursday we went to have a look round the Tithe Barn. We went through the woods and we saw a grey squirrel which jumped from a branch to a very thick branch. The trees were not all out, but the flowers were. The Tithe Barn is on Cupfield Hall Farm. The outside of the barn is made of flint and stone, and the tiles are very uneven. A lot of the barn is the arridginal material. At the tops of the roof there were nests, the tiles had moss and grass growing on them. There were holes in the roof. It was very dark in there.

Mary, aged 9

B What kind of world is a fish world? Imagine living in water all the time. There are many kinds of insect that crawl about the weeds and mud. Many are unearthly like creatures. Illustrated opposite is a caddis larvae made up of bits and bobs such as sticks and stones. Also there is the water scorpion which kills its enemys. First it kills them and then sucks out all the juices. Fish are streamlined for swimming. They breath by swallowing water and extracting the oxygen from the water and pushing it out through his gills.

Neil, aged 11

Quoted in Jones and Mulford, *Children Using Language*

- -

This writer of **Extract A** has a good command of punctuation and is beginning to use complex sentences with the help of relative pronouns like 'which'. Simple and compound sentences are still in the majority, however, and there is even one example of two simple sentences wrongly joined by a run-on comma (i.e. a comma used instead of a full stop).

Nevertheless, spelling is generally accurate ('original' is a difficult word to spell if you have not seen it written), and the beginning of a feel for style is shown in the use of the phrase *At the tops of the roof* to open a sentence.

The writer of **Extract B** begins well with an attempt to involve the reader: *Imagine living in water all the time*. Neil has a good command of spelling and punctuation and gets colour and drama into his writing with the help of emotive words and phrases like *unearthly*, *enemies*, *kills*, and *sucks out all the juices*. What the writing still doesn't have as yet, however, is the kind of smooth flow that adult writers achieve by using linking words and phrases to bind the writing into a harmonious whole. Compare the following:

> *Have you ever wondered* what kind of world is a fish world? *Just* imagine living in water all the time. *Under the surface* there are many kinds of insect that crawl about the weeds and mud, many of them unearthly looking creatures. Illustrated opposite, *for example*, is a caddis larvae made up of sticks and stones and other bits and bobs. Also there is the water scorpion, which kills its enemies *before* suck*ing* out all *their* juices. Fish are streamlined for swimming *in this watery environment*. They breathe by swallowing water, extracting the oxygen from *it* and pushing it out through their gills.

Using the word 'wondered' makes a link with 'imagine'; 'Under the surface' links with 'in water'; 'for example' relates back to 'many kinds of insect', and 'watery environment' links back to 'in water' and forward to 'swallowing water'. Notice too how using a participle like 'sucking' joins two sentences together without the need for repetitive conjunctions like 'and' and 'then'.

Extract B does have a coherent logical structure – that of question and answer. However, the techniques that more sophisticated writers use to weave clauses into longer, smoother sentences – subordinate clauses and linking words – are largely missing. For something much closer to adult writing, see the account written by a 14-year-old, below.

School trip to the South of France

After an exhausting eighteen hour journey by coach and ferry we arrived at Marseilles to meet the families we were going to stay with for the rest of the week. We were all called off the coach in pairs to be greeted by our very enthusiastic French families. We were kissed on the cheek twice by each person, a strange, but friendly experience! Despite the frenzied last minute practice of our French on the coach we found that, at first, all we could say was oui or non. However, over the next few days our French improved, especially when we realized we needed it to survive. The next day we set off early to the Camargue and St Marie de la Mer. At the Camargue, the landscape was very flat, marshy, and rather boring, until we spotted a group of pink flamingoes! Later on during the journey we saw herds of wild black bulls and the occasional white horse. In St Marie de la Mer we visited Arles and looked around two old Roman bull fighting rings, where bull fighting still sometimes continues.

Features to look for in children's writing

Stage 1

Lexis consists of simple common nouns (names of objects close to them), the names of friends and family (mummy, daddy, Gary, etc.) and basic verbs, e.g. *had, go, got, did*; these are always in the active rather than the passive voice (e.g. *for my birthday I got* rather than *for my birthday I was given*). Writers handle the present and future tenses correctly but may get things wrong when describing actions at different stages in the past. Modal verbs such as *might* are rare and are usually echoes of adult speech rather than spontaneous utterances.

Sentence structure consists mainly of simple declarative statements of fact, strung together by the co-ordinating conjunctions *and, but, then,* and *so*; occasional subordinating conjunctions such as *when* and *because* occur, but are exceptions that only serve to prove the rule. Phrases are not used at this stage; anaphoric pronouns (e.g. 'it' for a previously mentioned noun) are also absent.

Punctuation is almost entirely lacking.

Spelling: Most common words are correctly spelled; errors tend to occur only with polysyllabic words and words which are spelled differently from the way they sound.

Stage 2

Lexis is still largely concrete and simple, with little use of abstract nouns or words derived from Latin or Greek.

Sentence structure has become more varied: writers now use simple sentences correctly, with a full stop marking their ends, e.g. *There were holes in the roof. It was very dark in there.* They use conjunctions to join simple sentences into compound ones, e.g. *The trees were not all out, but the flowers were*, and they use relative pronouns and other subordinating conjunctions to form complex sentences, e.g. *We went through the woods and we saw a grey squirrel which jumped from a branch to a very thick branch.* Anaphoric pronouns are not yet commonly used to avoid awkward repetitions such as 'branch' in the preceding sentence, and the writing still has a rather stilted, clunky feel.

Punctuation: Full stops and commas are correctly used, though occasional lapses are made when run-on commas incorrectly link two unrelated sentences, e.g. *At the tops of the roof there were nests, the tiles had moss and grass growing on them.*

Spelling is now very accurate.

Stage 3

Lexis: Latinate words such as *exhausting, enthusiastic* and *experience* now appear.

Sentence structure: The monotonous simple sentence disappears; most sentences are now complex in form, e.g. *However, over the next few days our French improved, especially when we realized we needed it to survive* and *At the Camargue, the landscape was very flat, marshy, and rather boring, until we spotted a group of pink flamingoes!* Note how the use of the subordinate clause in the second of these sentences in particular helps the writing to flow: at Stage 2, writers would probably have said *At the Camargue, the landscape was very flat and marshy and it was boring and then we spotted a group of pink flamingoes and it* *got better.* The writing is also made smoother and more lively by the use of phrases (groups of words that differ from clauses because they don't have a main verb), e.g. *After an exhausting eighteen hour journey by coach and ferry; a strange, but friendly experience!* and *Despite the frenzied last minute practice of our French on the coach.* As a result, the writing is fully integrated at last, with all parts of the sentences working smoothly together and all the sentences flowing easily into one another.

Punctuation is good.

Spelling is totally accurate.

Just as with speech, then, the distinguishing marker between adult and childish writing is the ability to form sentences into smoothly flowing, natural-sounding sequences with the help of a wide range of linking words, phrases and clauses.

8 Language Change

All living languages change, and English has changed more than most. The historical and social events that transformed it from Anglo-Saxon – a sub-dialect of Old German – into the *lingua franca* of the modern world are outlined below.

External influence 1: Invasion by the Vikings

Thanks to Britain's position on the western edge of Europe (last stop before America) its past has been marked by successive waves of invasion from the Continent.

The Anglo-Saxons themselves entered England in this way in about 450, just after the Romans moved out of England for good. They swept the Celtic inhabitants (the Ancient Britons) out to the hills and the coasts and took over the major part of the country, only to be invaded later in their turn, first by Scandinavian Vikings – the Danes – then by the Norman French under William the Conqueror.

The language that evolved from the mingled dialects of Angles, Saxons and Jutes – Old English – was plainer and harsher than English today. It reminded the more civilized Romans of the cawing of crows, and the addition of Old Norse words like *brink*, *dregs*, *steak*, *skin*, *rotten*, *muggy*, *rake*, *scare*, *scowl*, and *thrust*, contributed by the Viking invaders, only heightened the impression of harshness.

In the tenth century, Old English looked like this:

> And hyrdas waerdon on þam ylcan rice waciende, and nihtwaeccan healdende ofer heora heorda. Þa stod Drihtnes engel wiþ hig, and Godes beorhtnes him ymbe scean; and hi him mycelum ege adredon.

A rough literal translation would be as follows:

> And shepherds there were in that same country on guard, and nightwatch keeping over their flocks. Then stood the Lord's angel before them, and God's brightness shone about them; and they feared him with much fear.

Note

The elongated letter þ here is the Anglo-Saxon letter called 'thorn', representing our *th*. Where we write *with* and *the*, they wrote *wiþ* and *þe*.

When the printing press was invented in the fifteenth century, printers had no letter to represent thorn, and for some inexplicable reason decided to replace it with a letter *y*. Therefore *þe* appeared as *ye*, *þæt* as *yat* – but in printed texts only; nobody ever said 'ye olde tea shoppe', because they knew *ye* was simply a method of writing *the*.

Based on the evidence of the billion-word Oxford English Corpus (OEC), analysis reveals that:

The vast majority of the words we use most frequently [today] are from Old English: the basic elements of nearly any sentence that any of us utters were in place before the Norman Conquest of England in 1066.

Look at the passage below, for example, and you will see how much of the oldest part of our language has survived into the present day. Words of Anglo-Saxon origin are printed in bold.

English is not merely **the** product **of the** dialects **brought to England by the Jutes, Angles, and Saxons. These** form **its** basis, **the** sole basis **of its** grammar, **and the** source **of by far the** largest part **of its** vocabulary. **But there are other** elements **which** entered **into it.**

Now look at what is left when these are removed:

merely	product	dialects	form	basis	sole basis
grammar	source	largest part	vocabulary	elements	entered

You will see that it would be impossible for us to speak or write intelligibly today without the help of Old English, simply because all the little function words that hold sentences together – like *a*, *the*, *in*, and *that* – are Anglo-Saxon.

Other indispensable Anglo-Saxon function words are:

- the personal pronouns *I, you, he, she, we, us*
- the demonstrative pronouns *this, that, these, those*
- the auxiliary verbs *can, shall*
- the conjunctions *as, and, but, so, then*
- the prepositions *on, in, under, over, down, up, to, by*
- the adverbs *when, while, where.*

Common nouns with Anglo-Saxon origins include those in the following table.

house (hus)	love (lufu)	heart (heorte)	wife (wif)
husband (husbonda)	father (fæder)	son (sunu)	friend (freond)
ship (scip)	food (foda)	grass (græs)	leaf (leaf)
fowl (fugol)	saddle (sadol)	water (wæter)	moon (mona)
sun (sunne)	winter (winter)	spring (spryng)	fall (feall)
day (dæg)	night (niht)	king (cyning)	

Common adjectives from Anglo-Saxon include:

good new first last long great little old big small large same
right evil cold busy next few own early young bloody bitter

Common verbs include:

be have do say get make go know take see come think
look want give find tell ask work seem feel leave call
eat drink sleep live fight

Interestingly, these monosyllabic Old English verbs are still among the most commonly used verbs in modern English. As the OEC comments, it seems that 'English prefers terse, ancient words to describe actions or occurrences'.

Most names for parts of the body, most numbers, and most strong verbs also come from Old English. (Strong verbs are those that form their past tense by changing the vowel, e.g. *speak/ spoke*; *ride/ rode*; *sing/ sang*; *think/ thought*; *fight/ fought*; *find/ found*; *sit/ sat*; *stand/ stood*; *drink/ drank*; *hold/ held*; *do/ did*.)

Finally, most 'rude' names for parts of the body and its functions – *arse* and *fart*, for example – are Anglo-Saxon in origin. So are most of the 'four-letter words' still sometimes written with initial and final letters and a row of asterisks in between: *sh*t*, *c**t*, and *f**k*, for example (although there are no written records of these last two before the twelfth century). Once probably used in normal colloquial speech, they have come to be considered obscene over the centuries and are now shunned (theoretically) before the 9 o'clock watershed on television.

Grammatical points to remember

Where modern English uses *you* in talking to another person, Anglo-Saxon used þu (pronounced *thu*) and Middle English *thou*.

Where modern English puts an *-s* ending only on the third-person singular of the verb – *I love*, *you love*, *he/she love*s, *we love*, *you love*, *they love* – Anglo-Saxon and Middle English had separate endings for the second- and third-person singular: *þu/thou lov**est***; *he/she lov**eth***.

It is important to know this, because if you don't it gets in the way of reading the work of older writers, and of Shakespeare in particular. The old second- and third-person singular endings such as *dost*, *doth*, *hast* and *hath* survived until the end of the eighteenth century and are still found in dialect forms today.

External influence 2: Invasion by the Norman French

Only after a second set of invaders, the Normans under William the Conqueror, had forced the English upper classes to speak French for a century or so did English really begin to modify its harsh and basically monosyllabic nature. Words like *melodye*, *corage* and *tendre* were brought into common use by writers such as Chaucer, lending a touch of grace to down-to-earth English. French brought more varied rhythms, too, thanks to the difference in its stress patterns. Whereas English speakers have always tended to stress the first or second syllable of words – *CHOC'lat*, *NEGligee*, *DEButante*, for example – the French tend to give an equal stress to each syllable:

```
 /  /  /        /  /  /        /  /  /
choc o lat     neg li gee     deb u tante
```

If you think about this, it's easy to see why iambic verse became the dominant stress pattern of modern English poetry.

The two languages gradually merged to create a new one, with Old English still predominant despite its modified vocabulary. The resulting language, known as Middle English, is far closer to the language we speak today than its Old English predecessor. It looked like this:

> And scheeperdis weren in the same cuntre, wakynge and kepynge the watchis of the nyzt on her flok. And lo! the aungel of the Lord stood bisidis hem, and the cleernesse of God schinede aboute hem, and thei dredden with greet drede.

Activity

Find the French borrowings that are equivalent to the following English words and phrases. The first letter of each French word is given in brackets as a guide.

a an illicit sexual affair (l)

b a secret meeting (r)

c remission given to a convict (p)

d hair grown on the upper lip (m)

e girl with dark brown hair (b)

f public eating place (r)

g an engaged person (f)

h what success brings (p.......e)

External influence 3: The Renaissance

If the English language was modified to some extent by French, it was almost swept off its feet by Latin. What invasions by physical force couldn't achieve, Latin managed without a shot fired in anger. Thousands of words from that language flooded into English over the next thousand years, many entering the language indirectly through French, others being absorbed directly from Latin texts when scholars rediscovered classical literature during the Renaissance and later periods. Half of our modern lexis, like the words listed below, is derived from Latin, partly because the new ideas and knowledge that came into England in the sixteenth century came in the form of words with Latin roots:

medium	demonstrate	prodigious	superintendent	external
meditate	urge	eradicate	decorum	calculate
hereditary	vagary	strict	interregnum	excursion
compendium	omen	expostulation	emulate	quarto
critical	horrid	militia	radius	sinus
pathetic	delirium	excavate	stratum	

The advantage of such borrowing is that it brings new words for new ideas (plus new models for poetry and drama).

A possible disadvantage is the loss of linguistic inventiveness. Old English used to coin new words out of existing elements before it gave up and began to borrow words from Latin instead. Anglo-Saxon clerics coined the composite word *hand-book*, for example, as a translation of Latin *manual*, from *manus*, 'hand'. It had the advantage of being perfectly clear and more easily understood by ordinary people than *manual*, as was *threeness* compared with *trinity*, but out of deference to the 'superior' language, the Latin words beat the English ones every time.

The indirect result was to cut off the common man and woman from many of the important new ideas that would shape their lives. Quite unintentionally, they were denied access to knowledge and new ideas by their ignorance of the sophisticated vocabulary in which these were typically expressed.

Glance at the leader pages of the *Sun* and the *Telegraph* and you will see that this linguistic apartheid still operates today. Well over 50% of the English lexicon now has a Latin base, making the transition from primary to secondary school, where academic education begins, a peculiarly painful one in England. Young children begin with simple English words like *brother* and *sister*, for example, and are suddenly confronted with the alien term *siblings*. The more academic children can handle it, but many just switch off. In a country like Germany, the move into higher education may be easier; modern German, although originally from the same linguistic roots as Anglo-Saxon, has kept the habit of making new words from native elements. For example, when German needed a word to express the concept of feeling and working together as a unified group, it came up with the coinage *Zusammengehorigkeitsgefuhl*, from:

zusammen = together

Gehorigkeit = belonging

Gefuhl = feeling.

Unwieldy and long, perhaps, but immediately understandable to every German reading it. English, in contrast, plumped for *solidarity*, from Latin *solidus*, 'solid' – not immediately understood by everyone in the land.

Activity

1 Write clear definitions of the following words derived from Latin:

   allegory   tolerance   contempt   conspiracy   simile   memento

2 What is the most striking difference between these words and your definitions of them?

3 Argue the case for and against Latin loan words by translating them into native English elements: e.g. *ungettatable* for *inaccessible; unseethroughable* for *opaque.*

Conflicting reactions to Latin influence

Reading great works in Latin gave many English writers of the sixteenth and seventeenth centuries an inferiority complex about their own language. Some disliked it for the meanness of its vocabulary, and welcomed Latin borrowings:

> Our English tongue of all languages most swarmeth with single money of monasillables which are the only scandall of it. Bookes written in them and no other, seeme like Shop-keepers boxes, that containe nothing else, saue halfepence, three-farthings and two pences.

> Thomas Nashe, *Christs teares ouer Ierusalem*, 1594

Others despised such borrowings as a form of showing off by people who wanted to be thought learned: *clerks and ſcholers or ſecretaries… not content with the vſual Normane or Saxon word.*

The way in which writers of this period organized (or failed to organize) their sentences also made reading hard work. Here is George Puttenham in 1589 complaining that Latin and Greek terms corrupt our native tongue:

> but now I muſt recant and confeſſe that our Normane Engliſh which hath growen ſince William the Conquerour doth admit many of the auncient feete, by reaſon of the many polyſillables euen to ſixe and ſeauen in one word, which we at this day uſe in our moſt ordinarie language: and which corruption hath bene occaſioned chiefly by the peeuiſh affectation not of the Normans them ſelues, but of clerks and ſcholers or ſecretaries

long ſince, who not content with the vſual Normane or Saxon word, would conuert the very Latine and Greeke word into vulgar French, as to ſay innumerable for innombrable, reuocable, irreuocable, irradiation, depopulation & ſuch like, which are not naturall Normans nor yet French, but altered Latines, and without any imitation at all: which therefore were long time deſpiſed for inkehorne termes, and now be reputed the beſt & moſt delicat of any other.

George Puttenham, *The Arte of English Poesie,* 1589

The most striking feature of this clotted writing is its syntax. The piece is effectively a one-sentence paragraph consisting of single main clause – *but now I muſt recant and confeſſe* – on to which is strung a series of eight dependent clauses and two phrases. The writer does not so much organize the sentence as allow it to pile up, reaching for a new clause every time another thought or quibble occurs to him. The result is so rambling and convoluted that by the time we get to the end of the sentence we may well have forgotten what the writer said at the start.

This is the downside of sixteenth-century writing. The upside is that, with no 'style police' looking over their shoulders, writers were free to bend language to suit their needs. Because no standard grammar books had yet been written, writers felt free to do what they liked with it; Shakespeare, for instance, frequently turns one part of speech into another. Conjunctions become verbs and nouns:

But [verb] me no buts [noun]

Adverbs turn into nouns:

in the dark backwards [noun] and abysm of time

Nouns turn into verbs:

stranger'd with an oath

As Baugh and Cable remark:

When Shakespeare wrote *stranger'd with an oath* he was fitting the language to his thought, rather than forcing his thought into the mold of conventional grammar. This was in keeping with the spirit of his age. It was in language, as in many other respects, an age with the characteristics of youth – vigor, a willingness to venture, and a disposition to attempt the untried. The spirit that animated Hawkins and Drake and Raleigh was not foreign to the language of their time.

Albert C. Baugh and Thomas Cable, *A History of the English Language*

Checklist of the inconsistencies of sixteenth-century prose

Most pieces of writing from the sixteenth century contain some or all of the following inconsistencies.

Spelling

- Redundant *-e* endings on random words, e.g. *worthe, claime*

- The doubling of a vowel at the writer's whim, e.g. *wee* (we); *bee* (be)

- The use of *u* and *v* interchangeably as a vowel, e.g. *euer, vſual*

- The use of *i* and *y* interchangeably as a vowel, e.g. *time, tym*

- The use of *i* and *j* interchangeably as a consonant, e.g. *iustice, justice*

- The use of double consonants at the whim of the writer, e.g. *naturall, uppon*

- The use of the long *-s* (ſ), so confusing to the modern eye

Grammar

- The retention of earlier forms, often alongside later ones, e.g. *(h)it* and *(h)its* (early); *hys* ('his', later)

- The third-person singular verb ending *-eth*, e.g. *hath, doth, signifieth, semeth*

Punctuation

- The rather random use of commas, not necessarily where logic demands

- The occasional use of colons and semi-colons within clauses rather than at their ends.

Activity

The passage below shows many of the inconsistencies referred to above.

1 Translate it into modern English, turning some of the minor clauses into separate sentences and modernizing spelling and punctuation.

2 Discuss the ways in which the writer expresses his feelings in this extract, then compare what you have written with the sample critique on page 145.

Since the tyme of Chaucer, more Latin & French, hath bin mingled with our toung then left out of it, but of late wee haue falne to ſuch borowing of woords from, Latin, French, and other toungs, that it had bin beyond all ſtay and limit, which albeit ſome of vs do lyke wel and think our toung thereby much bettred, yet do ſtrangers therefore carry the farre leſſe opinion thereof, ſome ſaying that it is of it ſelf no language at all, but the ſcum of many languages, others that it is moſt barren, and that wee are dayly faine to borrow woords for it (as though it yet lacked making) out of other languages to patche it up withall, and that yf wee were put to repay our borrowed ſpeech back again, to the languages that may lay claime vnto it; wee ſhould bee left litle better than dumb, or ſcarſly able to ſpeak anything that ſhould bee ſencible.

Richard Verstegan, *A Restitution of Decayed Intelligence*, 1605

3 Paraphrase Nashe's comments above (page 135) in modern English, doing your best to translate the money metaphor into ordinary terms.

4 Look up the meanings of the prefixes *homo-* and *hetero-* in preparation for the next section.

Advantages conferred by a heterogeneous language

Despite Verstegan's claim that to borrow words from other languages 'discredited' one's own, it is difficult to see how English could now do without them. It began as a homogeneous language with Germanic roots. By the middle of the sixteenth century, thanks to the mingling of Latin, French, and native Anglo-Saxon elements, it was rich in synonyms.

The French have a word for everything, we are told. English has at least three for everything, each with different qualities that fit it for different purposes in different contexts. Three major layers of vocabulary can be seen in English:

1 Anglo-Saxon words that are familiar and therefore homely in tone

2 French borrowings that are more formal and polite

3 Latin loan words that are heavier in sound and weightier in meaning, and that seem more remote from ordinary affairs.

In theory, therefore, we can always find the exact word we need to suit a particular context: the Anglo-Saxon word for ordinary situations; the French for more sophisticated contexts; the Latin for metaphysical concerns.

The distinctive qualities of these different kinds of words can be seen in the following triplets, where the first word is native English, the second French, and the third Latin in origin:

ask–question–interrogate	thin–spare–emaciated	folk–people–nation
help–aid–assistance	goodness–virtue–probity	fast–firm–secure
fire–flame–conflagration	holy–sacred–consecrated	time–age–epoch

Activity

1 Put the following groups of three into the same English–French–Latin sequence as above, judging which word belongs to which language purely on sound and connotations.

a impecunious–needy–financially distressed

b inept–incompetent–gauche

c residence–domicile–house

d reserved–close-mouthed–uncommunicative

e harden–solidify–coagulate.

2 Check that you are correct by consulting the *Concise Oxford Dictionary*.

3 Write sentences using all the words of each set.

4 Discuss the different tones of the sentences you have created out of each set of synonyms. What impression do they make on you? How do they sound?

Internal influences: The beginnings of modern prose, 1650–1800

In the sixteenth and early seventeenth centuries the English language was valued mainly as a means of self-expression, and writers were free to do pretty much as they liked with it. After 1650 people began to see it in a more utilitarian light: as an instrument that should be shaped to serve the purposes of society, or important groups within society, rather than individuals alone.

Language as a tool for thinking

It was considered that language should be made, for instance, into a tool with which to think. New ideas and discoveries in mathematics, science and philosophy were spreading through England and Europe, and *the old rambling complexities* of sixteenth-century prose were not thought suitable for expressing them. The Royal Society of London (set up in 1662) declared that something must be done to bring language *closer to mathematical plainness*, and it demanded that its own members should do their best to write without *amplifications, digressions, and swellings of style*.

John Evelyn was a member of the society and the following extract from his diary for June 1658 shows the influence of its ideas on his writing style.

June 2. An extraordinary storme of haile & raine, cold season as winter, wind northerly neere 6 moneths.

3. A large Whale taken, twixt my Land butting on ye Thames & Greenewich, which drew an infinite Concourse to see it, by water, horse, coach, on foote from Lond, & all parts: It appeared first below Greenewich at low-water, for at high water, it would have destroy'd all ye boates: but lying now in shallow water, incompassed with boates, after a long Conflict it was killed with the harping yrons, & struck in ye head, out of which spouted blood & water, by two tunnells like Smoake from a chimney: & after an horrid grone it ran quite on shore & died: The length was 58 foote: 16 in height, black skin'd like Coach-leather, very small eyes, greate taile, small finns & but 2: a piked snout, & a mouth so wide & divers men might have stood upright in it: No teeth at all, but sucked the slime onely as thro a grate made of yt bone which we call Whale bone: The throate yet so narrow, as would not have admitted the least of fishes: The extreames of the Cetaceous bones hang downewardes, from ye Upper jaw, & was hairy towards the Ends, & bottom withinside: all of it prodigious, but in nothing more wonderfull then that an Animal of so greate a bulk, should be nourished onely by slime, thro those grates.

Activity

1 Comment on the way Evelyn expresses his feelings in this extract, relating it to the influence of the new ideas about language, then compare what you have said with the critique on page 145.

2 Comment on any inconsistencies of expression in the writing of this extract.

Language as a tool for social harmony

Language was also seen as a means of bringing people together. After the violence and bloodshed of the English Civil War, all reasonable men and women were expected to conform to the norms of society in order to preserve it in a state of balanced harmony. Standardizing the language was thought to be one way of bringing this about, and a generalized style of writing aimed at pleasing the rising middle class came into being.

Popular magazines like *The Tatler* and *The Spectator* used the register of what Jonathan Swift called *the Learned and Polite Persons of the Nation*: by 'polite', as Dennis Freeborn explains in *From Old English to Standard English*, Swift means *polished, refined, elegant, well-bred*. In the attempt to entertain all and offend none, originality gave way to correctness of expression, passionate feeling to common-sense attitudes and balanced emotion. Since antithesis (setting off one statement directly against another) is a useful device for achieving neatness and balance, it became a favourite device of writers. In poetry, it is found in the heroic couplet, used by poets like Alexander Pope:

True wit is Nature to advantage dressed;
What oft was thought but ne'er so well expressed.

In prose, it is found in writing such as Joseph Addison's:

I… shall leave it to my readers' consideration, whether it is not much better to be let into the knowledge of one's self, than to hear what passes in Muscovy or Poland; and to amuse ourselves with such writings as tend to the wearing out of ignorance, passion, and prejudice, than such as naturally conduce to inflame hatreds, and make enmities irreconcilable.

The Spectator, no. 10, March 1711

The way Addison sets parallel clauses against one another here gives the reader a sense of balance and order that reinforces the idea of social harmony he is advocating:

to be let into the knowledge of one's self
to hear what passes in Muscovy or Poland

such writings as tend to the wearing out of ignorance, passion and prejudice
such [writings] as naturally conduce to inflame hatreds

Activity

1 Explain in your own words the points that Addison is making here. Say how far you agree with him, relating what you say to the kind of articles published in *The Spectator* magazine today. (You will find *The Spectator* in the reference section of your local public library.)

2 The following extract is taken from the preface to *The Lady's Polite Secretary, or New Female Letter Writer,* by the Right Hon. Lady Dorothea DuBois, written in 1771.

a Discuss what you understand to be the author's intentions in writing the book.

b Explain how the style of the author's writing helps to communicate the ideals of eighteenth-century society described above.

Amidst the varied improvements which engage the time and attention of our young ladies, the editor of these pages has been long surprised that EPISTOLATORY COMPOSITION should be so generally neglected; that, whilst a multiplicity of works had appeared to model the style of the other sex, hardly anything had been attempted which could be of any material service to her own. Convinced that in every age, every nation, it has been a confessed maxim that women are born with talents peculiarly adapted for this path of literature – with a liveliness of imagination, and a facility of expression, unknown to the lords of creation; she determined to exert her efforts to supply the deficiency – to collect, as taste or judgment directed, a variety of LETTERS which might form the manners, whilst they formed the style, of her fair readers; which might amuse them as GIRLS, and be worthy of their attention as Women. How far her labours deserve the patronage of the public, the public are now to determine; and, at any rate, it would ill become female delicacy to pronounce.

Language as an indicator of social class

English had come a long way by the middle of the eighteenth century, thanks to the standardizing influence of detailed grammar books and Samuel Johnson's *Dictionary of the English Language*. It was still felt to be imperfect, however, measured against Latin, and Latinate phrasing and vocabulary were still regarded as the mark of a good writing style.

Societies for the 'protection' of the language were proposed, first to lay down rules for how language *should* be written, then to 'fix' it – save it from being 'corrupted' by the *depraved language of the common people* (Swift). Linguistic snobbery was rife in eighteenth-century England – so much so that petitions addressed to Parliament by sections of the working class could be dismissed out of hand, ostensibly for not being written in *decent and respectful language*.

Extract A below is an example of the approved prose style of the period, as ponderous and heavy as its marble monuments to the dead; extract B illustrates the 'indecent' (offensive) and 'disrespectful' writing of the scarcely educated lower classes.

A This, my Lord, is my idea of an Engliſh dictionary, a dictionary by which the pronunciation of our language may be fixed, and its attainment facilitated; by which its purity may be preſerved, its use aſcertained, and its duration lengthened. And though, perhaps, to correct the language of nations by books of grammar, and amend their manners by diſcourſes of morality, may be taſks equally difficult; yet as it is unavoidable to wiſh, it is natural likewiſe to hope, that your Lordſhip's patronage may not be wholly loſt; that it may contribute to the preſervation of antient, and the improvement of modern writers; that it may promote the reformation of thoſe tranſlators, who, for want of underſtanding the characteriſtical difference of tongues, have formed a chaotick dialect of heterogeneous phraſes; and awaken to the care of purer diction ſome men of genius, whoſe attention to argument makes them negligent of ſtile, or whoſe rapid imagination, like the Peruvian torrents, when it brings down gold, mingles it with ſand.

Samuel Johnson, *Plan of a Dictionary*, 1747

B Whe right these lines to you who are the Combin'd of the Parish off Cheshunt in the Defence of our Parrish rights which you unlawfully are about to disinherit us of... Resolutions is maid by the aforesaid Combind that if you intend of inclosing Our Commond fields Lammas Meads Marches &c Whe resolve before that bloudy and unlawful act is finished to have your hearts bloud if you proceede in the aforesaid bloudy act Whe like horse leaches will cry give, give until whe have split the bloud of every one that wishes to rob the Inosent unborn. It shall not be in your power to say I am safe from the hands of my Enemy for Whe like birds of pray will prively lie in wait to spil the bloud of the aforesaid Charicters whose names and places of abode are as prutrified sores in our Nostrils. Whe declair that thou shall not say I am safe when thou goest to thy bed for beware that thou liftest not thine eyes up in the most mist of flames...

Quoted in E.P. Thompson's *The Making of the English Working Class*

Activity

1 Discuss the main features of the use of language in extracts A and B above.

2 Explain the ways in which each writer expresses his feelings.

Points to notice in seventeenth- and eighteenth-century writing

There was no system of standardized spelling until printing was widely established, but by the time the first English dictionaries were published in the mid 1600s, the spelling system of English started to stabilize, and by the 1800s most words had set spellings.

The more of the following features occur in a piece of seventeenth- to eighteenth-century writing, the earlier in the period it is likely to have been written.

Spelling

- The abbreviations *yᵉ* and *yᵗ* for *the* and *that*
- The letters *u* and *v* used interchangeably for both the vowel *u* and the consonant *v*, e.g. *euer, vſual*
- The letter *j* used interchangeably with the letter *i*; not yet used as a consonant in its own right, e.g. in *justify, iustify*
- Redundant *-e* endings on random words, e.g. *worthe, claime*
- The use of *i* and *y* interchangeably as a vowel, e.g. *time, tym*
- The use of *-ie* instead of modern *-y* at the end of words, e.g. *potencie*
- The use of the long *-s* (ſ)

Grammar

- The retention of earlier forms, often alongside later ones, e.g. *(h)it* and *(h)its* (early); *hy*s ('his', later)
- The third-person singular verb ending *-eth*, e.g. *hath, doth, signifieth, semeth*
- The use of the negative *not* after rather than before the verb, e.g. *I know not; I think not*, where modern English would reverse the order and use the auxiliary verb *do*, e.g. *I do not know; I do not think*.

Punctuation

- The rather random use of commas, not necessarily where logic demands

Activity

Swift's remarks (page 141) were written in 1712. George Bernard Shaw wrote *Pygmalion* (the original version of *My Fair Lady*, where a Cockney flower girl is taught to speak like a duchess) in 1912. In April 2007 – as mentioned in Chapter 3 – the press and the media were busy with reports that the romance between Prince William and Kate Middleton had foundered on issues of linguistic vulgarity. Discuss whether language use is still a marker for social class and/or intelligence today.

The Romantic period: Language as the expression of feeling

The period that followed – the Romantic – rebelled against social convention and 'artificiality'. Romantic writers such as Wordsworth dropped polish and refinement of expression in favour of simpler, native English *such as men* (i.e. 'real' people) *do use*.

In his poetry, Wordsworth wrote about particular flowers such as the lesser celandine rather than 'flowery meads', and Coleridge called the moon the moon, rather than the 'evening Cynthia [filling] her silver horn', as Alexander Pope had written in imitation of the Latin poet Virgil.

In prose writing, language took on a new force and energy in the hands of writers like William Cobbett. The bland vocabulary, smooth constructions and balanced clauses are gone; this is fighting talk:

> Here we found a parcel of labourers at parish work. Amongst them was an old playmate of mine. The account they gave of their situation was very dismal. The harvest was over early. The hop-picking is now over; and now they are employed by the parish – that is to say, not absolutely digging holes one day and filling them up the next; but, at the expense of half-ruined farmers and tradesmen and landlords, to break stones into very small pieces to make nice smooth roads lest the jolting, in going along them, should create bile in the stomachs of the over-fed taxeaters. I call upon mankind to witness this scene and to say whether ever the like of this was heard of before. It is a state of things where all is out of order.
>
> William Cobbett, *Rural Rides,* 1830

The end of Latin influence on English style

The nineteenth century saw the beginning of the end for Latin influence on English writing. There would always be writers after this who favoured the abstract, polysyllabic style that Latin lexis can provide, but the characteristic movement of English prose since the 1800s has been towards freer and more flexible expression in both speech and writing.

Today, after 300 years of striving to standardize, polish and protect the language against change, arguments are raging again about what is acceptable and what is not.

The revolt against linguistic authority began in the 1960s, when schoolchildren seemed to be voting with their feet against formal grammar teaching and educationalists changed their syllabuses accordingly. Liberal thinkers rejoiced at the resulting freedom; prescriptivists (those who believe that written expression should be governed by rule-books) blenched at the 'sloppy' writing that ensued. Letters of protest are still written to newspapers and the BBC complaining about errors of expression like the ones below, to the disgust of those who think such complaints are mere purist nit-picking:

> do like I do (instead of 'do as I do')
>
> the wines of France are different to Australia (instead of 'different from those of Australia')
>
> less tourists are coming to England than five years ago (instead of 'fewer tourists')
>
> H.G. Wells' short stories seem very modern (instead of 'Wells's')

There are still those who would die to prevent words from other languages (American English in particular) coming into Standard English, and others who would accept anything from anywhere in the name of universal brotherhood. Neither are books much help. Unlike sixteenth-century writers, we do have dictionaries and grammar books to guide us, but these tend to be descriptive rather than prescriptive in attitude; they tell us how language *is* used, rather than how it *should* be used. In an age democratic enough to pass the Human Rights Act, everyone's opinion is regarded as equally valid; there is no supreme authority to appeal to, and many people feel free to do more or less as they like with the language.

The situation is compounded by:

- modern technology, which floods our homes with foreign terms, acronyms, and, in the case of computers and the Internet, outlandish neologisms coined to describe their own functions

- immigration, which, depending upon the individual point of view, is either enriching or corrupting English with foreign words and idioms drawn from different cultures all over the world.

What should be done in the midst of such linguistic flux? Choose the middle way, perhaps, like the writer below.

Last week the think-tank Demos came up with a revolutionary new approach to the language – given the spread of hybrid forms of English, instead of insisting that new arrivals to this country learn standard English, it said, they should be taught such variants as Spanglish (Spanish-English), Hinglish (Hindi/ Punjabi/ Urdu-English) and Chinglish (Chinese-English).

Foisting a dollop of postcolonial guilt on to the mother tongue, the report argued that British attitudes to the language are 'better suited to the days of the British Empire than the modern world'. Rather than regard English as a uniquely British invention to be defended, the British should see themselves as 'just one of many shareholders in a global asset'.

I love the strange shapes into which English grows when transplanted into foreign soil, and the varieties of words that we import from the subspecies. 'Chuddies', the Hinglish for underpants, [for instance] is only one of the most recent adoptions from India...

But to leap from an appreciation of English in all its hybrid forms to the notion that these should be accorded equal status with standard English in England seems faintly perverse, and a misunderstanding of the organic way in which language evolves...

Maintaining and preserving a standard form of English is not merely 'Little Englishism': employers and governments need to know that there is a correct way to use English, as do new learners. Demos suggests abandoning the Oxford English Dictionary as the repository of true English, and replacing it with a website to which anyone could contribute 'English' words and definitions. Such a project would be fascinating, but not English: the outcome would be an informal lingua franca, a sprawling form of communication derived from English, but hardly a language...

If [hybrid forms like] Chinglish must be taught in English schools, then teachers should also instruct pupils on playground patois, internet argot, Glasgow patter or any of the countless subsidiaries into which English has evolved. These are all interesting and valuable children of the mother tongue, but children nonetheless.

To put that another way, there may be many shareholders in the English language, but there is only one CEO – Shakespeare.

Ben Macintyre, 'Books', *Times*, 24 March 2007

Activity

Discuss the way in which Ben Macintyre communicates his feelings in this article, then compare what you have written with the sample critique on page 147.

Sample critiques

Richard Verstegan (page 137)

Perhaps the most striking feature of this extract is its immediacy: the impression it gives of a man expressing himself directly to his audience, with genuine feeling. The tone is very much that of the speaking voice. This effect is achieved partly by the handling of grammar: Verstegan uses personal pronouns *our*, *wee*, and *vs*, as the main subjects throughout, thus inviting his readers to identify with him, involving them in the argument as if talking to them face to face, and working to persuade them to feel as he does.

Verstegan conveys his distaste for borrowings from other languages through the emotional connotations of the words he chooses. Not only is his lexis almost exclusively English, his use of the word *falne* suggests the depths to which we have sunk in preferring other languages to our own. He also uses overstatement to make his point, first in the claim that we have absorbed more Latin and French into English than we have left out (impossible), then in the complaint that the extent of our borrowing has been *beyond all ſtay and limit*. In addition, the emotive force of the words he uses to reveal foreign contempt for the English language – *ſcum* and *barren* – suggests that he is seeking to work up his readers and make them feel as indignant as he himself does on its behalf.

The passage is also interesting syntactically. The loose structure of its one sentence, moving in a rather disjointed way from one clause to another, reflects the rambling way in which we speak. The succession of minor clauses emphasizes just how far foreigners will go in insulting our native language:

> it is… but the ſcum of many languages

> it is moſt barren

> wee are dayly faine to borrow woords for it… out of other languages to patche it up withall

Working up to a grand climax, he claims that if we gave back all the words we've taken from other languages:

> wee ſhould bee left litle better than dumb, or ſcarſly able to ſpeak anything that ſhould bee ſencible.

John Evelyn (page 139)

Genre

This is a diary entry, presumably written for the writer's private reading. We can therefore expect the writer to be fairly casual in the way he expresses himself, leaving out anything he thinks is unnecessary for understanding.

Purpose and audience

The whole effect of the writing is to suggest Evelyn trying to remember all he can about the whale and jotting it down before he forgets, without time to worry about the finer points of style.

Approach and manner

The most striking feature of this extract is its lack of overt (openly expressed) emotion. Most people writing in their diaries would concentrate on describing how they felt when confronted by such an event, but Evelyn doesn't; he simply sticks to the facts. Evelyn's approach is that of an objective observer. The terse opening statements sound more like a daily weather report entered in a ship's log than an entry in a personal diary. He gives us very precise physical detail: the storm is a mix of hail and rain; the wind is still blowing from the north, as it has been doing for the past six months.

Lexis

The lexis of this first statement is accurate and objective; nothing is exaggerated: he tells us simply that the season is as cold as winter, avoiding extra descriptions such as 'freezing' or 'bitingly' cold. Even the one apparently emotive adjective he uses – *extraordinary* – doesn't have our modern meaning of 'to be wondered at', but the cooler seventeenth-century meaning, 'out of the ordinary' or 'unusual'. Evelyn writes about the whale and how it was *killed* (a modern writer would almost certainly have used the word *slaughtered*) in a similarly cool and objective manner. He describes it initially simply as *large* (a modern writer would probably have used *enormous, huge,* or *gigantic*), then goes on to give precise measurements in a scientific manner. Only towards the end of the piece does he express his wonder at the creature – *all of it prodigious* (i.e. amazing, marvellous) – and even then the wonder is focused on the strangeness of the fact that so large an animal can be nourished by feeding on what appears to him to be simply *slime*.

Grammar

Sentence structure: Evelyn's sentence structure is casual rather than conventionally correct. The first two 'sentences' lack a main verb: [There was/We had] *An extraordinary storme…*; *A large Whale* [was] *taken…* The third sentence does contain main verbs but is rather disjointed; it is made up of seven clauses and several phrases clumsily tacked together with the help of the conjunctions such as *but, after, & after.*

The physical details given in the fourth sentence are assembled in an even more haphazard way, with no attempt to keep the construction consistent. Having begun with the subject noun *the length*, Evelyn should, conventionally, have continued his list with more nouns, e.g. *the length was…*; *the skin was…*; *the eyes were…*; *the tail was…*; *the fins were small and only two in number.*

The next 'sentence' lacks a subject and main verb: [The whale had] *No teeth at all.* Evelyn continues his short-hand style, and the next three sentences are again joined together by colons (though beginning with capital letters) instead of being separated by full stops. Finally, he fails to make his subject and verb agree in number in the last, unconventionally constructed sentence: *The extreames of the Cetaceous bones… was hairy towards the Ends, & bottom withinside.* The comma before *&* here seems to have no logical function at all — again one of the inconsistencies of writing of this period.

Spelling: Evelyn's spelling reveals inconsistencies typical of early seventeenth-century writing. A redundant *–e* is tacked onto words like *storme* and *raine*; certain nouns are given initial capital letters for no reason that we can see (*Concourse, Smoake, Ends*); extra vowels are used in words like *Smoake* and *onely* and double consonants in *finns* and *wonderfull*. The printing symbol *-y* is still used here as an abbreviation of *-th*, e.g. *ye* (the) *boates*; *yt* (that) *bone*.

His punctuation also differs from that of modern writers. We use commas to separate words and phrases that should not be read together; Evelyn sometimes uses them unnecessarily between the subject and the verb, e.g. *in nothing more wonderfull then that an Animal of so greate a bulk, should be nourished onely by slime…*

Similarly, we use a colon to mark the end of a statement that we are going on to illustrate; Evelyn often uses a colon before a complete change of subject, yet follows it with a capital letter as if it had been a full stop, e.g. *The throate yet so narrow, as would not have admitted the least of fishes: The extreames of the Cetaceous bones hang downewardes…* The rest of the time he avoids the need for punctuation by tacking unrelated clauses together with *ands* and *buts*. You can also sense careless haste in the illogical placing of the comma in the clause *out of which spouted blood & water, by two tunnells like Smoake from a chimney*. By separating *spouted blood & water* from *by two tunnells*, the comma makes nonsense of the image.

Rhetorical devices: Evelyn uses only two images, both similes: *as thro a grate*, and *like Smoake from a chimney*. The word *grate* is probably the seventeenth-century version of modern *grating*, i.e. an iron grid. Both are very ordinary images drawn from everyday life, chosen to describe the visual impression he got as accurately as possible rather than to show off any literary skill.

Overall impression

The piece gives the impression of Evelyn hurrying to get things down on paper before he forgets them, jotting down each detail of the event as it occurs to him without bothering much about accuracy or style because, as a diary entry, it's intended only for his eyes. Had he been writing it up for other people to read it would have been considerably more polished and conventional.

Ben Macintyre (page 144)

Genre, audience and purpose

This piece is a newspaper article written to interest and entertain the largely well-educated and literature-loving readers of the 'Books' section of the *Times*.

Manner and approach

Macintyre treats his readers as equals, using the personal pronoun *I* to make it clear that he is giving his own opinions but laying out the argument in a reasonable and calm tone of voice. He takes care to show his lack of prejudice against new varieties of English by saying *I love the strange shapes into which English grows*, but balances the argument by asserting that if these strange new forms were given equal status with Standard English, chaos would result.

Lexis

For the most part, Macintyre uses the formal, conventionally polite vocabulary educated readers would expect in a discussion of language. To express disapproval of Demos's attitudes, for instance, he uses the following cool and impersonal phraseology:

> the notion that these should be accorded equal status with standard English in England seems faintly perverse, and a misunderstanding of the organic way in which language evolves…

Because Macintyre wants to keep the argument on a rational footing, he chooses his words carefully here to keep emotion firmly under control: *notion* has an inbuilt sense of 'mistaken', and so saves him from having to use a phrase like 'stupid idea'; *perverse* is a word with strong suggestions of deliberate wrong-headedness, but is watered down by the adverb *faintly* to avoid putting up opponents' hackles. The same skill in handling words can be seen in the phrase *Foisting a dollop of postcolonial guilt on to the mother tongue*. *Foisting* has connotations of unfairness, if not dishonesty; the colloquial term *dollop* suggests an over-the-top amount of something applied without discipline or judgement (as in 'He poured a dollop of tomato sauce over his chips'). By making his criticism implicit he keeps the emotional temperature low. He could have said something like, 'Because the writers of the report feel guilty about Britain colonizing other countries in the past, they're trying to get rid of their guilt by claiming that the hybrid Englishes developed in the former colonies are as valid as traditional English today.' This is much more aggressive and much less witty than the original.

Grammar

Macintyre's grammar is conventionally correct in every respect, including punctuation and spelling. Sticklers for old-fashioned rules might quarrel with his use of a dash instead of a more traditional colon in the first sentence, and with his use of the conjunction *But* to begin a sentence later in the piece, but these can be justified as a means of making the writing more lively.

Verbs

Macintyre uses the modal verbs *should* and *must* to flag up the think-tank's dogmatic attitudes: *new arrivals to this country… SHOULD be taught such variants as Spanglish*; *the British SHOULD see themselves as… shareholders in a global asset*; *Chinglish MUST be taught in English schools*. Both *should* and *must* are verbs implying obligation: they are forms of indirect command. Macintyre counters these with a modal of his own: *If Chinglish MUST be taught in English schools, then teachers SHOULD also instruct pupils on playground patois…*

Nouns

Macintyre keeps his approach impersonal by using abstract nouns rather than using specific people as subjects: *the think-tank, the report, postcolonial guilt, an appreciation of English, employers and governments* – these are all things that people are involved in, but the actual people are missing. So, therefore, are pronouns. Macintyre keeps himself modestly out of the picture by using *I* only once.

Adjectives and adverbs

His intention to keep overt emotion out of his writing means that Macintyre uses comparatively few adjectives, and hardly any that carry an emotional charge. They are used to make the nature of language itself more vivid.

There are even fewer adverbs in the article, and again, these are used to convey information rather than evoke emotion: *faintly*, for example.

Sentence structure

Macintyre varies the structure of his sentences so skilfully that the writing never becomes boring or the argument hard to follow. A glance at the beginnings of the first four paragraphs reveals that a different structure introduces each one:

Paragraph 1: an adverbial phrase: *Last week...*

Paragraph 2: a participial phrase: *Foisting a dollop...*

Paragraph 3: a subject pronoun and main verb: *I love...*

Paragraph 4: an infinitive used as a subject noun: *But to leap...*

Prosodic features

Macintyre also varies the rhythm of his sentences by varying the structures. For example, he balances one clause or phrase against another:

> Maintaining and preserving a standard form of English is not merely 'Little Englishism': employers and governments need to know that there is a correct way to use English, as do new learners.

This also has the effect of giving more force to what he says.

At times he makes us wait until nearly the end of a sentence before we get to the main verb and see what he is saying:

> But to leap from an appreciation of English in all its hybrid forms to the notion that these should be accorded equal status with standard English in England SEEMS [main verb] faintly perverse...

The fall of the voice after *seems* towards the full stop helps to add conviction to what he's saying.

Rhetorical effects

Macintyre uses two extended metaphors in this article: one drawn from organic farming, the other from financial investment.

Macintyre uses the metaphor of plant growth to describe language development, then extends it to show how a language with strong roots, like Latin or English, can cross-fertilize with another language to produce a striking new linguistic form.

Macintyre's obvious love and admiration of his native language contrasts strongly with the more practical and utilitarian attitudes of the members of the Demos think-tank. To them, English is simply money in the bank: a global asset that helps those who can speak it to profit in some way. In itself, it's nothing: just a means to a purely practical end. Macintyre extends their metaphor and counters their claims by saying that English may indeed be like a global company, but if it is, it has only one chief executive in control – the thoroughly English Shakespeare.

Overall impression

Macintyre writes as a calm, rational man able to take a balanced look at the world. On the one hand, he welcomes the added richness that new varieties of English can add to its traditional form; on the other, he makes the rational point that if each was given equal status and value with Standard English, chaos would result. Without making an overtly hostile attack on members of the Demos think-tank, he criticizes their idea that English should be seen as simply a useful tool for getting on in the world, and reasserts its claim to superiority by referring to the writer who has used it to greatest effect – Shakespeare.

9 Establishing a Context and Dealing with Data

For your coursework you need to carry out a language investigation, to show your ability to explore and analyse language data using a variety of methods. Your completed study will need to contain the following sections:

- Introduction
- Methodology
- Analysis
- Conclusion/evaluation
- Bibliography

All of these are explained below, in this chapter and the following one. You will also need to include Appendices, containing the data you have collected.

This chapter looks at the **Introduction**, **Methodology** and **Analysis** sections of your language investigation. It also considers the skills you will need for **investigating phonetics** (the sounds made by speakers), should you choose to do this kind of investigation.

Introduction

The English language is a huge subject, so the first thing you have to do is narrow down your approach to a particular **field of study**.

You might want to investigate an aspect of spoken English – the persistence of dialect in your own or some other region of the country, perhaps; or the different styles of writing to be found in the quality press and tabloid newspapers; or the different kinds of language to be found in British and American situation comedies (sit-coms).

The first heading in your Introduction section might be, therefore, 'Field of study'. Explain your reasons for choosing the focus of your study. This might look like the students' examples below.

Field of study

A My chosen field of study was spoken English, because speech is more spontaneous and natural than writing and gives everybody chance to express themselves. It is also more varied and individual than non-literary writing. Standard English, as its name implies, uses conventional forms of grammar and lexis and so makes most people sound much the same. As soon as people speak, however, they unconsciously reveal all kinds of things about themselves: the part of the country they come from, their social background, the extent of their education – even something about their social attitudes. I find this very interesting.

B My aim was to examine the nature of the language used in English and American situation comedies. Various people have claimed that we and the Americans are 'divided by a common language', and I was interested to see whether the similarities in the way 'ordinary people' (as represented by the characters) express themselves outweigh the differences.

- -

When you've outlined your chosen field, however, it will be very wide. This means that you will need to narrow it down even further – this time to the **specific subject area** you're going to focus on. The second heading of your report might therefore be 'Subject area' or 'Specific focus'. Look at the examples below.

Subject area

A The particular area I decided to focus on was dialect. I wanted to discover whether the traditional dialect forms of my own region were still in common use among people under the age of 30, or whether they were being replaced by more modern words and standard grammatical constructions.

B Since my investigation required the detailed analysis of language used in British and American situation comedies, I decided to restrict my investigation to two particular sit-coms only: one American – *The Simpsons* – and one English – *The Royle Family*.

Both families are dysfunctional when judged by conventional middle-class standards, yet both can be considered successful to some degree because, whatever their conflicts and disasters, their members are bound together by loyalty and love. Both families have an aged grandparent in the background, plus various friends and neighbours, but both focus mainly on the four most important family members: father, mother, daughter and son.

> **Note**
>
> When writing this you can use the present tense rather than the past if you prefer, e.g. *My aim in writing this report is to examine*, etc. The present tense is conventionally used when referring to books, plays and films, whose characters continue to exist after they are first created, e.g. *Bridget Jones worries about her weight*; *Romeo worships Juliet.*

Having told your readers what you intend to do, you now need to tell them what suppositions or assumptions you had in mind when you chose to investigate this particular subject. To put it in more technical terms, you should explain the **hypothesis** you were working on (or if there is more than one, the **hypotheses**). This will give you the third heading for your report, as in the examples below:

Central hypothesis

A When I began my investigation I assumed that the dialect expressions used by my parents and grandparents would largely have disappeared from the speech of people under the age of 30. For instance, when somebody asked my grandfather how he was, he usually replied 'Middling, thanks', and my mother's usual answer is 'I'm fine, thank you'. My friends and I are much more likely to say 'I'm good, how are you?'

I also wanted to test the idea that male speakers were more likely to use dialect forms than women, since some studies suggest that women, wanting to be thought 'respectable', prefer more conventional forms of speech.

B The main hypothesis in mind when I began my investigation was that there might be a distinct difference between the vocabulary and sentence structure of the British characters, the Royles, and the American characters, the Simpsons. I assumed that the language of the Royles would be ordinary, everyday English, and that of the Simpsons would be a distinctly different variety.

I also wanted to investigate the speech patterns of the male and female characters, since past studies have suggested that these vary significantly. Male speech has been shown to be domineering in nature, assertive and directive in style, intolerant of interruption, based on facts and focused on achieving goals; women's has been shown to be more tentative in contrast, stating what might be or what ought to be, given to suggestions rather than assertions and inviting co-operation through the use of inclusive pronouns.

Methodology

Having got this far, your readers will want to know how you set about testing your hypothesis or hypotheses. What methods did you use?

Methodology

A I interviewed 10 people over the age of 65; 10 between the ages of 50 and 65; and 10 between the ages of 35 and 50. There were 5 women and 5 men in each age group, giving me 6 sub-groups to listen to and record. Most were members of my own family or the families of friends. I explained the purpose of my investigation and asked if they would agree to take part in discussions and allow me to record them. Fortunately, they were all happy to agree.

To avoid the formality of direct questioning, I asked each group of 5 to sit around a multi-directional microphone attached to a tape recorder and discuss topics I thought likely to bring out any remaining local dialect names and constructions:

- their earliest memories of the house they grew up in, their family, and neighbours
- the environment surrounding the house – town or countryside
- going to school for the first time
- games they used to play: at home, in the school playground, in the street, etc.
- any pets they had or animals they were involved with.

If you were carrying out an investigation in this field, you could also go to your local library and/or museum and ask for any records of local dialect held there, or accessible by them. Armed with such information, you could do one of two things:

A Present your interviewees with a list of their local dialect terms – e.g. *cob* (Derby dialect word for Standard English *bread roll*) and record which age and sex groups use them

B Give the Standard English equivalents of the dialect words you have found, then ask your interviewees if they know any local terms for such things. For example, *alley* (Standard English) might elicit *snicket* or *ginnel* in the north of the country.

In this section, you will need to explain any difficulties you encountered in collecting the data for your investigation, and how you overcame these problems. See the students' examples below.

Difficulties encountered

A Technical difficulties included getting the microphone positioned so that everybody's speech was clear, and controlling the stop-start and play-back buttons when I needed to ask questions or go back in the recording to clarify a point.

The main difficulty, though, was in making a written transcript of the sentences containing the dialect words and phrases within the spoken discussion. It took hours of replay before I was sure I had made an accurate record, and if I had to do such a thing again I would definitely want to use a recorder that could download speech directly to my computer.

B The main difficulty I experienced was in finding episodes in both sit-coms with similar story-lines. In the end, I couldn't, and had to select a similar theme common to both instead.

There were also some technical difficulties. To test the truth of my hypotheses, I watched six recorded episodes of each programme, making notes on language use with the aid of the pause button. I don't have access to Sky or Cable, and so I had to fast-forward several times through certain episodes to find the dialogue I wanted to use as illustrations.

I also looked up reviews of each programme on the Internet to see if there was any critical support for my hypothesis. These reviews were taken from the websites of various newspapers and magazines and are listed at the end of my report.

Transcribing from the screen involves a lot of stopping, starting, and rewinding to check the accuracy of your quotes, and this is time-consuming.

Analysis

To introduce your analysis of the data you have collected, explain the key questions you formulated in order to test your hypothesis. If you were examining the relative frequency of dialect use among younger and older speakers in a particular town or region, for instance, your key questions would concern the non-standard lexis, grammatical structures, and pronunciation peculiar to the region. For example:

- What dialect words are common to both the younger and the older groups interviewed?
- Are there any dialect words used exclusively by older speakers, male and female?
- Are there any dialect words used exclusively by male speakers in any of the age groups?
- Are there any dialect words used exclusively by female speakers in any of the age groups?
- Are there any non-standard grammatical constructions exclusive to the speech of the older groups of people interviewed? (For example, variants of Standard English past tenses: *I seen her* for *I saw her*, *he done it* for *he did it*; variant adverbs, e.g. *happen* for *perhaps*, *while* for *until*; double negatives with verbs, e.g. *I ain't got no money left*.)

If you were investigating possible differences of language in British and American sit-coms, your analysis might be based on questions like these:

1 What is the predominant kind of lexis used in each sit-com?

   Nouns: Common; Anglo-Saxon; abstract/technical; Latinate?

   Verbs: Assertive; stative; directive; modal; subjunctive in mood; interrogative?

   Adjectives: Conventional; colloquial; from the slang register; vulgarisms/swear-words; original; stale?

   Adverbs: Precise; vivid; meaningless; repetitive?

2 What kind of sentence structures are found in each sit-com? Short; incomplete; elliptical; loose; rambling?

3 Is there any verbal humour in either sit-com? Use of puns; irony; bathos; mocking of pretentious language?

4 How far does the nature of the language used in each sit-com reflect the life style of the characters? In other words, do the characters speak as they do because of the way they live?

Conventions for marking conversation features

If you have been investigating spoken language *per se*, you will obviously have to include in your appendices transcripts of any conversations you have recorded and commented on. You will need to mark such things as pauses, overlaps and interruptions, and give some idea of the prosodic effects achieved by the speakers.

To mark where a speaker emphasizes a particular word, underline the relevant word:

I know the road you mean but I don't know if you can <u>park</u> there.

To mark where a speaker pauses briefly, use the symbol (.), as follows:

I think so (.) I could be wrong though.

Longer pauses should be marked in seconds, e.g. (1).

To mark organized turn-taking, in scripted conversations on the radio for example, use the symbol = at the end of one speaker's utterance and the same symbol at the beginning of the response:

A *We've had programmes about dysfunctional working-class families before, of course =*

B *= Yes we have (.) Till Death Do Us Part for instance (.) not to mention Steptoe & Son*

Transitions like this are technically called **latches,** because the two speakers latch on to each other so smoothly.

In more spontaneous spoken exchanges, turn-taking often takes the form of **overlaps**, where a respondent starts to talk in tandem with the speaker before he or she has finished. This sort of transition can be marked with vertical lines through the text as on page 26, or with double vertical lines ‖ as follows:

I'm <u>dying</u> to see Daniel Craig ‖ in the new Bond film

  Ooh ‖ Daniel Craig (.) I love him (.) me too

You will also need to mark prosodic features such as intonation and pitch, to point out how these enhance the speaker's meaning. Again, there are several symbols you need to use.

Mark rising tones with a small upward symbol / above the relevant words. These are used when a speaker asks a question, or enumerates a list of points:

/
so you'll be coming tonight

/   /   /
the acting was brilliant (.) *the script was brilliant* (.) *Daniel Craig was gorgeous* (.) *it was great*

Mark falling tones with a small downward symbol in the same way. These are used mainly:

                                               /

- when a speaker is coming to the end of an utterance, e.g. *as far as I'm concerned*

                                \

  (.) *this James Bond is much more sensitive than the others*

                        /   \

- when a speaker is saying something negative: *no* (.) *I don't think so*

The upward and downward symbols can be combined into one ^ to mark what is called a **falling–rising tone**. This is used when a speaker wants to indicate uncertainty; for example, when they're not sure whose voice it is on the other end of the phone:

  ^   ^
Tony (.) *is that you*

or when they are doubtful:

  ^
really

or incredulous about what they're hearing:

A *my dad's buying me a sports car if I get four As*

          ^   ^

B *a sports car* (1) *really*

In conversations where the speakers get excited or angry, or in commentaries on sports events, speakers' voices may rise and fall significantly in **pitch**. 'Pitch' simply means the level of the voice, whether it's high or low. 'Screaming pitch' is a fair description of some sports commentators' voice levels when a horse nears the finishing post or a footballer shoots at goal.

You should mark these significant pitch changes with vertical arrows, up and down, e.g.

and Beckham floats the ball over to Owen on the far side and Owen traps it (.) *takes it past the defender* (.) *runs it across the middle for Crouch and* ↑ *Crouch shoots* ↓ (.) *and it's one nil to England*

When speakers get excited, they raise the pitch of their voice. At the same time they begin to speak more rapidly, and your final task in transcribing will be to indicate this increased pace in the margin of your transcript. You can do this by using the following terms, borrowed from musical notation:

alleg (allegro)	fast	*lento* (lento)	slow
accel (accelerando)	getting faster	*rall* (rallentando)	becoming slower
forte (forte)	loud	*piano* (piano)	quiet
cresc (crescendo)	getting louder	*dimin* (diminuendo)	getting quieter
stacc (staccato)	short, clipped	*leg* (legato)	drawn out

For example:

[alleg] *and Beckham floats the ball over to Owen on the far side and Owen* [accel]
    /   /
traps it (.) *takes it past the defender* (.) *runs it across the middle for Crouch and*
               /   /   \
[cresc] ↑ *Crouch shoots* ↓ (.) *and it's one nil to England*

Investigating phonetics

If you are interested in **phonetics** (the study of the sounds made by speakers) you may prefer to investigate dialect **sounds** rather than dialect **lexis**. Use the same methods to get your interviewees talking; record what they say; and listen to the recording for evidence of pronunciations that vary from received pronunciation (RP). RP is the standardized system of pronunciation used by newscasters on radio and TV; the kind that mothers are referring to when they say they want their children to learn to 'speak properly'. It goes hand in hand with Standard English.

Making phonetic transcriptions of speech

The notation of transcripts looks very complicated at first sight, but if you take it bit by bit you'll soon find it a very useful tool.

There are three basic facts you need to know.

1 Every word in the English language is made up of units of sound called **phonemes**.

2 Each of these phonemes is represented by a phonetic symbol.

3 The sounds represented by these phonetic symbols are those of **received pronunciation** (RP for short).

The first thing you have to do, therefore, is get to grips with the phonetic symbols that represent the sounds of RP; not because it will teach you to speak in a prestigious accent (though it may), but because it provides a fixed and neutral standard against which to measure regional variations.

Don't try to learn all the symbols given in the following pages by heart. Just go through them slowly, practising the different sounds each one represents, until they become familiar.

Phonetic symbols for single vowels

Short Vowels		Long Vowels	
ɪ	p<u>i</u>t	ɪː	b<u>ea</u>n
ɛ	p<u>e</u>t	ɜː	b<u>ur</u>n
æ	p<u>a</u>t	ɑː	b<u>ar</u>n
ɒ	p<u>o</u>t	ɔɑː	b<u>or</u>n
ʌ	p<u>u</u>tt	uː	b<u>oo</u>n
ʊ	p<u>u</u>t		
ə	patt<u>er</u>		

Activity

Copy out the following paragraph, replacing all the ordinary vowel letters – a, e, i, o, u – with phonetic symbols that represent the way the word would be spoken by an RP speaker. You will find that some symbols, a and ɔ, for example, cut down the number of letters in a word because they sound like a vowel and a consonant combined: 'r', for instance, isn't needed in words like *yard*.

Whenever Willy was in trouble his thoughts turned towards planting seeds in his back yard. He resented his boss, was fed up with his work, and sad that Biff, his son, was just bumming along instead of planning ahead. For Willy, true success meant earning hundreds of dollars and winning respect from other men.

One very common vowel sound represented in the table is the one that looks like an upside-down *e*: /ə/. This is a sort of all-purpose sound found in words like *another* (/ənəðə/), and the many different words that end in *ent* or *ant*: /prezənt/, /kleimənt/. It is called **schwa**.

Not all the vowel sounds of RP can be represented by single vowels, however. When writing the paragraph for the Activity above, for instance, I couldn't use words like *out, around*, *thousands*, and *go*, because the sounds in these words are made up of combinations of vowels, called **diphthongs**. Say 'go' aloud and you will hear your voice glide from the neutral *schwa* sound to the more rounded vowel represented by /ʊ/.

Key words

Diphthong: Two vowel sounds combining to produce one syllable of a word; during the pronunciation of the syllable the tongue moves from one position to another, causing a continual change in vowel quality: as for instance in the pronunciation of the syllable *a* in *late*, during which the tongue moves from the position of *e* towards that of *i*.

Triphthong: As the name suggests, a triphthong combines three vowel sounds to form one syllable, e.g. fire (/faɪə/).

Diphthongs

aɪ	b<u>i</u>te		aʊ	h<u>ou</u>se
ɛɪ	b<u>ai</u>t		ʊə	p<u>oo</u>r
ɔɪ	b<u>oy</u>		ɪə	<u>ear</u>
əʊ	r<u>oe</u>		ɛə	<u>air</u>

Activity

Write out the following paragraph, representing all vowels and diphthongs with phonetic symbols.

Linda did not know what to say to her husband. She sighed and took up her darning. If only Biff would stop his bumming around and settle down. Willy would be happy then; it would give him something to cheer about. He cared so much for Biff, and she could not bear to watch his slow drift towards death. It was pure torment to her.

Consonants

Finally, look at the list of consonants. Apart from the fact that there are two different symbols for the two different sounds of *th*, these are quite straightforward and should give you little difficulty.

p	<u>p</u>i<u>p</u>	θ	<u>th</u>igh	dʒ	ju<u>dge</u>
b	<u>b</u>i<u>b</u>	ð	<u>th</u>y	m	<u>m</u>an
t	<u>t</u>en	s	<u>s</u>et	n	ma<u>n</u>
d	<u>d</u>en	z	<u>z</u>en	ŋ	si<u>ng</u>
k	<u>c</u>at	ʃ	<u>sh</u>ip	l	<u>l</u>et
g	<u>g</u>et	ʒ	lei<u>s</u>ure	r	<u>r</u>ide
f	<u>f</u>ish	h	<u>h</u>en	w	<u>w</u>et
v	<u>v</u>an	tʃ	<u>ch</u>ur<u>ch</u>	j	<u>y</u>et

Activity

Complete your practice of phonetic transcription by adding the symbols for consonants to the paragraphs in the two Activities above about Willy and Linda Loman. You will end up with something that looks like a foreign language.

Key deviations from the RP norm

Once upon a time, the concentration of political clout, wealth and education in the south-east of England made its accent king. Now that same part of the country is doing its best to destroy RP with the introduction of a new set of sounds known as Estuary English (i.e. English as it's pronounced in the area around the estuary of the Thames). Once, accents were peculiar to a small locality; you could go 15 miles down the road and hear distinct changes in the way people spoke. Now, television sprays the pronunciation of the London area across the whole country night after night and, almost without knowing it, we find ourselves joining in.

Changes to consonants

The letters 't' and 'd' have ceased to be pronounced by people all over the country, even in the north and Scotland. They use the glottal stop instead. To test whether you do so yourself, do the following:

1   Say the words 'party' and 'better' aloud, being careful to pronounce the /t/; notice that it's produced at the front of your mouth, with your tongue on the ridge above your teeth.

2   Now say the words again, being careful to keep your tongue away from your teeth; you will feel a movement in your throat (this is known as a **glottal stop**), as your tongue ends up below your bottom teeth.

The combined consonant /th/ has also been abandoned by many people in the south-east, in both its voiced form   (ð) and its unvoiced (θ). This may be partly due to the influence of black rappers and the teen glamour of black street talk:

Like I'm goin' down da street, like, an' da policeman stop me, like, right?

I was wiv my bruvver at da time.

Activity

Transcribe the above sentences into phonetic script.

Changes to vowels

The main change seems to be a tendency among younger people to reduce diphthongs and triphthongs into monophthongs: many young RP speakers and non-RP speakers now pronounce the word *our* as /aː/, and the same thing seems to be happening to words like *poor*, *fire* (formerly /fiəl/), and *mild* (now *mald*). Spelling 'our' as 'are' is already common in the south-east, and children will presumably soon be spelling *mild* as *marld*.

Investigating pronunciation

You now have the basic knowledge to transcribe and analyse the many different ways in which people in our society pronounce their words. Below are suggestions for some of the things you might do.

• Record yourself reading out a short passage from a book or newspaper and transcribe your speech into phonetic script; write notes on any deviations from RP pronunciation.

• Ask members of your family, male and female, young and old, to read the same passage; record each one; transcribe each into phonetic script, and write about any deviations from standard RP that you can hear. Be careful to write down the age of each speaker as well as the sex (names such as Sam and Chris can be misleading).

• Obtain or make recordings of popular media figures like Jonathan Ross and Chris Tarrant; transcribe and write up your findings.

• Obtain or make recordings of the Queen and other members of the Royal family and investigate any differences you can find between the Queen and the younger royals such as Princess Anne, Prince Charles, and Charles's sons.

• Investigate the pronunciation of Welsh or Scots speakers of English.

10 Drawing Conclusions and Presenting Findings

When you have presented and analysed all your data, you are ready to write about what you have discovered in the course of your investigation, taking care to provide evidence to support what you say. This chapter discusses the corresponding sections of your language investigation.

Findings

You need to present your findings in a clear and logical way. Make sure that you do the following.

- **Classify your evidence.** That is, assign it to a particular category. For example, if you wish to show evidence about changes in the way men (or women) were pictured in advertisements between 1950 and the present day, use a main heading such as *Evidence of Changes in the Presentation of Men* (or women) *in Advertisements between 1950 and the Present Day*.

- **Break your evidence down into sections.** Deal with each aspect of your evidence separately, under a relevant subheading, such as *Creating an Image through Pictures; Creating an Image through Graphology; Creating an Image through the Use of Language*. Include pointers to the readers as to the direction of the argument.

- **Give detailed examples and clear quotations** from your evidence to justify your comments and make your meaning clear. For example, quote the different kinds of lexis used in the captions and slogans accompanying advertisements to show any difference you may find in the attitudes and values suggested in the two periods under investigation.

- **Present evidence in a balanced way.** If your investigation produces contradictory evidence, take care to present it in such a way that you show both sides of the argument. For example, some people complain that men are being made to look like wimps in current ads; others complain that male images are too overtly sexual.

- **Link your evidence clearly to your main thesis.** If your investigation finds clear evidence for a particular point of view, try to provide links between each part of your evidence and your main thesis; you can do this by using phrases such as 'This idea is supported by the fact that...', 'This suggests that', 'This might lead us to suppose/ think/ speculate', 'Another piece of evidence for this is...' etc.

Activity

Slang is a rich field for language investigation, revealing attitudes towards all aspects of our social life: work, money, sex, class, and gender and age differences.

Design a structure for presenting the findings of an investigation into the evolution of slang from the 1940s (when even words like *blimey, golly* and *crikey* were frowned upon in school) to the present day (when anything goes), based on the advice above.

Use statistics set out in tables if appropriate. Take, for example, a student who has been investigating the differences in style between the editorials in upmarket newspapers like the *Times* and *Telegraph* and those in the *Sun* and *Mirror*, and has been surprised to find that the 'red-tops' cover the same ground as the 'quality' papers and express their opinions with greater clarity and force. To help make this point, the student could refer to the statistical results of a readability test (the Flesch Test) that she ran on her selected editorials in order to verify her findings.

A student who has been investigating dialect usage, on the other hand, may present findings like these:

General findings

As anticipated, dialect words and dialect forms were found in use mainly among the over-65 age group. Speakers aged between 40 and 65 were familiar with all the words used by the older group, but used them only in a jocular way when telling anecdotes about their younger days. Younger speakers used only one of the dialect words – 'mardarse' – with any frequency; they did not even recognize some of the others, like 'alleys', never having played at marbles in their lives.

Dialect words still in use

The following dialect words were found to persist in the speech of the older age group: 'shotties', 'alleys' (marbles); 'segs' or 'seggies' (shout for claiming second go at something); 'kecks' (trousers); 'lug'oles' or 'tabs' (ears); 'mardy-bum' or 'mardarse' (a sulky person); 'wench', 'our wench' (girl, sister); 'duck' (term of endearment); 'mithered' (upset, bothered); 'nesh' (wimpish).

Dialect constructions still in use

The following deviant constructions were also found: 'cos' (can you), 'dunna' (don't), 'wunna' (won't), 'cunna' (can't).

Dialect words used among the different age groups

The largest number of these dialect words were used by speakers in the oldest age group, however, as the table below shows:

Sex	Oldest group	Middle group	Youngest group
Male	8	3	1
Female	5	1	0

Dialect constructions among the different age groups

Sex	Oldest group	Middle group	Youngest group
Male	8	3	1
Female	3	1	0

If you had given your interviewees a selected set of dialect words and forms to respond to, you would of course have to do a count for each word and construction on your list.

Below are the findings of a different kind of investigation; the student investigated the lexis and sentence constructions to be found in use in *The Royle Family* and *The Simpsons*.

Findings

The language used by the characters in these two programmes was found to differ greatly in both lexis and sentence construction.

Lexical differences

The lexis of the Royle family, male and female, is English at its most basic. It consists mainly of the characters' remarks and questions about common physical objects – money, clothes, bills, 'ciggies', particular foods, chocolate, cake, and beer. The following is a typical telephone conversation between Barbara Royle and her mother, Norma (we can only hear Barbara's speech):

Barbara: 'ave you 'ad your tea? What did you 'ave? [Pause for reply] Oh, we had that. Dave 'ad corn beef 'ash.

Many of the common nouns used are at the extreme end of the colloquial scale, verging on the indecent, if not obscene: some are the names of bodily parts, like 'gob', 'arse' (from Old English *ers*) and the modern term 'knob' or 'nob'; some are the words for basic physical functions like farting and excreting (s**t and s**te are favourite expletives of Jim Royle) and for sexual acts. Occasionally two of these are combined to form the insulting term 'gobshite', used by Jim to describe anyone he thinks pretentious.

In the same way, slang terms are used by characters to insult one another throughout the episode: 'idle little sod', 'ikey [arrogant] little bleeder', 'knob-head', 'crabby arse', 'scruffy git'.

Only one example of a Latin-derived word – 'career' – was to be found in the length of one half-hour programme (episode 1 of series 6), and the only word with more than two syllables in the same episode –'catalogue' – referred to a physical object rather than to an abstract concept.

The vocabulary of *The Simpsons*, in contrast, was found to be much closer to the conventional lexis of educated English. Apart from using different names from Standard English for familiar things – 'bar' for pub; 'nightstand' for bedside-table; 'candy' for sweets; 'dumpster' for skip, etc. – every word in the episode 'Lisa's Wedding' is plain, familiar English.

Syntactical differences

My investigation found clear differences in the type and construction of the sentences used in both sit-coms.

In *The Royle Family*, four major sentence types were found to predominate:

- Assertive statements, e.g. 'He's been out grafting all day, she's been sat on her fat arse, and he's massaging her feet. I don't know what the world's coming to.'
- Directives, e.g. 'Mam, tell Anthony to shut his gob when he's eating.'
- Exclamations, e.g. 'Oh, here's the gobshite now! Just look at him, full of himself!'
- Questions, (a) interrogative, e.g. 'You got a gig tonight, Dave?' and (b) rhetorical, e.g. Jim: 'Anthony, which room are you in, this one or that one?' Anthony: 'This one.' Jim: 'Well what's the bloody light on in that one for?'

In the whole of the episode I examined most closely, only two complex sentences were found, and these both consisted of a simple conditional clause and a statement, for example, Denise to Norma: 'Well, if it's too tight, take one of the insoles out.'

The dialogue in *The Simpsons* on the other hand was found to be full of different sentence types and constructions. It too contained the minor (i.e. incomplete) sentences common in speech (such as 'Guess so'), but the majority of the sentences are either compound or complex, as in the examples below.

a) Compound, i.e. consisting of two main clauses (MC):

Homer: 'My dad gave me these cufflinks [MC] on the day I married Marge [phrase] and they brought us good luck.' [MC]

b) Complex, i.e. consisting of a main clause and at least one minor one:

Lisa: 'That man is easily the most annoying person [MC] [that] I've ever met.'

These are very ordinary and simple sentences, but they are more than any of the Royles ever manage to construct.

Grammatical differences

The characters in *The Royle Family* are made to speak in what is technically known as a **social-class dialect** (see Trudgill, p. 35, 'Sociolinguistics'). We find them using the third person past tense 'sat' in place of the Standard English present tense 'sits', or 'is sitting', e.g. 'she's sat here on her arse all day'. They also use the third person plural of the verb 'to be' where SE uses the third person singular, e.g. 'It were all right for you on Tuesday night, though, weren't it?'

In the episode I analysed, the Simpsons' grammar was that of conventional SE.

Differences in male and female speech patterns

A clear difference was noticed between male and female speech patterns in *The Royle Family*.

Jim Royle is made to speak in short, sharp bursts, often strongly emphatic and indignant; his voice rises in pitch and volume before subsiding to an angry mumble, e.g.

'You've been ringing bloody Mary next door? If she shouted you could 'ear 'er.'

'Who do you think I am, bloody Rockefeller?'

If Jim's consuming interest is saving money, his wife Barbara's is other people. She finds interest in every small detail of their lives: 'Dave will be 'aving his tea, won't 'e?'; 'Who's the father of them two [illegitimate children]?'; 'How's your mam's legs, love?'. Writer Caroline Aherne makes her stereotypically female in her inability to think logically – when asked the make of a car, she replies that it's a red one. Because she can't (or possibly refuses to) talk openly about the worries and tensions in her family life (her mother's increasing frailty and loneliness, Jim's lack of sexual interest in her), she takes refuge in long, rambling anecdotes about her colleagues at work.

Examples of verbal humour

Very little humour or inventiveness could be found in the Royle family's language. This is probably deliberate on the writer's part; perhaps she wants to show the ritual nature of her working-class family's life style, the way it relies on old sayings and clichés like 'these things are sent to try us', and 'who smelt it dealt it'. To say anything original in this circle would be to step out of line and find yourself condemned as either a 'nutter' or a 'smart-arse'. The best jokes are the old ones, so bits of rhyming slang, and obvious puns like 'tiers' and 'tears', are passwords that show you're all right and you belong. For example Jim, referring to a trip to the lavatory, says 'I'm going for a tom-tit.'

The only other form of humour found came from a kind of heavy irony: 'Oh aye, can't smile wide enough, me', Jim remarks when asked how he is. There are also a few touches of dramatic irony; for example, showing the jeans he's come to sell to the Royles, the character called Twiggy (because he's fat) claims they're 'top quality – ten quid a pair'. Similarly, Jim remarks that Twiggy's a 'scruffy get' and wonders why he doesn't smarten himself up – totally unaware that he's as bad as Twiggy himself.

10 Drawing Conclusions and Presenting Findings 165

Dialogue in *The Simpsons*

The language in the dialogue spoken by the Simpsons was found to differ very little from Standard English.

Lexical differences

No significant differences between English and American English were found in the course of the episodes I watched. The names for certain things differed, as mentioned above, but otherwise the vocabulary used was largely that of conventional English. 'Lisa,' Marge says to her daughter, 'I can't believe your wedding day has come so soon', a sentence that could have been spoken by any mother to any daughter in the same circumstances in England.

Even Homer, rumbustious as he is, was found to speak in good, plain English. Offering a pair of cufflinks to his prospective son-in-law, he tells him, 'My dad gave me these cufflinks on the day I married Marge and they brought us good luck. Nobody could have had a happier marriage.' Exceptions that may prove the rule are perhaps the adjectives 'Great!' and 'Alright!', modern versions of SE 'Oh good!', but this may be simply because British SE hasn't caught up with this usage yet; it's been a common slang idiom for some years now.

Syntactical differences

The dialogue spoken by the Simpsons in the episode entitled 'Lisa's Wedding' was found to be very different from that of the Royles. There are many sentences containing phrases and dependent clauses (DC):

'That man is easily [MC] the most annoying person [phrase] [that] I've ever met [DC].'

There are sentences with two main clauses followed by a dependent clause:

'We don't have many traditions in our family [MC] but I'd be delighted [MC] if you kept this one alive [DC].'

There is even a cumulative structure where one main clause is piled upon another to emphasize the idea of how much the two characters have in common: 'We're both studying the environment, we're both utterly unhumorous about vegetarians, and we both love the Rolling Stones.'

Grammatical usage

No deviations from SE grammar were noticed in my analysis of the two different programmes. I did however find that the Simpsons' dialogue contained more 'colour' words – modifiers such as adjectives and adverbs – than the Royles', whose all-purpose modifier seemed to be 'bloody'. Lisa has 'easily', 'most', and 'ever' in one sentence; Homer has 'happier,' 'good', and 'delighted' in one of his.

Differences in male and female speech patterns

The speech patterns of Jim and Barbara Royle were found to contrast strongly in the episodes I analysed. Barbara, for example, never swears, uses indecent words like 'arse', or makes explicit references to sex. Her daughter Denise, however, frequently refers to sex, using slang terms like 'knob' and punning on the word 'hard', which may be taken to illustrate the much greater freedom of speech and behaviour allowable to the younger generation of women.

Sentence constructions were also found to show gender differences. Where Jim's utterances are short, sharp, and aggressively assertive, Barbara's are warmer and softer in tone: 'Ah, come on in, love' – and are sometimes seen to be vague, rambling and pointless:

'Ooh, you know that Donna that works with me (3) well (2) she only works half days (1) afternoons (.) and her mam usually picks the kids up for 'er (.) anyway her mam's going into hospital so she won't be able to pick the kids up for her will she...'

Aherne also draws a contrast between male and female speech patterns by making Barbara and Denise use modal verbs to reveal their aspirations towards middle-classness. This is an example of how Barbara expresses the need she feels to be classier than they are:

'We **ought** to have some [corned-beef hash].'

Here is an example of Denise indulging in wishful thinking; 'going to have' here is a verb predicting what she hopes will happen, not the simple future tense stating what will happen:

'We're **going to have** a microwave in our new kitchen… and a dishwasher…'

In 'Lisa's Wedding', the question of male/female speech patterns is complicated by the fact that Lisa is much more intelligent and well-read than her father, Homer, and her brother, Bart. Her uttering of sentences like, 'He can make you laugh with no more than a frantic flailing of his limbs' can therefore be put down to education rather than gender difference, especially as her college boyfriend, Hugh, speaks in much the same way.

Marge, Barbara Royle's equivalent, was given very little to say in this particular episode, and it was therefore impossible to draw any firm conclusions about her speech patterns.

Verbal humour

The main verbal humour to be found in the *Simpsons* episode was in the contrast between the suffering that Homer and Bart put Lisa's fiancé through, and the impeccably polite way in which he responded to it. 'I'm sorry I left you alone with Homer and Bart,' Lisa tells him, and he, gash on forehead from where Homer has driven into a dumpster, simply replies 'That's all right, honey, I had a fine time.' Not until Lisa forces him to wear Homer's ghastly cufflinks for the wedding does he reveal that meeting her family has been awful for him, and then the humour comes from understatement: 'You're quite right… This has been quite trying.'

Verbal humour can also be found in Homer's habit of claiming credit for things he didn't do – 'You're my greatest achievement', he tells Lisa, 'and you did it all yourself' – and his tendency to talk in one way and behave in the opposite: 'It's so great to have the whole family under one roof,' he says beamingly to Marge, 'listen to the murmurs in the next room'; after which he hammers on the adjoining wall and yells 'Keep it down in there.'

> **Note**
>
> Since neither your findings nor your conclusions can be definitive (i.e. know all there is to know about the subject of your investigation), a good technique to use when writing up your report is to use tentative constructions like *seems likely that, may be the result of, suggests that.*

Conclusions

Your conclusions should follow logically from your findings.

If your investigation of dialect use, for example, found a significant drop in the number of young people using the dialect forms common among their grandparents' generation, and that they are used only rarely in family gatherings or when older people are telling stories, you might want to suggest that exposure to the media and youth culture may well be eroding older patterns of speech.

If your investigation into mixed-gender conversation showed a softening of traditional male dominance patterns, you might think it likely that increasing success in education and employment is gaining women increased respect from male colleagues and friends.

Your conclusions can only come from your findings, but they should be more than simple re-statements of what your findings say. Look at the example below.

A comparison of the lexis in a single episode of each sit-com suggests that, in spite of what many English people believe, Americans speak a version of English very close to SE, or at least Matt Groenig and the other writers of *The Simpsons* – all well-educated people – do. It would seem to be the Royles who deviate from this common standard and speak a sub-dialect of their own – or rather of the northern working class to which they belong.

Where male/female speech patterns are concerned, my investigation found clear differences in lexis and sentence construction between Barbara and Denise and Jim in particular. The distinction between them and the younger male speakers, Dave and Anthony, was not quite so marked; this may be because Anthony, being only 15, has no authority in the house, and Dave, being only engaged rather than married to Denise as yet, has to be nicer to her.

Evaluation

Having drawn your conclusions, you are now expected to reflect upon your work in the investigation and say how satisfactory you find it. Start by describing what you have achieved – what you and your tutor think you have done reasonably well – before going on to discuss the less successful aspects of your work.

You might want to use a heading such as 'Reflections on my investigation', followed by two sub-headings such as 'Strong points' and 'Weak points'. See the example below.

Reflections on my investigation

Reading through the final draft of my investigation, I became aware that I had given myself too much to do. Instead of working on two hypotheses, I should have chosen only one of the two; I would then have had more time to explore either the different kinds of language or the different linguistic gender patterns to be found in *The Simpsons*. Investigating the language of *The Royle Family* was easier because so much of the same material was found in each episode.

Strong points

I feel the strong point of my investigation is the detailed analysis of speech patterns in *The Royle Family*. Even though I did not have enough time to make a close study of every character's way of speaking, I feel I did enough to show the general nature of northern working-class conversation and to reveal the major ways in which it differs from SE and Standard American English.

Weak points

My investigation has two main weaknesses. One is the rather scanty analysis of general speech patterns in *The Simpsons;* the other is the failure to demonstrate anything about the difference between male and female speech patterns in this sit-com.

When you have highlighted the strengths and weaknesses of your work on the investigation, you still have two further tasks to do. The first task is to state what you feel are the limitations of your finished study. For instance, if you had been investigating the persistence of dialect forms among younger speakers, you might say something like this:

> My investigation was able to cover only a small number of speakers, so it can give information only about the use of dialect by those particular groups of people at that particular place and at that particular time.

The second task is to recommend further investigations that could usefully be carried out in the particular area you have been studying. Here you might say something like this:

> In order to discover whether dialect forms are dying out generally among the young, similar studies involving larger samples of speakers would need to be carried out by students working in their own localities across the whole country.

Don't lost sight of the fact that your work is valuable, however – your investigation might be able to play a small part in a much larger investigation into the same subject. Any collection of factual data, however limited, may turn out to be of value to someone else, later on.

Bibliography

Under this heading, you should list any books, articles or websites you have consulted or quoted from in the course of your investigation.

Books

The usual method of layout is to list information in the following order:

- author's surname
- author's initials
- year of publication in brackets
- title of work
- place published
- name of publisher.

For example:

Trudgill, P. (1974), *Sociolinguistics*, London: Penguin.

Websites

When using material from a website which does not name individual writers, use the following format:

- creator of the website
- date listed at the top of the first page of the article
- title of the article
- web address (URL).

For example:

British Library, 08/27/2007, 'Regional Voices' in *Learning*, http://www.bl.uk/learning/langlit/sounds/regional voices

Articles

For articles from magazines, journals or newspapers, use this format:

- author (surname and initials)
- title
- name of publication
- date of publication.

For example:

Rosewarne, D. 'Estuary English', *Times Educational Supplement*, 19 October 2006.

If you are quoting an article from a number gathered into one book, refer to it like this:

- writer's name and initials
- year of publication in brackets
- title of article
- name(s) of the general editor(s) of the book
- title of book
- place of publication
- name of publisher.

For example:

Swann, J. (1989) 'Talk control: an illustration from the classroom of problems in analysing male dominance in education', in J. Coates & D. Cameron (editors) *Women in their Speech Communities*, London: Longman

11 Media Texts

Preparing to write a media text

Your final task in Unit 4 will be to use the subject of your language investigation to produce a media text (such as a newspaper or magazine article) highlighting the language ideas and issues you have been investigating. The text should be between 750 and 1000 words long, and aimed at a non-specialist audience. The purpose of this task is to allow you to develop and build on the writing and editorial skills you have gained on your course.

In general, when you're setting out to write a non-fiction text, you have several options. You can aim:

- to inform, in which case your audience will be either highly educated and/or very interested in your subject matter, your lexis will be abstract and technical, and your style formal and impersonal
- to instruct, in which case you must cater for a mixed audience, some of whom may not read well; you will avoid technical language in favour of plain, clear words; you will write in a series of simple, short sentences; you will use imperative rather than modal verbs in the active rather than passive mode, and you will write each instruction in chronological order
- to advise, which is a gentler, indirect form of instruction; your language should still be plain and clear, your sentence structure a mixture of simple, compound and complex, but you should use modal rather than imperative verbs and phrases, such as *might be better, should perhaps*
- to persuade, in which case you must attack your readers' feelings with emotive words, rhetorical appeals and carefully modulated sentence structures (e.g. cumulative ones) that give impact to what you're saying
- to entertain, in which case you must be able to spin a lot of stylish comment out of very little subject matter, dazzling readers with your wit and word-play as you go along.

In other words, to recap what was said at the beginning of this book, your purpose and the kind of audience you are writing for dictate the lexis and style you will use.

Taken singly, each of the above involves only one genre of writing, for only one specialized kind of audience. Media texts, on the other hand, are aimed at a wider potential audience made up of some of the members of all these narrower audiences. Their appeal needs to be as wide as possible, and so the most successful examples are often combinations of information, persuasion, and entertainment.

Most media texts take their subject matter from current issues discussed in radio and TV news bulletins. Today, changing speech patterns are again a key issue, with articles turning up almost every day in all kinds of newspapers.

To be able to clarify the important concepts that underlie, for example, the undermining of received pronunciation by Estuary English, journalists have to read and digest expert linguistic explanations of the phenomenon, before turning them into the kind of clear and entertaining report that will appeal to the majority of readers.

You will be asked to go through the same sort of process in the final part of your coursework. In preparation for this particular writing task, and to help you present your ideas succinctly for a non-specialist audience, the examiners suggest you should study:

> the evaluation and synthesis of complex ideas and concepts from a range of specialized source materials

A small sample of such source materials is given below to give you practice in:

- reading serious academic material
- abstracting from it the main points made by each writer.

Activity

1 Read each of the passages below carefully, making notes of their salient points.

2 For each, write one or two sentences re-expressing these main points about language in your own words.

As you do so, remember the following points.

- Writers often introduce ideas which they disagree with simply in order to show that they think they're wrong. These ideas are not therefore relevant to the main argument, and you can safely leave them out (this applies to Extract A).

- Writers often use analogies to make their meaning more plain. These analogies may clarify meaning but may not be strictly relevant to the main point and so can be left out of your notes (this applies to Extract C).

When you have finished, consult page 179 and compare your summary sentences with the suggested versions there.

A The distinction between *langue* and *parole* was made famous in the work of the Swiss linguist Ferdinande de Saussure...

Saussure regarded *langue* as a system or code which is prior to actual language use, which is the same for all members of a language community, and which is the *social* side of language, as opposed to *parole*, which is individual. For Saussure, *parole*, what is actually said or written, is determined purely by individual choices, not socially at all. Linguistics, according to Saussure, is concerned primarily with language, not *parole*.

Language use (*parole*) is, as Saussure was aware, characterized by extensive linguistic variation, and it is the account of this variation given by modern sociolinguistics which has done most to undermine the Saussurean concept of *parole*. Sociolinguistics has shown that this variation is not, as Saussure thought, a product of individual choice, but a product of social differentiation – language varies according to the social identities of people in interactions, their socially defined purposes, social setting, and so on. So Saussure's individualistic notion of *parole* is unsatisfactory, and in preferring the term *discourse* I am first of all committing myself to the view that language is socially determined...

In so far as homogeneity is achieved – as it is to some extent in the case of standardization [*the author is thinking here of Standard English, the official language of the nation*] – it is imposed by those who have power.

Norman Fairclough, *Language and Power*

B Estuary English is a social rather than a regional dialect, mirroring the supposed reduction in differences between the social classes.

Sara Thorne, *Mastering A Level English*

C If you are an English-speaker you will be able to estimate the relative social status of the following speakers solely on the basis of the linguistic evidence given here:

Speaker A	Speaker B
I done it yesterday.	I did it yesterday.
He ain't got it.	He hasn't got it.
It was her what said it.	It was her that said it.

If you heard these speakers say these things you would guess that B was of higher social status than A, and you would almost certainly be right. How is it that we are able to do this sort of thing?

The answer lies in the existence of varieties of English which have come to be called *social-class dialects*. There are grammatical differences between the speech of these two speakers which give us clues about their social backgrounds. It is also probable, though this is not indicated on the printed page, that these differences will be accompanied by phonetic and phonological differences – that is to say, there are also different *social-class accents*. The internal differentiation of human societies is reflected in their languages. Different social groups use different linguistic varieties, and as experienced members of a speech community we… have learnt to classify speakers accordingly. Why does social differentiation have this effect on language? We may note parallels between the development of these social varieties and the development of regional varieties: in both cases *barriers* and *distance* appear to be relevant… It seems to be the case that the greater the geographical distance between two dialects the more dissimilar they are linguistically: for instance, those regional varieties of British English which are most unlike the speech of London are undoubtedly those of the north-east of Scotland – Buchan, for example. The development of social varieties can perhaps be explained in the same sort of way – in terms of *social* barriers and *social* distance. The diffusion of a linguistic feature through a society may be halted by barriers of social class, age, race, religion or other factors. And social distance may have the same sort of effect as geographical distance: a linguistic innovation that begins amongst, say, the highest social group, will affect the lowest social group last, if at all. (We must be careful, however, not to explain all social differences of language in these entirely mechanical terms since… *attitudes* to language clearly play an important role in preserving or removing dialect differences.)

P. Trudgill, *Sociolinguistics*

In order to write your media text, the examiners also require you to have studied:

editorial skills including *paraphrase* and *summary*, the control of *register* and *style*, including *tone* and *voice*

Read the example of a media text below, then read the summarized version of the same text that follows.

Ain't nuttin' to wor' abaht, me old mate

Estuary English

[1] The moment an Englishman speaks he makes another Englishman despise him. Tony Blair must be reflecting wryly on Henry Higgins's adage in *My Fair Lady* after the howls of scorn that greeted his 'dumbed down' performance on Des O'Connor's World Cup Party last week. In contrast with Eliza Doolittle, who had to re-engineer her accent to become socially acceptable, the prime minister descended into estuary English in an attempt to reach out to the masses.

[2] Viewers who witnessed the transformation of Blair's modulated tones into a starburst of dropped aitches, glottal stops and missed final letters, could be forgiven for suspecting a medical explanation. Wasn't there a recent case where a Scottish woman went to bed with a headache and woke up speaking like Winnie Mandela? And a cockney policeman who came out of a two-week coma drawling in an American accent? Had Blair joined William Hague's judo classes and bumped his head?

[3] The following day's newspapers offered a less charitable interpretation. Blair had dumbed down in a blatant attempt to win public support, in much the same way that he had exploited Cool Britannia and thrown open the doors of No 10 and Buckingham Palace to hordes of meritless youth icons. He was a shameless chameleon, harping on his Irish roots in Ireland and even willing to try his hand at golf to ingratiate himself with Bill Clinton.

[4] What had he done to deserve the green slime douche of opprobrium? Describing a reception with a local mayor in France, Blair recalled: 'They pu' on a lit'le show for us with the mayor of the lit'le village.' The mayor had brought in a horse as a gift. Asked what had become of it, Blair replied: ''E's come back to England.'

[5] He also recounted how he had called the Spanish prime minister, his host on holiday, to apologise for his delay in joining his family. 'I rang 'im up. He says, "Well, look, I will put 'em up in my house".' In addition, Blair produced that stock-in-trade of cockney comedians, the mother-in-law joke, and as a final flourish he offered to sing with O'Connor if England win the World Cup.

[6] For a former public schoolboy educated at Fettes College, Oxford, and the law chambers of Derry Irvine, this was a right old 'ow's yer farver. Blair is the most truly middle-class prime minister Britain has had since Clement Atlee and can 'talk proper' when he wants to. But he has evidently decided that when it comes to courting the electorate, the wise course is to bot'le out.

[7] In attempting the 'high cockney', or estuarine English, spoken by Ben Elton, Jonathan Ross and Paul Merton, Blair risks joining Kavanagh QC in the dock, charged with dealing in counterfeit accents. Residents of Norfolk recently complained that the television series was taking liberties with their distinctive dialect. Particular exception was taken to the pronunciation of 'nothing' as 'nuttin'. A local explained: 'Nutting is something we do in woods. It's not something we do here.'

[8] But in down-shifting to estuary English, Blair no doubt hoped to ride its swelling tide. The new dialect, characterised by swallowing the 't' in words such as 'Ga'wick' and the 'l' in expressions such as 'St Pauw's Cathedral', has spread way beyond its traditional heartlands on the banks of the Thames in Essex and north Kent. It has pushed as far as Norwich and Cambridge, and has snaked down the M4 to Devon and Cornwall.

[9] Back in 1994, David Blunkett complained that he was fighting a losing family battle over estuary English, which was infiltrating his sons' speech. 'If it goes on I will have to emigrate to Scotland,' he said. Just as well he was joking. The classless cockney has now invaded Scotland, creating a new Glaswegian dialect known as Jockney. Suddenly, the deeply accented 'mither' has been replaced by 'muvver', 'tuth' has become 'toof' and 'bruvver' has supplanted 'brother'.

[10] Politicians have always sought populist devices for beaming down to the lower orders. Harold Macmillan was not averse to reciting music hall lines with great aplomb, but when James Callaghan sang a verse to the TUC in 1978, it back-fired badly. 'There I was waiting at the church, waiting at the church, waiting at the church,' he warbled. He was being enigmatic about the date of the general election, but when he called it, he was voted out of office. His successor, Margaret Thatcher, never descended into the vernacular, but developed a taste for wowing chat show audiences with unconscious double entendres ('Every prime minister needs a Willy [Whitelaw]').

[11] Ted Heath, from Broadstairs at the estuary's eastern extremity, made few linguistic concessions to the patois of his constituents, having developed a unique variety of his own. He was celebrated for his pronunciation of 'House' ('Heowse') and 'now' ('neow'). No previous prime minister in living memory had mangled the language of Shakespeare in quite that way.

[12] John Major, a Brixton boy, was famously responsible for switching his vowels, as in 'I wunt', which proved a gift to comic impersonators. More importantly, it reinforced the view that a lack of standard English, or the 'received pronunciation' which even the BBC was hastily abandoning, was no longer a barrier to advancement.

[13] A dropped letter can be used to devastating effect, but Blair's endeavours fell far short of the immortal line by Margot Asquith, as explained by T.S. Matthews: 'Jean Harlow kept calling Margot Asquith by her first name, or kept trying to: she pronounced it Mar*got*. Finally Margot set her right. 'No, no, Jean. The t is silent, as in Harlow.'

[14] Blair's reverse elocution may have struck commentators as patronising and even hypocritical, but it is a trick resorted to increasingly by the middle classes in their efforts to remain credible. To avoid having the mickey taken, lah-di-dah public schoolboys and girls switch to something more streetwise when they go home. Teenagers want to be cool, and older people do not want to sound like toffs.

[15] Even the young royals are not immune to the trend. According to linguists, current pronunciation owes more to 'Prince Andrew than the Queen'. Diana Princess of Wales, who was accused of dressing like an Essex girl, was particularly estuarial in speech. She shared the Duchess of York's partiality to Sloanisms such as 'ghastly' or 'absolutely', but largely conformed to estuary expressions such as 'in yonks' (for ages), 'bog' (lavatory) and 'chuffed' (pleased).

[16] In a corresponding shift, the upwardly mobile have discarded aspects of their dialects and moved closer to 'proper English'. The middle ground the British share is estuary English. No wonder this seems such a promising constituency to Tone, architect of 'the people's party'. Why crunch demographic statistics in search of Sierra man or Mondeo woman when the key is something as simple as speech?

[17] But the spectacle of a politician trying to prove that he is one of us gets up a lot of people's hooters.

[18] Hague was also at it last week, saying that he reads Hello! 'to look at the weekly picture of Ffion', that he enjoys watching Bond films and 'is obviously quite proud of *The Full Monty*' because he comes from the Rotherham and Sheffield area. The one asset he lacks is estuary English.

[19] Ironically, Hague owes public acceptance of his Yorkshire vowels to television soap operas such as Coronation Street and Emmerdale, which are seen as fashionable and helping to preserve regional patterns of speech.

[20] Democratisation of the English language is one thing. Nobody wants to sound like the Prince of Wales any more: 'There's a mace dane at the hace.' ('There's a mouse down at the house.') And there is no doubt that the plain speech of Mo Mowlem, the Northern Ireland secretary, helped to break down suspicions after the patrician tones of her predecessor, Sir Patrick Mayhew.

[21] But should our leaders be 'plumbing down' in this estuarine way? Do we really want the commissioner of the Metropolitan police to sound as if he has stepped out of The Bill? Or university professors who sound like Chris Evans? Leav'it aht, Tone.

Sunday Times, 7 June 1998

(1,344 words)

Summarized version

In contrast with Eliza Doolittle, who had to re-engineer her accent to become socially acceptable, former Prime Minister Tony Blair descended into Estuary English in an attempt to reach out to the masses.

Blair dumbed down in a blatant attempt to win public support, in much the same way that he had exploited Cool Britannia and thrown open the doors of No 10 and Buckingham Palace to hordes of meritless youth icons.

Blair was the most truly middle-class prime minister Britain had had since Clement Atlee, and could 'talk proper' when he wanted to. But he had evidently decided that when it comes to courting the electorate, the wise course was to bot'le out.

In down-shifting to Estuary English, Blair no doubt hoped to ride its swelling tide. The new dialect, characterized by swallowing the 't' in words such as 'Ga'wick' and the 'l' in expressions such as 'St Pauw's Cathedral', has spread way beyond its traditional heartlands on the banks of the Thames in Essex and north Kent. It has pushed as far as Norwich and Cambridge, and has snaked down the M4 to Devon and Cornwall.

The classless cockney has now invaded Scotland, creating a new Glaswegian dialect known as Jockney. Suddenly, the deeply accented 'mither' has been replaced by 'muvver', 'tuth' has become 'toof' and 'bruvver' has supplanted 'brother'.

Blair's reverse elocution may have struck commentators as patronizing and even hypocritical, but it is a trick resorted to increasingly by the middle classes in their efforts to remain credible. To avoid having the mickey taken, lah-di-dah public schoolboys and girls switch to something more street-wise when they go home. Teenagers want to be cool, and older people do not want to sound like toffs.

Even the young royals are not immune to the trend. According to linguists, current pronunciation owes more to 'Prince Andrew than the Queen'.

In a corresponding shift, the upwardly mobile have discarded aspects of their dialects and moved closer to 'proper English'. The middle ground the British share is Estuary English.

Democratization of the English language is one thing. Nobody wants to sound like the Prince of Wales any more: 'There's a mace dane at the hace.' ('There's a mouse down at the house.') And there is no doubt that the plain speech of Mo Mowlem, the Northern Ireland secretary, helped to break down suspicions after the patrician tones of her predecessor, Sir Patrick Mayhew.

But should our leaders be 'plumbing down' in this estuarine way? Do we really want the commissioner of the Metropolitan police to sound as if he has stepped out of The Bill? Or university professors who sound like Chris Evans? Leav'it aht, Tone.

(446 words)

The structures and conventions of media texts

If you carefully compare the full text with the summarized version, you will see examples of:

- how to précis a piece of writing (i.e. cut it down in length while retaining all the important points)
- the techniques you need for producing a media text.

You will also get an object lesson in control of lexis and tone of voice.

Look carefully at each paragraph in turn and you will see that what has been taken out is precisely:

- what makes it entertaining
- what differentiates it from the formal tone and register of the academic writing at the beginning of this section.

The writer uses the following techniques:

- allusions to popular TV programmes to appeal to a wide range of readers, e.g. *Coronation Street*, *Emmerdale*, *Kavanagh QC*
- references to funny stories in the news (see the incongruous connection between different events in paragraph 3)
- imagery to spice up the writing, e.g. *starburst* (paragraph 2), *chameleon* (paragraph 3), *green slime douche* (paragraph 4), *swelling tide* and *snaked* (paragraph 8)
- gossipy anecdotes about many subjects – people who live in Norfolk, earlier prime ministers, Tony Blair himself, David Blunkett and his sons, Princess Diana and Sarah Ferguson, William Hague's judo classes and Yorkshire vowels, etc.
- risqué jokes about dignitaries, e.g. Margaret Thatcher and Margot Asquith (paragraphs 10 and 13)
- pseudo-phonetic transcriptions that sound either silly – e.g. *bot'le* (paragraph 6) and *hace* (paragraph 20) – or ugly, e.g. *neow* and *Heowse* (paragraph 11)
- addressing the readers as if talking to friends
- avoidance of technical language, e.g. writing *talk proper* instead of referring to RP
- slang where appropriate to capture different people's attitudes, e.g. *lah-di-dah*, *cool*, *toffs*, *hooters*
- asking readers for their opinions having indicated his own (paragraph 21).

Writing media texts

Media texts by their very nature set out to entertain, inform and, albeit gently, persuade.

They are also by their very nature aimed at a wide and varied audience: not all *Times* readers are highly educated, and not all *Sun* readers are less well educated. The audiences for media texts do all have one thing in common, however: they bore easily. It's your job to interest them enough to make them keep on reading once they've begun.

Anglo-Saxon writers used to begin with a loud 'Hwæt' – equivalent probably to our 'Oi!' – and though you can't do that, you do need a catch-all starter to get readers interested. The writer of the article you've just read managed that very well with his quotation from *My Fair Lady* – most of his readers will have seen the film, if not the play, and most will have thoughts of one kind or another about the linguistic snobbery described.

Checklist of techniques for writing a media text

- Write in a friendly, accessible style, using inclusive pronouns if they seem appropriate, e.g. 'We all know'.
- Avoid abstruse technical vocabulary; translate it into ordinary terms even if it takes twice as long to describe.
- Try to find an arresting opening sentence. It needn't be directly about the topic you're discussing; you could lead in with an allusion or a quotation or a wider reference of some kind. For example, if you had been writing about Estuary English, you could have begun with a reference to the list of 'youf' slang Tesco is giving to its older employees so that they can understand the younger members of staff coming into the organization.
- People like people, so try to work in something about well-known people – actors, politicians, characters in films or TV programmes – as long as it's appropriate. But don't just drag them in because you like them.
- Expand the scope of your piece by bringing in examples and illustrations that contrast with the points you're making, as well as ones that support them. For instance, if you were writing in praise of the democratization of English through Estuary English, you could talk about the prescriptivists who can't bear any deviation from SE and RP and think that it will corrupt the language and morals of the nation.
- Allow your readers to make up their own minds: ask them rhetorical questions, e.g. *Can we be sure that Estuary English won't make it harder to produce and appreciate good writing?* Use modal verbs like *may* and *might* and *ought* and *should*, together with the tentative little word *perhaps*. Avoid making dogmatic assertions, e.g. *This can only end in disaster.*
- Try to avoid clichés such as *the best thing since sliced bread* and trendy words and phrases like *any time soon*, and do your best to avoid exclamations marks!

Remember that your article should have a clear beginning, middle and end, in that order; just as you need an arresting opening so you need a convincing conclusion – preferably one that leads off into the future, e.g. *There are fashions in language as in every other aspect of life, and Estuary English may disappear as rapidly as it has spread.*

References

Finally, don't forget to include a bibliography listing the materials you used – both sources of information and style models – to help you prepare your media text. See page 168 for guidance on how to present your bibliography.

Activity

Write a media text of roughly 750 words on the spread of Estuary English, using the information in the extracts in this chapter but putting any slant on it that you wish.

Suggested summaries for Activity on page 172

A: The various ways in which people express themselves is determined by their ideas about their social position and the way they want other people to think about them.

B: Speaking Estuary English is thought to spring from the wish to do away with old class distinctions and make society more democratic.

C: If people express themselves in a variety of different ways in our society, it may be because they live in different social hierarchies, separated by such barriers as class, age, religion, and ethnicity. Attitudes towards language, however, may also play a part.

Index